Millionaire Expat

Millionaire Expat

How to Build Wealth Living Overseas

Third Edition

Andrew Hallam

WILEY

Published by John Wiley & Sons, Inc., Hoboken, New Jersey.

Published simultaneously in Canada.

For general information on our other products and services or for technical support, please contact our Customer Care Department within the United States at (800) 762-2974, outside the United States at (317) 572-3993 or fax (317) 572-4002.

Wiley also publishes its books in a variety of electronic formats. Some content that appears in print may not be available in electronic formats. For more information about Wiley products, visit our web site at www.wiley.com.

Library of Congress Cataloging-in-Publication Data:

Names: Hallam, Andrew (Teacher), author. | John Wiley & Sons, publisher.
Title: Millionaire expat : how to build wealth living overseas / Andrew
    Hallam.
Other titles: Global expatriate's guide to investing
Description: Third edition. | Hoboken, New Jersey : Wiley, [2022] |
    Includes index.
Identifiers: LCCN 2021044853 (print) | LCCN 2021044854 (ebook) | ISBN
    9781119840107 (paperback) | ISBN 9781119840152 (adobe pdf) | ISBN
    9781119840145 (epub)
Subjects: LCSH: Finance, Personal. | Investments. | Retirement
    income—Planning.
Classification: LCC HG179 .H238 2022 (print) | LCC HG179 (ebook) | DDC
    332.024—dc23
LC record available at https://lccn.loc.gov/2021044853
LC ebook record available at https://lccn.loc.gov/2021044854

Cover Design: Wiley
Cover Images: U.K. passport © Jeff Fullerton/Getty Images; U.S. Passport © S.Perry/Getty Images

SKY54C1AF35-D8E2-4CCF-A131-81B3CFADCCDA_121321

Only a fool would take his wife on a multi-month cycling tour . . . while trying to write a book. An even bigger fool would attempt the same thing during a 17-month adventure in a camper van (trying to drive from Canada to Argentina). I have done both. Note to all single women: if you believe your future spouse might try such a stunt, run. Fortunately for me, my wife didn't just stick around she helped with every aspect of this book's production (and every other book I've written). Named after the Hawaiian fire goddess, Pele sometimes spewed lava in my general direction while I pretended it was normal to write books from bicycles and vans. And although I'm not fully rehabilitated, I'm a better man for it. So Pele Hallam-Young, this book is dedicated to you. You're amazing. I love you more every day.

Contents

Acknowledgements

If I were hit by a bus, I can imagine my wife eventually venturing back onto the dating scene. But I'm pretty sure she wouldn't date a writer. I can hear the checklist in her head right now: adventurous, check; handsome, check; caring, check; intelligent, check; writer . . . oh shit. Writing is an anti-social gig. The best part (for me, anyway) is gleaning stories from people that I can share and learn from. But then, as all writers do, I spend thousands of hours trying to make sense of it all. Only 0.01 percent of authors earn enough compensation to exceed a minimum hourly wage. I made that up. But it's probably true.

So, I have to thank my wife, Pele Hallam-Young, for helping me with this book. She encouraged me. She helped with edits and ideas. And she worked tirelessly as my time manager, taking on tasks that I was "too busy" to do because I was writing a book. OK, so writing this thing did have some perks.

I would also like to thank the publishing team at John Wiley & Sons, with an especially deep bow to Kevin Harreld. I don't really know what to call Kevin. Is he my publisher? My editor? My marketing specialist? After writing that last sentence, I looked up his title on LinkedIn (and no, I'm not lying). It reads, Senior Acquisitions Editor. All I know is that he's my man on the ground at John Wiley & Sons who seems to put everything into motion.

Thanks also to John S. Woerth, Senior Communications Advisor at Vanguard. John always helps me with charts and he cheerleads my efforts. He's one of those behind-the-scenes brilliant guys whom Vanguard founder, John Bogle often praised. John Woerth also co-wrote *More Straight Talk on Investing*, with former Vanguard CEO, John J. Brennan.

Thank you, also, to Vanguard's Mike Nolan, who John introduced me to. Upon request, Mike sent me charts faster than I could make my next cup of tea.

I would also like to thank the American fee-based financial advisor Tony Noto. He was my go-to guy for information on US taxes, with respect to IRAs for American expats. The Australian financial advisor, Jarrad Brown, also helped me with tax information for Australian expats. Thank you for your help, Jarrad.

Several Financial Independence (FI) warriors also deserve my heartfelt thanks. Several years ago, I met the impossibly good-looking Sebastien Aguilar in Dubai. He founded SimplyFI a UAE-based financial education group. Jen Lincoln began a Facebook group by that name and encouraged reams of people to join and organize events with Sebastien and his FI-minded friends. This is now the largest FI-oriented expat organization in the world. I profiled several of the group's members in this book. I couldn't include everyone who volunteered their time and stories, but I wish I could. Reading posts from SimplyFI's Facebook group continues to help me understand what questions people have.

The group includes several warriors for the cause, of which there are far too many to list. But I want to acknowledge Tuan Phan, whose name alone likely draws shivers from the creeps who sell investment linked assurance schemes. The tireless Facebook poster and presenter might know more about these products than anyone in the Middle East. He knows far, far more, in fact, than the people who sell them. I'd bet my portfolio on that.

Elie Irani and Steve Cronin are also indefatigable activators who inspire me to keep moving forward. Elie created a fabulous *Getting Started Guide* for the SimplyFI community and Steve (who organized my first public talk in Dubai) continues to help people on the Facebook group, and with his blog and workshops at, *Dead Simple Saving*.

To say I've also been inspired by PlanVision's Mark Zoril is a serious understatement. After introducing Mark to the expat community, he has worked tirelessly as an angel on their behalf. Knowing how many thousands of people Mark has helped also pushes me to try and keep up.

If there's something I want to convey more than anything else, it's this: we need each other. I'm not just talking about writing a book or managing money. We can all help each other in every capacity: socially, physically, emotionally and financially. So thank you, everyone, who contributed to inspire and help me. I'll keep doing my best to pay that forward.

Introduction

Our taxi crawled along the 3-lane highway. But from what I could see, Egyptians don't care much for lanes. Five cars squeezed, side-by-side, along a road designed for three cars abreast. I wondered if there was an accident ahead or whether this was normal mid-afternoon traffic. We were on the outskirts of Cairo, Egypt, driving into the old city. "Hey, check this out!" my wife laughed. Ahead of us, to our right, a bus driver yelled at a guy in a car. It was hot, and our taxi's air-conditioner was on its last legs. But at least now we had entertainment to keep our minds off the heat and the clogged traffic jam.

Tempers soared between the two drivers. And when the clogged traffic stopped, each guy sprang from his vehicle to wage a verbal war. Fueled by anger, they gesticulated and spat as they screamed at one another. I thought a physical fight would start. But before it could, passengers in the bus began screaming at their driver because, in his rush to jump from the bus, he had forgotten to pull his emergency brake.

Traffic was now moving, and the driverless bus gained speed on the downhill grade. The driver then sprinted for his bus, barely getting to the door and jumping in. He slammed on the brakes and averted smashing into a stopped car ahead.

Almost every traveler has a story (or ten) to share. The world, after all, is filled with wondrous sites, people, cultures and quirks. But expats witness far more than most. When choosing to leave their home countries, they enter other worlds. Some prefer ultra-modern cities like Hong Kong, Singapore or Dubai. Others seek African, Asian or South American cities with a bit more grit. These often contrast old ways of life with a growing modern touch. You might see a woman in Hanoi, Vietnam driving a top-of-the line Mercedes Benz, followed by a guy carrying a fridge on the back of his scooter. Plenty of expats move from place-to-place. Others settle down, sometimes moving to Europe from North America, Australia, New Zealand or South Africa.

But expats often face financial risks when moving overseas.

You might wonder what I'm smoking if you're on a cushy expat package. After all, there's a large league of expats in Southeast Asia and the Middle East who make bucket loads of cash.

They left their home countries to teach at international schools or work abroad in industries such as banking, information technology, oil, cosmetics, pharmaceuticals, and shipping. Many work for firms like Coca-Cola, Facebook, American Express, Johnson & Johnson, Google, Microsoft, and Exxon Mobil.

Not all expats (including millions in Europe) make massive sums of money. But even those that do face financial risks.

In 2003, when I left Canada to teach in Singapore, I kissed good-bye to a defined benefit pension. Had I continued with my former job, I could have paid off a home, contributed modestly to investments, and received pensionable income for life.

By comparison, most expats run naked. Many don't realize they would need more than a million dollars in the stock market or multiple mortgage-free rental properties just to equal, for example, the retirement benefits earned by most public-sector workers in the United States, Britain, Australia, or Canada.

Such benefits are globally waning. But they're still a reality. Governments offer additional monthly cash: Social Security (for Americans), Canadian Pension Plan for Canadians. In fact, most developed world countries offer retirement benefits for their respective home-country workers. But it's different for expats. Few expats contribute to their home-country social programs once they've moved abroad. Without maximizing contributions to these plans, they can't fully open their mouths to such morsels once they've retired.

One of my former colleagues learned this the hard way. She's American. But she taught overseas for most of her career, so she contributed little to US Social Security. While working abroad, she earned a lot of money. She furnished her large apartment with fine carpets. She bought beautiful jewelry. She enjoyed flashy holidays—often flying business class to five-star resorts. Unfortunately, she didn't save much. Today, my friend is back in the United States, renting a room in somebody else's home. She's 73 years old and struggling far below the US poverty line. As Warren Buffett says, you only know who's swimming naked when the tide goes out.

In sharp contrast, I also taught with a couple that retired with about $5 million in their investment account. That's a lot of money—especially for teachers. They paid for their two daughters to go to college. They own a mortgage-free home. They lived well as expats and retired fully clothed. But they were great planners.

In this book's first two editions, I described the most common investment products sold to expats in Asia, Africa and the Middle East. These rank among the world's worst financial schemes. They pay eye-watering commissions to the folks who sell them, which is why they're so prolifically sold. Over the past few years, I've given plenty of talks in Europe. With Europe's strict financial regulations, you might feel protected walking into a European bank and asking them to manage your money. But to my horror, banks in countries like Germany and Switzerland (just to mention two) also typically sell the same crap. These schemes are great for the banks. But investors get burned. And these investors are often trapped. If they want to sell, they are required to pay massive penalties (which, in the end, are almost always worth paying).

This book explains how to avoid these stinky schemes, explaining how to invest in a diversified portfolio of low-cost index funds or ETFs. I'll show where you can open your investment account, while describing how to make investment purchases for different nationalities. The strategy I describe beats the returns of most professional investors. Best of all, you won't have to watch the stock market, follow the economy, or read the dull business pages of *The Wall Street Journal*.

This strategy takes about 60 minutes a year. Don't believe me? Good. Don't believe anyone who talks to you about money. That goes double for a financial salesperson. Consider everyone a shark, until proven otherwise. Use the Internet as you read this book. Confirm all my sources.

Does 60 minutes a year sound like too much time to spend on your investments? No problem. You could hire a scrupulous financial advisor or a robo advisor firm. I list some in this book. They would build you a portfolio of low-cost index funds or ETFs. Nobel Prize winners in economics recommend these products. Warren Buffett does too. In fact, Mr. Buffett says that when he dies, his estate will be invested in index funds.

I'll explain what index funds are and how they work. I'll also show you how to buy them.

Millionaire Expat (3rd edition) outlines how to plan for your future. How much money should you invest, based on *your* future needs? How much of your investment portfolio can you afford to sell during each retirement year?

Several expats, however, might say, "I would love to retire, but I can't afford it." In some cases, they didn't save enough. Others saved well, but they were rooked into long-term investment schemes that didn't make them decent profits. But such people shouldn't fret. I'll describe some desirable locations where you could retire on a shoestring. You could live (full-time or part-time) in a low-cost country, spending a fraction of what it would cost to live in the United States, Canada, Australia, New Zealand or much of Europe. I also provide tips for younger, global nomads who are keen to travel the world while working online.

As an expatriate, you can build lifetime memories by experiencing more of what the world has to offer. You can live better, earn more, and provide for a generous retirement. You'll just need a plan. Fortunately, you're reading it.

Chapter 1

Grow Big Profits
Without Any Effort

O nce upon a time, in a land far away, there lived a young
farmer. His name was Luke Skywalker. Don't get confused
by his *Star Wars* namesake. That was just a movie.

Luke had a farming mentor, an awkward little guy with a massive
green thumb. His name was Yoda. "Use the Force you must, young
Skywalker," he said. "Add new seeds to your crop fields every year.
The Force will grow those seeds. They will flower and spread more
seeds and those seeds will grow."

"Which seeds should I plant?" asked Luke. "Buy the bags that
contain every type of seed for every type of vegetable," replied Yoda.
"You'll never know which vegetables will grow the best in any given

year," he said. "Plant them all, you should. Let the Force look after the rest. But watch out for the dark side."

Luke wasn't sure what Yoda meant by *the dark side*. He just knew that Yoda was a mysterious little dude. So Luke bought a bag that contained every seed. He planted every one, and his crops began to flourish. Some years, his carrots grew best. Other years, his lettuce, parsnips, or beets took center stage. Sometimes, droughts and a searing sun hurt his crops. But his crops always came back, stronger than ever.

This is how the stock market works. You can buy a single fund called a global stock market index fund. Like a bag of seeds representing multiple plants, it contains thousands of different stocks, representing dozens of different markets. It contains American stocks, British stocks, Canadian stocks, Australian stocks, and Chinese stocks. In fact, a global stock market index contains about 7,400 stocks from at least 49 different countries. Nobody trades those stocks. With a global stock market index, you own all of those stocks. You would also have access to that money, any time you want.

Some years (much like the garden during a drought), the proceeds recede. But just like that garden, the stock market always comes back stronger than before.

Imagine if someone had invested a lump sum of $1,200 in the global stock market, starting in 1970. They then saved an additional $3.29 per day, adding that amount to their investment at the beginning of each year. Between January 1970 and December 31, 2020, that person would have added a total of $61,200 (see Figure 1.1 and Table 1.1). If they equaled the return of the global stock market index during those 51 years, that initial $1,200 investment—plus a further commitment equal to $3.29 per day—would have grown to more than $1.8 million. Between January 1970 and January 2021, global stocks averaged a compound annual return of 10.07 percent per year.

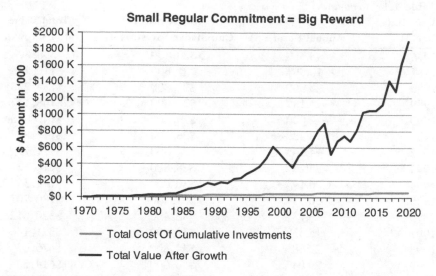

Figure 1.1 Global Stock Market Growth
SOURCE: Morningstar Direct.

Table 1.1 Global Stock Market Growth

Year Ended Dec 31	Annual Return	Total Cost of Cumulative Investments	Total Value after Growth
1970	−2.25%	$1,200	$1,173
1971	18.52%	$2,400	$2,812
1972	28.21%	$3,600	$5,144
1973	−8.96%	$4,800	$5,776
1974	−21.09%	$6,000	$5,505
1975	32.44%	$7,200	$8,880
1976	8.97%	$8,400	$10,984
1977	3.32%	$9,600	$12,588
1978	24.22%	$10,800	$17,128
1979	12.33%	$12,000	$20,588
1980	21.85%	$13,200	$26,548
1981	−3.19%	$14,400	$26,863
1982	6.61%	$15,600	$29,918
1983	25.37%	$16,800	$39,013
1984	6.47%	$18,000	$42,815
1985	51.83%	$19,200	$66,827

(*continued*)

Table 1.1   (*continued*)

Year Ended Dec 31	Annual Return	Total Cost of Cumulative Investments	Total Value after Growth
1986	45.35%	$20,400	$98,878
1987	10.06%	$21,600	$110,146
1988	20.56%	$22,800	$134,238
1989	24.15%	$24,000	$168,147
1990	−12.00%	$25,200	$149,025
1991	18.42%	$26,400	$177,897
1992	−4.10%	$27,600	$171,754
1993	25.25%	$28,800	$216,624
1994	6.19%	$30,000	$231,308
1995	20.73%	$31,200	$280,707
1996	13.73%	$32,400	$320,612
1997	15.33%	$33,600	$371,146
1998	27.58%	$34,800	$475,039
1999	29.04%	$36,000	$614,539
2000	−13.80%	$37,200	$530,767
2001	−17.86%	$38,400	$436,958
2002	−18.75%	$39,600	$356,003
2003	38.08%	$40,800	$493,226
2004	18.27%	$42,000	$584,758
2005	11.52%	$43,200	$653,460
2006	23.11%	$44,400	$805,953
2007	11.16%	$45,600	$897,231
2008	−41.72%	$46,800	$523,605
2009	30.40%	$48,000	$684,346
2010	8.62%	$49,200	$744,640
2011	−7.99%	$50,400	$686,248
2012	18.34%	$51,600	$813,526
2013	26.59%	$52,800	$1,031,361
2014	2.02%	$54,000	$1,053,419
2015	−0.44%	$55,200	$1,049,979
2016	6.53%	$56,400	$1,119,821
2017	−2.25%	$57,600	$1,394,068
2018	18.52%	$58,800	$1,258,000
2019	28.21%	$60,000	$1,595,348
2020	16.61%	$61,200	$1,895,913

SOURCE: Morningstar Direct.

Your Investment Time Horizon Is Longer Than You Think

A few years ago, I met a 50-year-old Canadian woman who lives and works in Ethiopia. "I need to take bigger risks with my money," she said, "because I'm only going to be investing for 15 years. I want to retire when I'm 65." She failed to realize, however, that if she retires at age 65, her investment duration isn't 15 years. If she lives until she's 85, her investment duration would be 35 years. Investment lifetimes have two phases. That's why she shouldn't take unnecessary risks.

The first is an accumulation phase. This is when we're working and adding money to our investments. The second stage is a retirement (or distribution) phase. The day we retire isn't the day we sell our investments, hold a massive party with the proceeds, and drink tequila until we puke. We need to keep our money invested, so we can sell pieces of it to cover our costs of living. That money should keep growing so we can continue to live off its proceeds (see Chapter 14).

That's why a 50-year-old investor's time horizon could be 35 years or longer. A 40-year-old investor's time horizon could be more than 45 years.

Why Average Returns Aren't Normal

If we look at various 30-year investment periods, global stock markets have averaged 9 to 11 percent per year. But individual calendar year returns that land precisely within that range are about as normal as a two-headed poodle.

During my lifetime, it has happened once. Global stocks gained 10.06 percent in 1987 (See Table 1.1).

It's much the same for the US stock market. Between 1970 and 2020, US stocks recorded calendar year gains between 9 and 11 percent just twice. In 1993, they gained 10.1 percent and in 2004, they earned 10.9 percent. The rest of the time, stocks soared, sank, or sputtered.[1]

US stocks averaged 10.68 percent between 1970 and 2020, but single-year performances were schizophrenic. On 10 occasions, US stocks recorded annual losses. On the flip side, stocks gained 25 percent or more during 12 other calendar years. Stock market volatility is normal and it always will be.

What Is the S&P 500?

The S&P 500 is a common measurement of the US stock market. It includes 500 selected large-company stocks. The composition of the index doesn't change much year to year. Some people measure the growth of US stocks by the Dow Jones Industrials. It represents 30 massive stocks, selected for their size and robustness. Sometimes, people reference the Wilshire 5000. It tracks more than 6,700 publicly traded US stocks. It's the most complete measurement of how US stocks perform. But over long periods of time, the S&P 500, the Dow Jones Industrials, and the Wilshire 5000 produce similar results.

When the Stock Market Beats Real Estate

I'm a huge fan of investment real estate. Buy a two-, three-, or four-unit home and reap income from every tenant (single family homes are far less efficient). Once you've saved for the down payment, let the tenants pay your mortgage.

This isn't a book about real estate investing. To do the topic justice would require a whole new book. But I do want to show how stock market growth might be better than you think.

Take one of the world's hottest real estate markets: Vancouver, British Columbia. Referencing figures from the Real Estate Board of Greater Vancouver, CBC News reported that the average detached Vancouver home sold for $368,800 CAD in 1994. By 2021, it was worth $1.83 million.[2] That's a massive gain of 396 percent over 27 years.

In contrast, if someone had invested $368,800 in a Canadian stock index, it would have grown to $2,865,576 by December 31, 2020, measured in Canadian dollars.[3]

If you had invested $368,800 in a US stock index, the money would have grown to $4,853,408 by December 31, 2020, measured in Canadian dollars.[4]

I'm not suggesting that stocks were a better investment than Vancouver real estate over the past 27 years. Investors can borrow to buy real estate and leverage their gains. They can also rent their properties, creating cash flow in the process.

But anyone who kept a cool head, kept investment fees low, and invested regular sums in the stock market over the past 27 years would have done a lot better than most people think. I'll show you how to do that.

What's Inside a Global Stock Market Index Fund?

A global stock market index represents the entire world's stocks. Roughly 55 percent of its holdings are US stocks. Roughly 20 percent are European stocks, 15 percent are Pacific stocks, and about 10 percent comprise emerging market stocks. This isn't a strategic composition. It represents a weighting based on something called global market capitalization. For example, if we had the power to sell every single stock market share in the world, about 55 percent of the proceeds would come from US stocks, 20 percent from European stocks, 15 percent from Pacific stocks, and about 10 percent from emerging-market stocks. That's why a global stock market index holds global shares in these proportions.[5]

Undressing Stocks with 50 Shades of Gray

You might wonder how money grows in the stock market. Such profits derive from two sources: capital appreciation and dividends. Let me explain with a story.

Imagine you've started a business called Fifty Shades, designing and manufacturing sexy underwear for men and women. After signing seductive advertising deals with Madonna and Miley Cyrus, sales thrust upward across every female age demographic. But as the company's CEO, you recognize a problem. Fruit of the Loom is spanking you silly in sales to aging Baby Boomer males. Only one solution makes sense: Sign Sylvester Stallone to a multiyear television-advertising contract. He could dance around a boxing ring, wearing Fifty Shades skivvies while pounding away at Siberian-sized strawberries and apples.

Such advertising should increase sales, but then you'll need to meet the product demand. New factories will be required; new distribution networks will be needed. They won't be cheap. To make more money, you're going to *need* more money.

So you hire someone to approach the New York Stock Exchange, and before you know it, you have investors in your business. They buy parts of your business, also known as shares or stock. You're no longer the sole owner, but by selling part of your business to new stockholders, you're able to build a larger, more efficient underwear business with the shareholder proceeds.

Your company, though, is now public, meaning the share owners (should they choose) could sell their stakes in Fifty Shades to other willing buyers. When a publicly traded company has shares that trade on a stock market, the trading activity has a negligible effect on the business. So you're able to concentrate on creating the sexiest underwear in the business. The shareholders don't bother you, because generally, minority shareholders don't have any influence in a company's day-to-day operations.

Your underwear catches fire globally, which pleases shareholders. But they want more than a certificate from the New York Stock Exchange or their local brokerage firm proving they're partial owners of Fifty Shades. They want to share in the business profits. This makes sense because stockholders in a company are technically owners.

So the board of directors (who were voted into their positions by the shareholders) decides to give the owners an annual percentage of the profits, known as a dividend. This is how it works. Assume that Fifty Shades sells $1 million worth of garments each year. After paying taxes on the earnings, employee wages, and business costs, the company makes an annual profit of $100,000. So the company's board of directors decides to pay its shareholders $50,000 of that annual $100,000 profit and split it among the shareholders.

The remaining $50,000 profit would be reinvested back into the business—so the company can pay for bigger and better facilities, develop new products, increase advertising, and generate even higher profits.

Those reinvested profits make Fifty Shades even more profitable. As a result, the company doubles its profits to $200,000 the following year, and increases its dividend payout to shareholders.

This, of course, causes other potential investors to drool. They want to buy shares in this hot undergarment company. So now there are more people wanting to buy shares than there are people wanting to sell them. This creates a demand for the shares, causing the share price on the New York Stock Exchange to rise. The price of any asset, whether it's real estate, gold, oil, stock, or a bond, is entirely based on supply and demand. If there are more buyers than sellers, the price rises. If there are more sellers than buyers, the price falls.

Over time, Fifty Shades' share price fluctuates—sometimes climbing, sometimes falling, depending on investor sentiment. If news about the company arouses the public, demand for the shares increases. On other days, investors grow pessimistic, causing the share price to limp.

But your company continues to make more money over the years. And over the long term, when a company increases its profits, the stock price generally rises with it.

Shareholders are able to make money two different ways. They can realize a profit from dividends (cash payments given to shareholders usually four times each year), or they can wait until their stock price increases substantially on the stock market and choose to sell some or all of their shares.

Here's how an investor could hypothetically make 10 percent a year from owning shares in Fifty Shades:

Warren Buffett has his eye on your business, so he decides to invest $10,000 in the company's stock at $10 a share. After one year, if the share price rises to $10.50, this would amount to a 5 percent increase in the share price ($10.50 is 5 percent higher than the $10 that Mr. Buffett paid).

And if Mr. Buffett receives a $500 dividend, he earns an additional 5 percent because a $500 dividend is 5 percent of his initial $10,000 investment.

So if his shares gain 5 percent in value from the share price increase, and he makes an extra 5 percent from the dividend payment, then after one year Mr. Buffett would have earned 10 percent on his shares. Of course, only the 5 percent dividend payout would go into his pocket as a *realized* profit. The 5 percent "profit" from the price appreciation (as the stock rose in value) would be realized only if Mr. Buffett sold his Fifty Shades shares.

Warren Buffett, however, didn't become one of the world's richest men by trading shares that fluctuate in price. Studies have shown that, on average, people who trade stocks (buying and selling them) don't tend to make investment profits that are as high as those investors who do very little (if any) trading. What's more, to maximize profits, investors should reinvest dividends into new shares.

Doing so increases the number of shares you own. And the more shares you have, the greater the dividend income you'll receive. Joshua Kennon, a financial author at About.com (a division of the New York Times Company), calculated how valuable reinvested dividends are. He assumed an investor purchased $10,000 of Coca-Cola stock in June 1962. If that person didn't reinvest the stock's dividends into additional Coca-Cola shares, the initial $10,000 would have earned $136,270 in cash dividends by 2012 and the shares would be worth $503,103.

If the person had invested the cash dividends, however, the $10,000 would have grown to $1,750,000.[6]

Let's assume Mr. Buffett holds shares in Fifty Shades while reinvesting dividends. Some years, the share price rises. Other years, it falls. But the company keeps increasing its profits, so the share price increases over time. The annual dividends keep a smile on Buffett's face as he reinvests them in additional shares. His profits from the rising stock price coupled with dividends earn him an average return (let's assume) of 10 percent a year.

The Stock Market Stars as the Great Humiliator

Choosing a company to invest in isn't easy, even if you think you can predict its business earnings. Over the long term, stock price increases correlate directly with business earnings. But over a short period of time (and 10 years is considered a stock market blip), anything can happen. This is why the famous money manager Kenneth Fisher refers to the stock market as the Great Humiliator.[7] Over a handful of years, a company's business profits can grow by 8 percent per year, while the stock price stagnates. Or business earnings could limp along at 4 percent per year, while the stock market pushes the share price along by 13 percent.

Such a disconnection never lasts. Ultimately, a company's stock price growth will mirror its business' profit growth. If a stock's price appreciation outpaces business earnings, the stock price will either flatline or fall until it realigns with business earnings.

If business profit growth exceeds the stock's appreciation, at some point the stock will dramatically rise, realigning share price growth with that of business profits.

Connections between stock and business profits correlate strongly over long time periods—15 years or more. But over shorter periods, markets are mad because people are crazy.

Those trying to buy individual stocks need to forecast two things: future business earnings and people's reactions to those business earnings. For example, if financial analysts and the general investment public felt that Google's business earnings would grow by 15 percent next year, and the company's earnings grew by 13 percent instead, many shareholders would sell. No, I'm not suggesting such a move would be rational. It wouldn't be. But people aren't rational. Such selling would drop Google's share price, despite the impressive 13 percent business growth rate.

Predicting the general direction of the stock market is just as difficult. Even with a solid eye on the economy, human sentiment moves stock prices in the short term, not government policies or economic data. The existence of more buyers than sellers increases demand, so stock prices rise. Having more sellers than buyers increases supply, so prices fall. That's it—nothing more, nothing less. The stock market isn't its own entity, moving up and down like some kind of mystical scepter. Instead, its movements are a short-term manifestation of what people do. Are they buying or are they selling? We move stock prices: the aggregate activities of you, global institutional investors, and me. Our groupthink is so unpredictable that most economists can't determine the market's direction. To do so accurately, they would have to predict human behavior. And they can't.

For example, imagine if every US economist were rounded up on January 1, 2020, to listen to a creepy soothsayer in a cave. "The world will face a global pandemic in 2020," utters the cloaked, eyeless figure, as spit flies from his mouth onto the cold wet walls. "The US economy will shrink by 3.5 percent."

This happened in 2020 (except the soothsayer dude is fiction).[8]

But even if such a soothsayer really told economists this, they would never have predicted that the US stock market would soar 20.96 percent in 2020.

However, over the long term, there's always a direct correlation between business earnings and stock prices. Warren Buffett's former Columbia University professor, Benjamin Graham, referred to the stock market as a short-term voting machine or popularity contest, but a long-term weighing machine.[9] Business earnings and stock price growth are two separate things. But in the long term, they tend to reflect the same result. For example, if a business grew its profits by 1,000 percent over a 30-year period, the stock price, including dividends, would perform similarly.

It's the same for a stock market in general. If the average company within a stock market grows by 1,000 percent over 30 years (that's 8.32 percent annually), the stock market would reflect such growth.

Over the long term, stock markets predictably reflect the fortunes of the businesses within them. But over shorter time periods, the stock market is nuts.

Fast-Growing Economies Can Produce Weak Returns

Adding to the difficulty of predicting stock market growth is the fact that emerging stock markets don't seem to follow the same rules. For example, everybody knows that China's economic growth has run circles around US growth for the past 20 years. But here's a trivia question to ask a friend. Knowing what you know now, if you went back 27 years in a time machine with $10,000 to invest, would you want to spread your money among 100 randomly selected Chinese stocks or 100 randomly selected US stocks?

Most people would choose China. But they might end up feeling foolish. If $10,000 were invested in Chinese stocks in 1993, it would have been worth about $23,898 by March 31, 2021 (the time of this research). If, on the other hand, the same $10,000 were invested in US stocks, it would have grown to about $155,398.[10]

Such disparity between economic growth and stock market growth isn't prevalent just in China. Emerging markets (India, Thailand, Indonesia, etc.) have definitely benefited as villagers have migrated to cities, worked at better jobs, and spent higher wages. In some cases, their bathrooms were outhouses. Many of those same people now fart through silk. But shadier legal frameworks and poor corporate governance sometimes leave stains.

As Yale University finance professor David Swensen writes in his book *Pioneering Portfolio Management*, "A particularly prevalent problem in many Asian countries involves family-controlled companies satisfying family desires at the expense of external minority shareholder wishes."[11] Most global expats are aware of the corruption among many emerging-market businesses. Such palm greasing is one of the reasons strong economic growth doesn't always manifest itself in the stock market.

While emerging-market economic growth has run circles around US growth, the developed world's stock markets haven't been left behind.

If $100,000 were invested in US stocks in 1985, it would have grown to about $5.75 million by March 31, 2021. If it were invested in developed-world stocks (excluding the United States), it would have grown to roughly $2.36 million. If it were invested in emerging-market stocks from January 1985 until March 31, 2021, it would have grown to about $2.47 million.[12]

Don't, however, commit to believing US stocks will continue to win in the years or decades ahead. They might. But often, one time period's winner is the next time period's loser. Nobody knows which stock markets are going to do well this year or over the next decade. That's why smart investors are like the young gardener I mentioned at the beginning of this chapter. They sow every type of seed. They invest in a representation of the entire world's market so they don't get caught with their pants down when a sector takes off (or when a specific stock market sector falls off a cliff).

Many people hire advisors to guess which investment sectors they think will do well. But speculating is silly, as I'll show in later chapters. Instead of rolling the dice with a soothsayer, trying to predict which market will outperform, it's better to diversify money across every sector at the lowest possible cost.

Unfortunately, many global expatriates fail to do so. They chase whatever market has performed well lately (or over the past 15 years) to the detriment of everything else. And their retirements often pay the price.

Bonds Are Protective Nets for Jumpers

Besides investing in stocks, smart investors choose bonds as well. When investing in bonds, individuals loan a government or corporation money in exchange for a fixed rate of interest. Bonds underperform stocks—not every year or every decade, but over the long haul, they do. But they aren't as volatile. An investor, for example, with the majority of his or her money in bonds issued by a developed country's government wouldn't suffer a 50 percent investment loss if the stock market dropped by half. In some cases, such an investor might gain money when stocks drop.

Investment portfolios composed of stocks and bonds are less volatile and more diversified than those made up solely of stocks. So they're safer. In the short term, investments get yanked about based on supply and demand. When demand for stocks is especially high (many more buyers than sellers), stocks rocket. But for stocks to rise so quickly, people would be buying them with abandon. Where do they get such money for their stock market purchases? Many pull proceeds from savings accounts, mattresses (if they're nuts), gold, real estate, and bonds. If enough money is pulled from gold, real estate, and bonds, these asset classes fall in price.

Their supply would exceed their demand. When stocks are roaring, investors selling bonds can force bond prices to drop. Always remember that short-term asset class movements are a result of supply and demand. If more people are selling bonds than buying, supply outweighs demand. So bond prices fall. If more people are buying bonds than selling, bond prices rise.

You don't have to know the intricacies of how bonds work. Just make sure your portfolio includes a government bond index (which I'll explain later in the book). If, however, you want to know how bonds work, here it is in a nutshell.

There are a few different types of bonds, but I'll explain the most common with a story. Assume your eccentric Uncle James wants you to save, so he makes you a deal. If you give him $10,000, he'll invest the money for himself however he sees fit. You arrange for him to keep the money for five years. In the meantime, he gives you cash interest. He promises 5 percent per year. This is called a 5 percent coupon.

In this case, the yield is also 5 percent. Uncle James promises to pay you $500 annually. He pays it twice a year, $250 each time.

At the end of the five-year term, Uncle James will return the $10,000. You will have recouped the $10,000, plus earned $500 for every year your uncle held your money.

But what if you had asked him to return the $10,000 before the end of the five-year term? This is where Uncle James's quirkiness shines. He may decide to return just $9,800. Or he may give you a gift, handing over $10,300.

Uncle James guarantees he'll return exactly what you give him only if he's able to hold the money for the duration agreed upon. If you want the money early, the strange duck might return more than you gave him, or less.

Here's where Uncle James gets weirder. Assume that one year after you invested your initial $10,000 with him, your friend Amy wants in on the action. She approaches your uncle, who makes her a deal. "Amy, you can buy into the same scheme, but it expires in four years. This means you have only four years to earn interest, not five. I'm returning all of the money four years from now—yours (if you choose to invest) and my nephew's." But bank interest rates have risen, so Amy starts wondering why she would invest with your uncle when the interest rate he promises is now lower than what she can earn elsewhere. "I'll tell you what," says Uncle James. "If you invest just $9,500, I'll pay you $500 per year (equivalent to 5 percent of $10,000), but when the term expires in four years, I'll give you $10,000 instead of just the $9,500 you invested."

In such a case, the investment's coupon is 5 percent of $10,000. It was the set interest rate on the initial $10,000 investment deal you made with Uncle James. But the investment yield is higher for Amy because she gets her $500 per year at a discount. She invests $9,500, will earn $500 per year in interest, and will receive $10,000 back at the end of four years. Consequently, her investment yields 5.3 percent per year.

If bank interest rates had dropped instead, Uncle James would have done something different. Realizing what a great deal he was offering compared to the dropping interest rates of the banks, he would have told Amy, "You can invest in this scheme. You will receive a 5 percent coupon on $10,000 but it will cost you $10,500, not $10,000. Therefore, your yield would be 4.8 percent, not 5 percent, because I'll return less than what you invested. It would still be profitable, of course, because you would receive $500 per year. But it would be less so."

If you followed this strange little story, then you'll understand how most bonds work. Newly issued bonds have an expiration term and a fixed rate of interest. Investors purchasing such bonds when they're launched earn the same coupon and yield. If the interest paid amounts to 3 percent per year, this is what investors will make each year if they hold the bonds to maturity. If they sell early, they would receive more or less than what they deposited, depending on current bond prices. If they hold the bonds to maturity, they would receive exactly what they had invested, plus the cash interest they had earned twice a year.

Other investors can jump into a bond after the initial launch date. But if demand for bonds is high, they'll pay a premium for the bond. So their yield will be lower than the coupon rate that was advertised when the bond was launched. If demand for bonds is lower (this occurs when bank interest rates rise), bond prices drop. This increases the yield for new investors jumping into the same bond.

Can You Lose Money with Bonds?

Those buying low-grade corporate bonds from companies with shaky financial foundations can certainly lose money. To entice investors, such companies offer higher than average interest rates. For example, assume a new technology company needs money for research and development. It might issue a bond with a 10 percent coupon, which is well above typical rates. But if the company goes bankrupt, investors might lose some or all of their original capital. It could get flushed down the toilet, along with the company's future.

Likewise, investors loading up on long-term bonds can lose money in *real* terms. Remember that a real return is the profit made after inflation. If investors bought bonds maturing in 20 years with coupons of 3 percent per year, inflation could devour the profits. Sure, they would still earn 3 percent per year on their investment. But if inflation averaged 4 percent, the investor's real return would be negative. Such interest payments would lose to the rising price of a box of corn flakes.

That's why I recommend shorter term or broad market government bond index funds. Every year you'll see a "Bonds Are Going to Crash" headline. They might quote some crazy banker whose mother dropped him on his head.

In Figure 1.2, you can see the sleepiness of a broad US government bond index. The roller-coaster line on top is the S&P

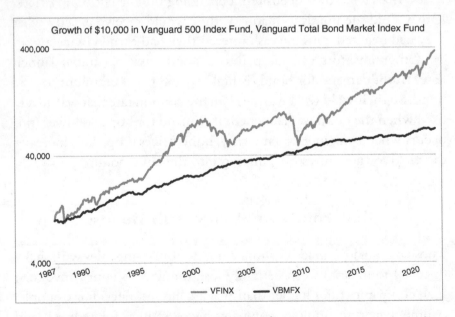

Figure 1.2   Bonds Are More Stable Than Stocks
SOURCE: Vanguard.com.

500 (VFINX). You should be able to see the stock market crash of 1987, the crash of 2002–2003, the crash of 2008–2009 and the mid-2020 dip. The line below it represents Vanguard's US Bond Market Index (VBMFX) with all interest reinvested. Compared to the stock market's movement, government bond index funds don't crash.

Patience, diversification, and low investment costs are keys to large profits in the stock and bond markets. To earn such returns, however, investors must avoid the industry's traps. Let me show you how.

Chapter Take-Away

1. Stocks earn strong, long-term returns. Historically they have averaged about 10 percent per year. But calendar year returns are wildly inconsistent. Stocks almost never record a calendar year gain between 9 percent and 11 percent.
2. Investors shouldn't focus on short time periods. Even for someone who's 60 years old, returns over a 30-year duration are far more relevant.
3. Nobody can consistently predict how stocks will perform, so it's best not to try.
4. Fast-growing economies don't always produce the best returns, which is why smart investors include exposure to the entire world's markets.
5. Bonds add safety to a portfolio, increasing stability.

Notes

1. "S&P 500 Index," Bogleheads. Accessed August 19, 2021. www.bogleheads .org/ wiki/S%26P_500_index; Morningstar.com.
2. "Why detached home Prices in Greater Vancouver have been rising, while condo prices have remained stagnant," *CBC News,* February 3, 2021: https:// www.cbc.ca/news/canada/british-columbia/pandemic-real-estate-vancouver-1.5898782, accessed August 10, 2021.
3. Moneysense.ca (1976–2010 data), Portfoliovisualizer (2010–2021 data, using iShares ETFs, XSP, XBB, XIC).

4. Stingy Investor, Asset Mixer Portfolios: http://www.ndir.com/SI/articles/Asset-Mixer-Portfolios.shtml
5. Vanguard.com (using prospectus from Vanguard's Global Stock Market Index). Accessed February 10, 2021. https://personal.vanguard.com/us/funds/snapshot?FundId=0628&FundIntExt=INT
6. Joshua Kennon, "Reinvesting Dividends vs. Not Reinvesting Dividends: A 50-Year Case Study of Coca-Cola Stock." Accessed May 1, 2017. www.joshuakennon.com/reinvesting-dividends-versus-not-reinvesting-dividends-coca-cola/.
7. Kenneth L. Fisher, Jennifer Chou, and Lara Hoffmans, *The Only Three Questions That Count: Investing by Knowing What Others Don't* (Hoboken, NJ: John Wiley & Sons, 2007).
8. Rachel Siegel, Andrew Van Dam and Eric Werner, "2020 was the worst year for economic growth since World War II," The Washington Post, January 28, 2021, accessed August 10, 2021, https://www.washingtonpost.com/business/2021/01/28/gdp-2020-economy-recession/
9. "The Voting and Weighing Machines," *Morningstar News*. Accessed May 1, 2017. http://news.morningstar.com/classroom2/course.asp?docId=142901&page=7
10. "China Wealth Proves Elusive as Stocks Earn 1% in 20 Years," Bloomberg.com. Accessed May 1, 2017. www.bloomberg.com/news/2013-07-14/china-wealth-eluding-foreigners-as-equities-earn-1-for-20-years.html
11. David F. Swensen, Pioneering Portfolio Management: An Unconventional Approach to Institutional Investment (New York: Free Press, 2000).
12. Portfoliovisualizer.com

Chapter 2

Don't Start a Fight with an Escalator

A dmit it. When you were a kid, you were tempted at least once to run up an escalator that was heading down. Sure, it was tougher than taking the stairs, but mastering the mechanical monster was part of the fun.

Unfortunately, most global expatriates trudge against an escalator full-time with their investments.

I could use any of the world's stock markets to explain this. But in honor of roast beef, Yorkshire pudding, and mushy peas, let's give a nod to the British.

During the decade ending September 30, 2021, the typical UK stock earned 95.52 percent.[1]

This means £10,000 invested in the average British stock grew to £19,552. Did most British investors make such profits? Not even close. Instead, most financed the lavish lifestyles of those working in the financial services industry.

If every stock on the British market were sold, most of the direct recipients would be pension funds, unit trusts (mutual funds), college endowment funds, and hedge funds. The money would then be paid to investors with stakes in such products. Because the vast majority of the money in the markets is professionally managed, when the UK market earns 95.52 percent over a given decade, it means the average professional fund earned roughly 95 percent—before fees.

The same premise applies to other countries' stock markets. As a group, because institutional and unit trust money represents the vast majority of assets invested in a given market, the average institutional investor and unit trust will earn (on average, before fees) the market's return. William F. Sharpe explained this in the *Financial Analysts Journal* in 1991, one year after he won the Nobel Prize in economic sciences.[2]

It's easy to visualize with a story. Imagine 100 students in a school called Unit Trust. Assume all 100 take an exam, and the school invites four or five kids from outside the district to join them. If the average exam score were 80 percent, the average Unit Trust student would have earned close to 80 percent. The four or five students from outside the district would not affect the average.

In the same vein, because institutional and unit trust money comprises nearly all of the assets in the British market, the return of the stock index will be close to the average British professional's stock market performance.

Yes, the Financial District Loves You!

You don't need to be Stephen Hawking to know that those in the British financial district don't work for free. Instead, they're among the highest-paid people in Britain. Who pays them? British investors, of course. If you invest in a pension or a unit trust, you're paying their salaries.

Most retail investors buy actively managed unit trusts. In North America, they're called actively managed mutual funds. In most cases, they're purchased through an intermediary advisor or broker. The broker then puts the money into a mutual fund. Once there, the cash gets pooled with money from other investors, like your Aunt Lucy, your friend Bob, and the strange homebound bloke with the telescope.

A fund manager then trades stocks within the unit trust. A large brokerage house charges commissions for each trade. But neither the fund manager nor his or her firm is generous enough to pay those commissions. Instead, the costs are skimmed from the mutual fund's proceeds. Can you see where this is headed?

The brokerage firm incurs other costs as well: salaries for employees, research expenses, electricity expenses, advertising expenses, lease expenses, and often a commission for the broker selling the products. Owners of the firm, as well, demand their share of profits. Where does this money come from? It all gets siphoned from the investment assets. Can you hear that escalator whirling?

Recall that the typical British stock earned 95.52 percent for the decade ending September 30, 2021. This means the typical professional investor (in British stocks) earned about the same. But that's before fees.

Add the plethora of costs, and the escalator starts smoking. It's a mathematical certainty that the average retail investor earns nothing close to the return delivered by the average stock, also known as the market average. Whether investors are Canadian, American, European, or Australian, they pay insidious fees to the financial services industry. Such costs jeopardize their futures.

Most of these fees, of course, are hidden from your investment statement. But they're real. And they're punishing. They also draw the ire of many.

Global Investors Getting Fleeced

Warren Buffett says, "Full-time professionals in other fields, let's say dentists, bring a lot to the layman. But in aggregate, people get nothing for their money from professional money managers."[3] David Swensen, Yale University's endowment fund manager, suggests that the government needs to stop the mutual fund industry's exploitation of individual investors.[4]

"Talk about irony!"

Illustration by Chad Crowe: Printed with permission.

Jack Meyer, the leader of Harvard University's endowment fund, says, "The investment business is a giant scam. It deletes billions of dollars every year in transaction costs and fees."[5]

Perhaps you're shaking your head right now. "These blokes are Americans," you're thinking. "We all know Wall Street gouges the typical Yank."

Table 2.1 Single-Year Profits Siphoned by Financial Industry When Markets Earn 6 Percent

Country	Average Mutual Fund Costs	Percentage of Annual Profits Lost by the Investor
Australia	1.26%	21.0%
Belgium	1.75%	29.16%
Canada	2.23%	37.16%
China	1.73%	28.83%
France	1.76%	29.37%
Germany	1.46%	24.33%
Hong Kong	1.72%	28.66%
India	2.22%	37.0%
Italy	2.07%	34.5%
New Zealand	1.38%	23.0%
Singapore	1.74%	29.0%
Spain	2.0%	33.3%
Taiwan	1.91%	31.83%
United Kingdom	1.28%*	21.37%
United States	0.67%*	11.16%

NOTE: The average US and UK and Australian mutual fund costs are lower because they include index mutual funds, which I discuss in the following chapter.
SOURCE: Morningstar, Global Fund Investor Experience Study.

Do investors in other countries pay such fees? The answer is no. Most non–Americans pay *much more*.

Morningstar's Global Fund Investor Experience Study compares mutual fund costs around the world. As seen in Table 2.1, British investors pay 91 percent more than Americans pay. Canadians pay 132 percent more than Americans pay.[6]

Understanding the impact of fees is important. If you're paying 2 percent in annual fees each year to have your money managed, you may see this as a paltry sum. But it isn't. If the markets make 6 percent in a given year and you're paying 2 percent in fees, then you're giving away 33 percent of your profits to the financial services industry.

Table 2.1 shows the percentages of annual fees paid by international investors. More important, note the annual profits that investors would lose if their respective stock markets earned 6 percent next year.

During years when stock markets don't perform well, the industry takes an even bigger chunk of your profits. Assume the German stock market earns 3 percent in a given year. The typical German fund investor pays a 1.46 percent annual fee. In this case, the average mutual fund (unit trust) investor relinquishes 48.6 percent of his or her annual profit.

High fees create a maddening process of two steps forward and one step back. Fortunately, there's an alternative. And by choosing it, global expats give less to the financial services industry and much more to themselves.

In the chapters ahead, I'll show how to bypass a fight with a downward-heading escalator.

Chapter Take-Away

1. The financial services industry's main goal is to make money from you, not for you.
2. The typical investor loses substantial sums over time to hidden investment fees.
3. When stocks don't perform well, hidden fees take an even bigger bite from the profits you would have earned.

Notes

1. "MSCI UK Index," iShares UK. www.ishares.com/uk/individual/en/products/253739/ishares-msci-uk-ucits-etf
2. William F. Sharpe, "The Arithmetic of Active Management," *Financial Analysts Journal*, 1991. Accessed August 4, 20121. www.stanford.edu/~wfsharpe/art/active/active.htm
3. Warren Buffett and Janet Lowe, *Warren Buffett Speaks: Wit and Wisdom from the World's Greatest Investor* (New York: John Wiley & Sons, 1997).
4. David F. Swensen, *Unconventional Success: A Fundamental Approach to Personal Investment* (New York: Free Press, 2005).
5. John C. Bogle, *Don't Count On It*, (New York, John Wiley & Sons, 2010), pg. 89.
6. Morningstar.com, Global Investor Experience Study. Accessed December 30, 2019, https://www.morningstar.com/lp/global-fund-investor-experience

Chapter 3

Where Are the Customers' Yachts?

An out-of-town visitor was being shown the wonders of the New York financial district. When the party arrived at the Battery, one of his guides indicated some handsome ships riding at anchor. He said,

"Look, those are the bankers' and brokers' yachts."

"Where are the customers' yachts?" asked the naïve visitor.

—Fred Schwed, *Where Are the Customers' Yachts?*[1]

If you've never read an investment book before, chances are you've never heard of index funds. Financial advisors rarely like to discuss them. Index funds are flies in caviar dishes for most financial advisors. From their perspective, selling them to clients makes little sense. If they sell index funds, they make less money for themselves. If they sell actively managed mutual funds, financial advisors make more. It really is that simple.

Most expats, however, should be interested in funding their own retirement, not somebody else's.

The term *index* refers to a collection of something. Think of a collection of key words at the back of a book, representing the book's content. An index fund is much the same: a collection of stocks representing the content in a given market.

For example, a total Australian stock market index is a collection of stocks compiled to represent the entire Australian market. If a single index fund consisted of every Australian stock, for example, and nobody traded those index fund shares back and forth (thus avoiding transaction costs), then the profits for investors in the index fund would perfectly match the return of the Australian stock market before fees. Stated another way, investors in a total Australian stock market index would earn roughly the same return as the average Australian stock.

Global Investors Bleed by the Same Sword

Now toss a professional fund manager into the mix—somebody trained to choose the very best stocks for the given fund. Unfortunately, the fund's performance will likely lag the stock market index. Most active funds do. And the actively managed funds that do beat their benchmark indexes over one measured time period usually lag the index during the next time period. That's why buying actively managed funds (especially those with strong recent track records) doesn't make sense. Regardless of the country you choose, actively managed mutual funds sing the same sad song.

Recall why from the previous chapter. Professionally managed money represents nearly all of the money invested in a given market. Consequently, the average money manager's return will equal the return of the market—before fees. Add costs, and we're trying to run up that downward-heading escalator.

Consider the UK market. According to Morningstar's Global Fund Investor Experience Study, the average mutual fund in Great Britain costs 1.28 percent each year.[2] Regardless of the market, the average professionally managed fund will underperform the market's index in equal proportion to the fees charged. Often, the reality is even worse.

Ron Sandler, former chief executive for Lloyds of London, reported a study for *The Economist*, suggesting that the average actively managed unit trust in Great Britain underperformed the British market index by 2.5 percent each year. Fees contributed to those poor returns.[3]

You might think that's nothing...a bit like a waiter's tip. But it's more like the tip of an iceberg. Here's an example. A 30-year-old investor might have an investment time horizon of 55 years. She would start selling parts of her portfolio once she retires. But she would keep most of the money invested, selling portions of the portfolio each year to cover retirement living costs.

If someone invested £5000 and it averaged 8 percent per year, it would grow to £344,569. But if £5000 averaged 5.5 percent per year, it would grow to just £95,028.

Not all actively managed funds fall behind their benchmark indexes. But most of them do. According to the SPIVA Scorecard, 83.22 percent of US actively managed stock market funds underperformed the broad US stock market index over the 10 years ending December 31, 2020.[4]

Canadians shouldn't feel smug after seeing these results. Canadians pay the second-highest investment fees in the world (after the expats who buy offshore pensions). During the 10-year period ending December 31, 2020, the broad Canadian stock index beat 84.29 percent of actively managed Canadian stock market funds. Canadian mutual fund companies also created funds that focus on US stocks.

Over that same time period, 95 percent of Canada's actively managed funds that focus on US stocks underperformed the broad US stock market index.[5]

Other countries' actively managed funds don't perform any better. Over an investment lifetime, beating a portfolio of index funds with actively managed funds is about as likely as growing a giant third eye.

American Expatriates Run Naked

Unlike most global expats, Americans can't legally shelter their money in a country that doesn't charge capital gains taxes. And actively managed mutual funds attract high levels of tax. There are two forms of American capital gains taxes. One is called *short-term*, the other *long-term*. Short-term capital gains are taxed at the investor's ordinary income tax rate. Such taxes are triggered when a profitable investment in a non-tax-deferred account is sold within one year.

I can hear what you're thinking: "I don't sell my mutual funds on an annual basis, so I wouldn't incur such costs when my funds make money." Unfortunately, if you're an American expat invested in actively managed mutual funds, you sell without realizing it. Fund managers do it for you by constantly trading stocks within their respective funds. In a non-tax-sheltered account, it's a heavy tax to pay.

Stanford University economists Joel Dickson and John Shoven examined a sample of 62 actively managed mutual funds with long-term track records. Before taxes, $1,000 invested in those funds between 1962 and 1992 would have grown to $21,890. After capital gains and dividend taxes, however, that same $1,000 would have grown to just $9,870 in a high-income earner's taxable account.[6] American expats, as I'll explain in a later chapter, must invest the majority of their money in taxable accounts. If that sounds depressing, it's good to know that index fund holdings don't get actively traded, so they trigger minimal capital gains taxes until investors are ready to sell. And when such holdings are sold, they're taxed at the far more lenient long-term capital gains tax rate, as opposed to the higher short-term capital gains tax rate paid by investors in actively managed funds.

Why Brokers Want to Muzzle Warren Buffett

Most financial advisors wish to muzzle the brightest minds in finance: professors at leading business universities, Nobel Prize laureates in economics, the (rare) advisors with integrity, and billionaire businessmen like Warren Buffett. Brokers make more when experts are mute.

Warren Buffett, chairman of Berkshire Hathaway, is well known as history's greatest investor. And he criticizes the mutual fund industry, suggesting, "The best way to own common stocks is through an index fund."[7]

That's why Warren Buffett instructed his estate's trustees to put his heirs' proceeds into index funds when the great man dies.[8]

Nobel laureate Sharpe explains it's delusional for most people (and most advisors) to anticipate beating market indexes over the long term. In a 2007 interview with Jason Zweig for *Money* magazine, he stated his view:

Sharpe: The only way to be assured of higher expected return is to own the entire market portfolio. You can easily do that through a simple, cheap index mutual fund.

Zweig: Why doesn't everyone invest that way?

Sharpe: Hope springs eternal. We all tend to think either that we're above average or that we can pick other people [to man- age our money] who are above average . . . and those of us who put our money in index funds say, "Thank you very much."[9]

Daniel Kahneman, another famed Nobel Prize–winning economist, echoed the sentiment during a 2012 interview with the magazine *Der Spiegel*:

"In the stock market . . . the predictions of experts are practically worthless. Anyone who wants to invest money is better off choosing index funds, which simply follow a certain stock index without any intervention of gifted stock pickers . . . we want to invest our money with somebody who appears to understand, even though the statistical evidence is plain that they are very unlikely to do so".[10]

Merton Miller, a 1990 Nobel Prize winner in economics, says even professionals managing money for governments or corporations shouldn't delude themselves about beating a portfolio of index funds:

Any pension fund manager who doesn't have the vast majority—and I mean 70 percent or 80 percent of his or her portfolio—in passive investments [index funds] is guilty of malfeasance, nonfeasance, or some other kind of bad feasance! There's just no sense for most of them to have anything but a passive [indexed] investment policy.[11]

In the documentary program *Passive Investing: The Evidence the Fund Management Industry Would Prefer You Not See*, many of the world's top economists and financial academics voice the futility of buying actively managed funds. But as the title suggests, it's the program most financial advisors will never want you watching.[12]

Financial Advisors Touting "The World Is Flat!"

Your financial education is the biggest threat to most globetrotting financial advisors seeking expatriate spoils. Consequently, many are motivated to derail would-be index investors from gaining financial knowledge.

Self-Serving Argument Stomped by Evidence

Here is one of the most common arguments you'll hear from desperate advisors hoping to keep their gravy trains running:

Index funds are dangerous when stock markets fall. In an active fund, we can protect your money in case the markets crash.

This is where a salesperson tries scaring you—suggesting that active managers have the ability to quickly sell stock market assets before the markets drop, saving your mutual fund assets from falling too far during a crash. And then, when the markets are looking safer (or so the pitch goes), a mutual fund manager will then buy stocks again, allowing you to ride the wave of profits back as the stock market recovers.

There are problems with this smoke screen. First, nobody should have all of his or her investments in a single stock market index fund. They should own a global representation of stocks and a bond market index for added stability. Bonds are loans investors make to governments or corporations in exchange for a guaranteed rate of interest.) If the global stock markets dropped by 30 percent in a given year, a diversified portfolio of stock and bond market indexes wouldn't do the same.

Have some fun with self-proclaimed financial soothsayers. Ask which calendar year in recent memory saw the biggest stock market decline. They should say 2008. Ask them if most actively managed funds beat the total stock market index during 2008. If they say "yes," you've exposed your Pinocchios.

SPIVA published detailed proof. In 2008, US stocks plunged 37 percent. But despite that horrible year, the US stock index beat 64.23 percent of actively managed US stock market funds.[13]

Global stocks fell 40.11 percent in 2008. Yet the global stock market index still beat 59.83 percent of actively managed global stock market funds during that calendar year.[14]

Warren Buffett wagered a $1 million bet in 2008, unveiling more damning evidence against expensive money management. A few years previously, the great investor claimed nobody could handpick a group of hedge funds that would outperform the US stock market index over the following 10 years.

Hedge funds are like actively managed mutual funds for the Gucci, Prada, and Rolex crowd. To invest in a hedge fund, you must be an accredited investor—somebody with a huge salary or net worth. Hedge fund managers market themselves as the best professional investors in the industry. They certainly have plenty of flexibility. Hedge funds (according to marketing lore) make money during both rising and falling markets. Managers can invest in any asset class they wish; they can even bet against the stock market. Doing so is called "shorting the market," where fund managers bet that the markets will fall, and then collect on those bets if they're right.

Buffett, however, doesn't believe people can predict such stock market movements, charge high fees to do so, and make investors money.

Hedge Fund Money Spanked for Its Con

Grabbing Warren Buffett's gauntlet in 2008, New York asset management firm Protégé Partners bet history's greatest investor that five handpicked hedge funds would beat the S&P 500 index, a large US stock index, over the following 10 years. Protégé Partners selected five hedge funds with index-beating track records (each was actually a fund that contained winning hedge funds within it). But historical results are rarely repeated in the future.

The bet began in 2008. Stocks crashed that year, so it should have been a great year for hedge funds. If the fund managers could have predicted the crash, they would have pulled far ahead. But that didn't happen. In the years that followed, the S&P 500 ran like an Olympic Kenyan marathoner from a pack of pudgy men.

By January 2018, Buffett had won. Vanguard's S&P 500 Index gained 98 percent. The hedge funds were up just 24 percent. In fact, none of the funds of hedge funds kept pace with the S&P 500.[15]

If you've read Simon Lack's book, *The Hedge Fund Mirage*, these results won't surprise you. He says hedge funds produce horrible returns. Lack reveals that a portfolio balanced between a US stock index and a US bond index would have beaten the typical hedge fund in 2003, 2004, 2005, 2006, 2007, 2008, 2009, 2010, and 2011.[16] After his book was published, hedge funds continued to underperform the balanced stock and bond index in 2012, 2013, 2014, 2015, 2016, 2017, 2018, 2019 and 2020. In other words, a balanced stock market index beat the Masters of the Universe for 18 straight years . . . and counting.[17]

In fact, the hedge fund managers' shortfall was so poor that the managers could have worked for free (not charging their usual 2 percent per year plus 20 percent of any profits) and a balanced US index fund would have still given them a beating.

The global stock market index (which includes US and international stocks) also beat hedge funds to a pulp. Consider the hedge fund industry's failure to beat portfolios of market indexes. If they can't do it, what chance does your financial advisor have? If your advisor has Olympian persistence, you might hear this:

You can't beat the market with an index fund. An index fund will give you just an average return. Why saddle yourself with mediocrity when we have teams of people to select the best funds for you?

If the average mutual fund had no costs associated with it, then the salesperson would be right. A total stock market index fund's return would be pretty close to average. In the long term, roughly half of the world's actively managed funds would beat the world stock market index, and roughly half of the world's funds would be beaten by it. But for that to happen you would have to live in a fantasy world where the world's bankers, money managers, and financial planners all worked for nothing—and their firms would have to be charitable foundations.

If your advisor's skin is thicker than a crocodile's, you might hear this next:

I can show you plenty of mutual funds that have beaten the indexes. We'd buy you only the very best funds.

The SPIVA Persistence Scorecard proves that selecting mutual funds based on high-performance track records is naïve. Twice a year, the firm looks at the top performing actively managed funds: those that are among top 25 percent of performers. Then they wait a couple of years and determine what percentage of those winning funds remains among the top 25 percent of performers. Typically, about 75 percent of those "top-performing" fall from grace after just two years.[18]

Neither you nor your advisor will be able to pick the funds that will win over the next year or decade.

If the salesperson's tenacity is tougher than a foot wart, you'll get this as the next response:

I'm a professional. I can bounce your money around from fund to fund, taking advantage of global economic swings and hot fund manager streaks, and easily beat a portfolio of diversified indexes.

Sadly, many investors fall victim to their advisor's overconfidence. Instead of building diversified accounts of index funds, they build portfolios with actively managed funds that are on a hot streak. But the results typically lead to underperformance or disaster.

Why Most Investors Underperform Their Funds

If you're countering your advisor's market-beating claims with proof, he or she might start to panic. When the advisor's desperation peaks, you might hear this:

We use professional guidance to determine which economic sectors look most promising. With help from our professionals, we can beat a portfolio of index funds.

Colleges hire some of the brightest finance minds in the world to manage their endowment funds. They look at current trends, interest rates, corporate earnings and the economic landscape. But most of them lose to diversified portfolios of index funds. And those that win during one time period often lose the next. The publication,

Pensions & Investments compiled 10-year performances for 34 college endowment funds to June 30, 2020.[19] However, these US fund managers could have saved a lot of effort if they bought Vanguard's Balanced Institutional Shares Index (60 percent stocks, 40 percent bonds). It beat 77 percent of American college endowment funds over the previous 10 years.

That's a small case sample. But researchers Sandeep Dahiya and David Yermack studied a larger case sample of 35,262 US non-profit endowment funds. The researchers averaged their returns based on Internal Revenue Service filings from 2009–2018. On average, a balanced stock market index beat them by 3.97 percent per year.[20]

Armed with such knowledge, you should be able to fend off financial advisors selling inefficient investment products and saying that they (or their firm) can see the future (see Figure 3.1).

Are Most Financial Advisors Bad People?

When faced with evidence that conflicts with our beliefs, each of us should be able to change our mind. Several years ago, I thought financial advisors who built portfolios of actively managed funds fell under two categories: they were either naïve or evil (especially those selling offshore pensions to unwary expats). While some evil ones exist, most are just undertrained salespeople trying to make a buck from commissions and trailer fees. Their bias hurts investors, but it can hurt the advisors too. The most respected accreditation for financial advisors is a CFP (Certified Financial Planner or Chartered Financial Planner). Most financial advisors without this qualification are glorified salespeople with questionable training. But even the CFP training (which takes a fraction of the time to complete compared to a nurse, teacher, social worker or plumber's training) leaves most financial advisors woefully unqualified to build portfolios based on economic science.

One of these two dresses in an elaborate costume to make
you think he can predict the future. The other wears a turban.

Figure 3.1   Financial Advisors Can't Predict the Future
Illustration by Chad Crowe: Printed with permission.

I asked one of Canada's top financial planners, Benjamin Felix. He's a CFP with the firm, PWL Capital. "The CFP education program is designed to ensure that CFP professionals have a broad understanding of 12 topics core to the financial planning process," said Felix. "Investments is one of those topics . . . but there is no requirement to fully understand the evidence in favor of buying and holding low-cost index funds."[21] Edward Goodfellow, a CFP with PI Financial echoed the sentiment: "If advisors understood, from an academic perspective, how markets actually worked, they would be much more suited to provide advice. The problem is, markets are noisy and the advisors, investors and media get lost in the noise."[22] Olivia Summerhill, a Certified Financial Planner (CFP) with Summerhill Wealth

Management, in Washington State says the same thing: "During the Certified Financial Planning extensive training, the focus is not on investment vehicles. A CFP candidate does not get any training in their program if actively or passively managed funds are better for clients."[23] That's why, if you have a financial advisor who built you a portfolio of actively managed funds, don't be too upset. After all, most advisors pee in their own drinking water.

Finance researchers Juhani T. Linnainmaa, Brian T. Melzer, and Alessandro Previtero gained access to portfolio performances for 4,688 Canadian financial advisors and about 500,000 the advisors' clients between 1999 and 2013. It was no surprise to see that most of the advisors bought actively managed funds for their clients. But they bought similar funds for their personal portfolios.

When comparing their performances to an equal-risk adjusted portfolio of index funds or ETFs, the advisors underperformed by about 3 percent per year. Sure, the advisors paid fees that were higher than those charged by index funds or ETFs. But the advisors also chased past performance. They bought funds that were "doing well." But they didn't read the SPIVA Persistence Scorecard. They didn't learn that funds that perform well during one time period usually lag the next.

That's why the advisors' personal money, and their clients' money, underperformed by 3 percent per year. Compounded over the 15-year study, they unperformed similarly allocated portfolios of index funds by about 55 percent.

Chapter Take-Away and Tips

1. Index funds (or ETFs) beat most actively managed funds over time.
2. While some actively managed funds beat their counterpart index funds, you'll never know which will win ahead of time.
3. Nobody can predict what stocks or what economic sectors will perform well in the future. Most active mutual fund managers,

hedge fund managers and college endowment fund managers try. But as a result, they lose to similar, risk-adjusted portfolios of index funds.

4. Most people buy funds with hot track records or they follow a guru with a "winning record." Don't do that. Funds that win during one time period typically underperform the next, whether they're actively managed mutual funds, hedge funds or college endowment funds.

5. If you mention index funds to most financial advisors, most of them will try to fight you. Hold your ground. And remember that most financial advisors are not bad people. They are just undertrained and dealing with a conflict of interest.

Notes

1. Fred Schwed, *Where Are the Customers' Yachts? Or, A Good Hard Look at Wall Street* (New York: John Wiley & Sons, 1995), 1.
2. *Global Investor Experience Study*, Morningstar. Accessed August 11, 2021, https://www.morningstar.com/lp/global-fund-investor-experience
3. "Actively Cheated," *The Economist*, July 13, 2002. Accessed May 5, 2014. www.economist.com/node/1224513
4. "SPIVA US Scorecard," Accessed August 11, 2021, https://www.spglobal.com/spdji/en/documents/spiva/spiva-us-year-end-2020.pdf
5. "SPIVA Canada Scorecard," Accessed August 11, 2021, https://www.spglobal.com/spdji/en/documents/spiva/spiva-canada-scorecard-year-end-2020.pdf
6. Burton G. Malkiel, *A Random Walk Down Wall Street: The Time-Tested Strategy for Successful Investing*, 11th ed. (New York: W.W. Norton, 2012), 399.
7. Warren E. Buffett, "Chairman's Letter—1996." Accessed August 11, 2021. www.berkshirehathaway.com/letters/1996.html
8. "Berkshire Hathaway Inc., 2006 Annual Report." Accessed August 11, 2021, https://www.berkshirehathaway.com/letters/2006ltr.pdf
9. Jason Zweig, "The Man Who Explained It All," *CNNMoney*, July 6, 2007. Accessed May 5, 2014. http://money.cnn.com/2007/05/21/pf/sharpe.money mag/index.htm?postversion=2007070616
10. "Spiegel Interview with Daniel Kahneman: Debunking the Myth of Intuition," Spiegel Online. Accessed May 5, 2014. www.spiegel.de/international/zeitgeist/interview-with-daniel-kahneman-on-the-pitfalls-of-intuition-and-memory-a-834407-2.html

11. Peter Tanous, "An Interview with Merton Miller," Index Fund Advisors, February 1, 1997. Accessed May 5, 2014. www.ifa.com/Articles/An_Interview with_Merton_Miller.aspx

12. *Passive Investing: The Evidence the Fund Management Industry Would Prefer You Not See* (documentary), Sensible Investing. Accessed May 5, 2014. www.sensibleinvesting.tv/ViewAll.aspx?id=8B9BC346-E853-475D-9050-889E41CE0289 .

13. "Standard & Poor's Indices versus Active Funds Scorecard, Year End 2008," April 20, 2009. Accessed May 21, 2017. http://www.spindices.com/docu ments/spiva/spiva-us-year-end-2008.pdf

14. Ibid.

15. Andrew Hallam, "The Embarrassing Side of Buffett's Million-Dollar Bet," January 11, 2018. Accessed March 26, 2019. AssetBuilder. https://assetbuilder .com/knowledge-center/articles/the-embarrassing-side-of-buffetts-million-dollar-bet

16. Simon Lack, *The Hedge Fund Mirage: The Illusion of Big Money and Why It's Too Good to Be True* (Hoboken, NJ: John Wiley & Sons, 2012), 175.

17. Andrew Hallam, "The Couch Potato Portfolio Makes Hedge Funds Look Silly," November 19, 2020, accessed August 11, 2021. https://assetbuilder .com/knowledge-center/articles/the-couch-potato-portfolio-makes-hedge-funds-look-silly

18. "SPIVA Persistence Scorecard," accessed August 11, 2021, https://www .spglobal.com/spdji/en/spiva/article/us-persistence-scorecard/

19. *Pensions & Investments*, accessed August 11, 2021, https://www.pionline .com/section/endowments?field_emphasis_image=&title=&year=2020& order=field_pub_date&sort=desc

20. Sandeep Dahiya and David Yermack, "Investment Returns and Distribution Policies of Non-Profit Endowment Funds, accessed August 11, 2021, https:// papers.ssrn.com/sol3/papers.cfm?abstract_id=3291117

21. Interview with Benjamin Felix. E-mail interview by author, April 10, 2020.

22. Interview with Edward Goodfellow. E-mail interview by author, April 8, 2020.

23. Interview with Olivia Summerhill. E-mail interview by author, April 12, 2020.

Chapter 4

Expats Should Avoid Snakes In Suits

Thirty-seven year old Daniel Rix walked away from almost $19,000. No, he didn't decline a $19,000 payday to kiss a python on the mouth. Instead, he just sold his investment scheme. After doing so, his investment firm slapped Daniel with a $19,000 penalty.[1] You might ask, "Why would he sell everything and pay that penalty?" After all, his portfolio showed a gain of about $1000. He didn't need the money for a medical emergency, nor did he lose his job and need that money for food. But mathematically, he says it was the right move to make. That might sound crazy, so let me explain. Daniel had bought an investment-linked assurance scheme called a Zurich Vista plan. It's one of several similar schemes sold prolifically to expats.

If you're an expat, you or someone you know has almost certainly bought one of these products. They are the most commonly sold investment schemes in the Middle East, Asia, Africa and (surprisingly) mainland Europe. Such schemes pay financial salespeople sky-high commissions. Investors pay those commissions—without realizing that, at first.

These aren't the run-of-the mill, actively managed mutual fund products that I described in Chapter 3. These are much worse. They're insurance policies wrapped up as investment schemes. And typically, the salespeople who sell them and the firms that create them make out like bandits. Sam Instone is the CEO of the financial services company, AES International. He says such products are aggressively sold because brokers earn sky-high commissions for doing so. For example, Daniel began investing $1000 a month in a 25-year Zurich Vista policy in 2015. Instone explains: "As soon as Daniel signed the contract, his brokerage would have received a commission of about $13,500 from the Swiss insurance firm, Zurich International. Of that $13,500 commission, Daniel's advisor would have netted about $8,500. Whether Daniel's broker sold him a Zurich Vista policy, or an investment-linked assurance policy from Generali International, Friends Provident, Old Mutual [formerly Royal Skandia] or RL 360, the commissions paid to the brokerage and advisor would be similar on a 25-year plan. And who pays for that commission? Daniel does."[2]

The monthly sums that Daniel contributes over his first 18 months essentially pay for those commissions. That's why, if he tries to cash in his policy within the first 18 months, he receives nothing. Yes, you read that right. Daniel could contribute $1000 a month for 18 months. An extortionist could kidnap Daniel's Egyptian Sphinx cat (a super-ugly breed) and demand a $15,000 ransom. Assume Daniel's account statement said his investments were worth $18,800 after 18 months of contributions. That's money he could use to save his ugly cat. Now assume Daniel sees his advisor and begs, "Please, sell $15,000 so I can get my cat back." Unfortunately, the advisor would say something like this:

> "No Daniel, we realize your account says you have $18,800. However, the account's "surrender value" is the only one that matters. That's the money you have access to."

Distraught, Daniel might ask, "And what is my account's surrender value?" The advisor might smile sheepishly. "It isn't worth a penny," he says. "You can't have access to any of the money you contributed over the first 18 months."

Daniel doesn't really own an ugly cat. If he did, and he had no other funds, he might crowdsource that money to get his freaky feline back. Daniel did, however, cancel his policy after about 3 years. By then, the account's market value was $40,182.40. That's roughly $1000 more than what Daniel contributed. But his surrender value was about $21,000. In other words, after closing his account in December 2018, Daniel paid about $19,182.40 in early redemption penalties.

At first brush, you might ask yourself, "Why didn't he stick it out? If he kept his money with the firm for 25 years (the length of the policy) he wouldn't have to pay a redemption fee!" That's true. But Daniel says he saved more money by closing the account, compared to what it would cost him if he stayed. And Daniel is correct based on how much he would have paid in fees.

First, Daniel's policy charges him 4 percent per year on the money he contributed over the first 18 months. His first 18 deposits (one per month for 18 months) are known as "initial units." Secondly, Zurich International levies an additional annual charge of 0.75 percent per year on the total value of the account every year. Adding a cup of acid to an open wound, the mutual funds within Daniel's account charge additional expense ratio fees of about 1.75 percent per year. When such schemes include "mirror funds," which they often do, Zurich charges another 0.75 percent per year. You can access information on these charges with the referenced link to Zurich International in this chapter's endnotes.[3]

When we total Daniel's fees, he paid 8 percent per year on the money he contributed over the first 18 months. Those contributions (known as "initial units) would continue to be charged 8 percent annually over the duration of the 25-year plan. But to access the money Daniel contributed over the first 18 months, he would have to keep the money invested for the full 25 year term. If that money earned an 8 percent annual return (before all fees) Daniel wouldn't make a dime on his "initial units." The insurance company counts on that.

The $1000 a month that Daniel planned to keep contributing (after the first 18 months) would carry total annual charges as high as 4 percent per year (platform fees, actively managed fund fees and possible mirror charges).

Daniel had about 22 years left on his policy when he cashed in. He received about $21,000, after paying about $19,182.40 in "re-demption penalties." Assume he invested the remaining $21,000 in a diversified portfolio of low-cost index funds or ETFs. Assume a diversified portfolio (without fees) averaged 8 percent per year over those 22 years. If Daniel paid annual fees of 0.20 percent for his portfolio of index funds or ETFs, he would average 7.8 percent per year. Let's assume he invested his surrender value ($21,000) and added another $1000 a month for the next 22 years. In this case, Daniel would end up with about $785,840.

Now assume, instead, that he kept his high-cost investment policy. His initial units ($18,000) would likely be worth about $18,000 after 25 years, so we can add that on the end.

If his Zurich Vista policy cost him about 3.5 percent per year (on money deposited after the first 18 months) Daniel would average gains of about 4.5 percent per year, assuming the markets averaged 8 percent. In other words, as with the index fund investor, he would earn the return of the stock and bond market allocation, minus the fees charged.

Table 4.1 shows the breakdown of Daniel's portfolio, assuming a diversified allocation averaged 8 percent per year (before fees) over the next 22 years.

However, if a diversified allocation earned less than 8 percent per year over the next 20 years, Daniel would likely have less than $522,607.59. In this case, his initial units ($18,000) would be worth less than $18,000 because the market's gains wouldn't exceed the 8 percent fees charged on the initial units every year.

In contrast, Table 4.2 shows how Daniel's money would grow after cutting his losses and reinvesting what remained (his surrender value) in a portfolio of low-cost index funds or ETFs. Instead of ending up with about $522,607.59, he would have about $785,840.10.

I don't mean to pick on Zurich International. But based on Nobel Prize winner, William F. Sharpe's explanation in his Stanford based publication, "The Arithmetic of Active Management," Daniel would earn the market's return, minus the fees he paid. It's tough to argue against the laws of mathematics. Years after buying these schemes, investors often feel hoodwinked. But they shouldn't be embarrassed. Daniel Rix, who works as a finance director at a multi-national company in Dubai says, "I know several people who have been burned on these schemes, including me. It happens at all levels of the employment spectrum and the salespeople are so convincing. It's easy to get sucked in."[4]

Thirty-eight year old IT professional, Farai Patrick Dunduru agrees. The Dubai-based expat, originally from Harare, Zimbabwe, bought a 15-year scheme through Hansard International. Farai added money for six months before pulling the plug and licking his wounds. Because he was still in the "initial units" phase, he lost everything he invested. Like Daniel Rix, Farai knew the longer he remained with the plan, the higher the long term opportunity costs would be. "Smarter people [than me] have fallen for the same schemes," he says. "The hunters [financial salespeople] know the right buttons to push and they are very manipulative, so other victims should not feel embarrassed."[5]

Table 4.1   Daniel's Zurich Vista Account: If He Stayed The Course Assuming A Diversified Allocation (Before Fees) Averaged 8 Percent Per Year

Zurich Vista Policy

Approximate Market Value After 3 years	$40,182.40	This was approximately Daniel's "current value" as of December 2018.
Initial unit contributions	$18,000	This money would attract fees of about 8% per year over the remaining 22 years of Daniel's policy plan. As a result, if a diversified portfolio averaged 8% per year, the initial units would be worth about $18,000 after more 22 years.
Approximate value of Daniel's regular contributions that he made after the first (18 months)	$22,182.40	This is the amount of money Daniel added to his account after the "initial unit" (first 18 month) period. This money would attract annual fees of about 3.5% per year for the remainder of the policy's term (25 years).
Continued Monthly Contributions for the next 22 years	$1000 per month	
Annual interest rate (after 3.5% annual fees) assuming portfolio returned 8% annually before fees	4.5%	
Approximate Account Value after 22 more years (not including initial units value)	$504,607.59	
Approximate Account value after adding $18,000 of initial units	$522,607.59	We added what Daniel contributed over the first 18 months (his initial units) to the total, but based on their sky-high fees of 8% per year, they would not likely make money.

Table 4.2 The Growth of Daniel's Money In A Low-Cost Portfolio Assuming A Diversified Allocation (Before Fees) Averaged 8 Percent Per Year

Diversified Portfolio of Low-Cost Index Funds or ETFs		
Approximate Market Value After 3 years	$21,000	This was Daniel's redemption value, after "losing" $20,000 to early redemption fees
Monthly Contributions	$1000 per month	
Annual interest rate (after 0.20% annual fees) assuming portfolio returned 8% annually before fees	7.8%	
Approximate Account Value After 22 More Years	$785,840.10	

Mark Gray, a 48-year old British physician working in Doha, Qatar bought a Zurich International Vista scheme in 2017. He invested £5,500 per month (about $7,800 USD) through a wealth manager at HSBC. He had hoped to get solid financial advice from one of the world's biggest banks. But instead, the wealth manager stuffed Dr. Gray's money into an investment-linked assurance scheme. Dr. Gray, who walked away from his account after making just six payments says he's one of the lucky ones. He also offers advice for people who bought similar products: "Get out now. You may lose money, but it will likely be much less than your potential loss if you continue to pay in."[6]

As previously mentioned, other offshore investment-linked assurance schemes include those from Generali International, Friends Provident, Old Mutual (formerly Royal Skandia) or RL 360. Some of them offer loyalty bonuses to investors who stay the course. They show up on the brokerage statement. But firms that offer such bonuses typically charge even more than the Zurich Vista policy, so the firms recoup those bonuses over time by charging extra fees.

Unfortunately, expats fall into these traps every single day. Financial salespeople rarely (if ever) reveal the entire truth. In 2015, *The Telegraph's* Katie Morley wrote *Exposed: The Rip-Off Investment "Advisors" Who Cost British Expats Billions.*[7]

She profiled a former employee of a large international advisory firm. He didn't have any financial training, beyond that of a week-long course. He alleged that the course included training to "psychologically manipulate customers into handing over their money." He added, "We were told to prepare clients' paperwork and put it in blue folders. But after [the customer] had signed on the dotted line we'd slip extra pages into the folders that they hadn't seen before, which included details of the charges."[8]

But they don't just target Brits. In 2015, a broker from The deVere Group approached Australian Tuan Phan in Abu Dhabi. The guy said Tuan should buy a Friends Provident Premier investment scheme. Its costs would have been more than 9 percent per year for the first 18 months (the initial units). After that, costs dropped to about 4 percent per year. On average, that's 20 times higher than the cost of a global stock market index fund. Tuan didn't know that, but as he began to sign the documents, he knew something wasn't right.

The documentation said it was an investment scheme with an insurance wrapper. But he didn't want insurance. "I told the advisor it wasn't a suitable product for me," he said. "I told him I didn't want it."

The advisor then recommended another product. "What's the difference between this one and the other one?" Tuan asked.

The salesperson replied, "This is more suitable for you. It doesn't contain an insurance wrapper." Unfortunately, Tuan says the guy performed a bait and switch. He used Tuan's original documents for the product he didn't want. Tuan had assumed that the previous documents (which contained his signature) were scrapped when Tuan said he didn't want the product. Without his knowledge, he had signed up for the original product—the one he had told the advisor he didn't want.

When Tuan learned that he had been duped, he complained to the regional head of the brokerage. According to Tuan, the regional leader said, "*We have your signature and we got our commission from Friends Provident. Deal with them if you want a refund!*"

Unfortunately, Friends Provident told Tuan to complain to deVere.[9]

The deVere Group Faces Trouble

In May 2017, Bloomberg profiled deVere. Journalists Zeke Faux, Benjamin Robertson, and Matt Robinson published "Firm Targeting Nest Eggs of UK Expats Faces SEC Probe." The story explains how the US branch of the deVere Group was being investigated by the SEC (Securities and Exchange Commission) for charging commissions on products without having a license to do so.

Bloomberg also says a Singapore subsidiary of deVere was fined in 2008. They were using unlicensed advisors and selling insurance products without a license.

In 2016, a former deVere subsidiary in Hong Kong was fined for using unlicensed advisors and for failing to provide information to a local regulator.

In Japan, deVere is on a list of firms that are not authorized to solicit investors.

Bloomberg also reports that South African authorities are investigating deVere over undisclosed fees and commissions.[10]

The deVere Group is one of the world's biggest sellers of expensive, inflexible, offshore investment schemes.

Such salespeople might fall under one of two categories:

1. Those with extremely low levels of financial education. They don't fully understand the products that they're selling.

   Or

2. Psychopaths or Machiavellians. They might understand the products. But they make them sound amazing so they can earn a big commission.

British Expats: Can I Trade You That Diamond for a Big Lump of Coal?

Imagine that you're entitled to a British government defined benefit pension. Before moving abroad, you worked in education, the military, nursing, or had a different public-sector government job. The British government says, "We'll give you a fixed monthly payment for life when you retire."

Then you move abroad. A snake in a suit slithers up to your gate. "You don't want that pension; let me offer something better."

You might wonder, "Who would want to get rid of their government pension?" But these snakes in suits possess septic silver tongues.

For a small number of people, it makes sense to cash them in and put the proceeds in a QROPS (qualified retirement overseas pension scheme).

But for most former government public sector workers, a QROPS doesn't make sense. Sarah Lord, head of financial planning at Killik & Co., a British FCA-regulated firm, was quoted in *The Telegraph* saying, "The operation of offshore advisers, in the main, is totally unscrupulous."[11]

I've visited plenty of international British schools. Sadly, most of the teachers had cashed in their UK government defined benefit pension plans. One teacher, who worked at Abu Dhabi's Brighton College, cried when she told me. "I transferred £300,000," she said, "but it's now worth only £180,000." Other times, investors lost everything when the money was directed into a UCIS (unregulated collective investment scheme).

UK-based financial advisor Ben Sherwood joined Hillier Hopkins in 1997 and became a partner in 2002. He's a Certified Financial Planner and Chartered Financial Planner for high-net-worth clients. He also holds investment and taxation qualifications and he's a co-author of *The 7 Secrets of Money: The Insider's Guide to Personal Investment Success* (SRA Books, 2013).

He was horrified to learn that many British expats cashed in their UK government teachers' pensions for QROPS schemes.

"The idea that most teachers with rights under the UK Teachers Pension Scheme should transfer is simply scandalous." He says transferring to a QROPS rarely makes sense. "The right QROPS can be the right answer for the right client in the right circumstances. But in our experience the likelihood of these stars aligning is very rare."[12]

I also asked Simon Glazier. The Chartered Financial Planner works for A+B Wealth. He won the United Kingdom's financial advisor of the year award in 2015.

"A pension transfer of this type is effectively a transfer of risk, from the government to the member," he says. "For many people such a transfer of risk is unacceptable, especially where they do not have significant financial resources in addition to their pension scheme. Moving money into a high charge, poorly regulated substitute pension, recommended by an 'adviser' who is incentivised to sell one to you, will almost always be a poor choice."[13]

Fortunately, the UK government has limited such transfers. Investors wanting a QROPS now pay a 25 percent tax. But for many expat teachers and former public-sector workers, the damage has been done.[14]

The 10 Habits of Successful Financial Advisors . . . Really?

Former expatriate financial advisor Frank Furness created a series of training videos for advisors. One of them is titled "The 10 Habits of Successful Financial Advisors." Not one of the habits deals with investors' welfare. Instead, the video outlines strategies expatriate advisors use to make millions of dollars a year in commissions. As Furness says, "For me, it's the best job in the world. Where else can I go out and meet somebody, drink their coffee, eat their cake, and walk out with $5,000 in my pocket? No other business."[15]

Much like car salesmen, many measure success by how many deals they can close. In a different video, Furness interviews Steve Young, a representative working for International Financial Services (Singapore). Furness describes Steve Young as one of the region's top advisors—one of "the true tigers in the industry." The advisor explains that his team puts prospective clients in front of him "to let me do what I'm good at, which is closing the deals out."

Young adds, "If I can delegate the paperwork, all I want to do is see the checks from the clients." The advisor is so good at selling, in fact, that he once established 198 new clients in a single calendar month, claiming to set a world record in the process. Furness closes the video by saying to the camera, "If you live anywhere in Asia, especially in the Singapore area, and you want to deal with the best... why not contact Steve?"[16] Unfortunately, "the best" advisor in sales lore isn't necessarily the best advisor for clients. Many advisors, in fact, consider the sales process a war between themselves and their clients.

When Your Advisor is a Sales Commando

In April 2014, online publication International Adviser highlighted quotes from Doug Tucker's book, *Sales Commando: Unleash Your Potential* (PG Press, 2014). Tucker, a former offshore pension seller, says that to generate clients "you have to go into full-frontal attack mode. This means huge, massive action. To do this you need a strategy, a plan of attack, and the absolute certainty you are going to win."

Before a prospective client can object to a product, Tucker suggests to advisors: "Create a mental picture of each objection as a small monster being born and figuratively popping out of the client's mouth. The minute you pay attention to the fledgling monster you will be feeding it with energy, because this little monster thrives on encouragement. The more you acknowledge its presence, the more it will grow and grow."[17]

Welcoming Sharks into the Seal Pool

Few expatriate employers understand how offshore pensions work. Yet many invite sharks into the company seal pools. Chip Kimball, superintendent at The International School of Prague, says, "Many international schools don't have any form of regulation, and little to no vetting or oversight regarding the financial products that salespeople try selling on campuses." Some schools embrace expensive, inflexible official providers, while encouraging staff to use them. "This is dangerous," adds Kimball. "High fees and commissions for poor financial products cost teachers dearly."[18] International teachers aren't the only expats at risk.

Here's how the process often begins. A representative from a brokerage firm slides into a workplace.

The broker convinces management to endorse the broker's firm, resulting in a ready-made customer base. Such brokers are intermediaries for offshore pension providers, many of which are based in the British Channel Islands, Luxembourg, or the Isle of Man.

This is what happened, years ago, at the Western Academy of Beijing (WAB). The administration, at the time, didn't know the difference between a legitimate financial advisor and a shark in a suit. I spoke at the school in 2015. The administration had offered to match part of the employees' savings into an investment plan. But the plan had to be on the school's approved list. Unfortunately, that list included brokerage firms that sold expensive offshore pensions. None of the firms on the list charged low fees. In each case, they sucked teachers and administrators into long-term, expensive offshore investment schemes.

After the teachers had learned what they had done, there was little they could do. Such firms pay huge commissions to the brokers who sell the products. To recoup that commission, firms like Friends Provident, for example, must keep the investor's money as long as possible. Doing so allows the company to reap more fees over time. As an investor adds more money, fees mount. But investors awakening to the tyranny of costs find their private parts stuck in a zipper. Early redemption penalties might cost 80 percent (or more) of the investor's total proceeds.

Jon Williams, formerly a British information technology (IT) worker in Dubai, explains how these offshore pensions can gain traction away from the workplace. "A friend of mine gave my contact information to an advisor working for PIC [Professional Investment Consultants]. It's an affiliate of the deVere Group." Jon met the representative in his apartment. "I wanted a breakdown of costs," says Jon, "so the advisor promised to send it the following day."

In return, the advisor wanted the names and contact details for 10 of Jon's friends or colleagues. "I felt Jedi mind-tricked by the guy and did what he asked." The following day, Jon received the breakdown of fees, entered the particulars into an Excel spreadsheet, and was horrified by the costs. "I didn't sign up, even though the rep told me he was offering a special one-time offer—one that needed an immediate decision." Promises of urgent, one-time offers should always raise red flags, whether you're buying financial products or a holiday time-share. Jon also asked the advisor not to contact his friends. "I made a lucky escape. But many of my friends weren't as fortunate."[19]

Let Me Offer You a Free Trip to the Maldives

One financial salesperson gunning for a huge commission sent Matthew Backus an unusual e-mail. She offered the Canadian a free trip for two to the Maldives.[20]

Matthew and his wife are educators. They live in Dubai. The Maldives would have offered a nice break from their giant urban sandbox. He just needed to introduce the financial advisor to some of his friends. She wanted a list of 10 names that included e-mails and phone numbers. If Matthew had agreed, he and his wife would have been on their way to the Maldives, with all expenses paid.

But Matthew didn't bite. He feared that if he gave her the names of his friends (even if he had warned his friends ahead of time), she might have convinced one of them to invest in an offshore investment scheme. If that actually happened, it would have been Matthew's fault.

Some financial advisors (I prefer to call them salespeople) earn more in a week than the typical teacher earns in a year. That's why they sometimes offer concert tickets, hotel stays, iPads, or free trips to the Maldives in exchange for phone numbers.

Fees of 4.5 Percent per Year? Really, That's Nothing!
An ever-increasing number of complaints about offshore investment schemes have been reported to The National (a media network based in Abu Dhabi). Many of the people calling in have lost a lot of money. The National's reporters, including Alice Haine, can relate to their complaints. She lost money too.

In 2017, the media network invited me to a roundtable discussion. As Alice Haine and Gillian Duncan wrote, "Insurers that operate the plans—Zurich International, Generali Worldwide, Friends Provident International, RL 360, and Hansard International—were all invited to attend the event but declined."[21]

Fortunately, representatives from deVere and Globaleye (two offshore investment scheme sellers) were present. The National recorded everything. At one point, they recorded me saying:

"If we have financial products that, all in, are costing 4.5 percent per year—and that is what we are seeing, 4.5 percent, 5 percent, sometimes higher—if you are looking at costs of 4.5 percent per year and you are looking at the advisor not doing anything silly and building a globally diversified platform and if markets end up making, let's say, 7 percent a year, and the investor is losing 4.5 percent in fees, what do we have left? We have 2.5 percent.

(*continued*)

"But we have inflation historically, which has run 3 to 3.5 percent per year. So it is my belief that you cannot retire effectively with the platforms that are sold prolifically throughout the Middle East."

Tim Searle sat across from me. He's the chairman of Globaleye. His firm's sales team flogs plenty of investment schemes, such as those offered by Friends Provident, Generali, Aviva, Royal Skandia (Old Mutual), Zurich International, and RL 360.

He responded to my claim that investment fees of 4.5 percent per year were outrageous:

"The guys at Goldman Sachs wouldn't get out of bed
for that kind of money, okay?"

Goldman Sachs is an American multinational finance company. They offer dozens of investment funds for stateside American retail investors. The Goldman Sachs Focused International Equity Fund (GSISX) is one of their most expensive funds. It costs 1.41 percent per year. Stateside Americans can buy it without any additional costs: no up-front sales charge, no cancellation penalty, no additional 18-month administrative charges, and no ongoing account fee.

Goldman Sachs also offers stateside Americans diversified portfolios wrapped up in a single fund. The firm's Target Date Retirement Funds, for example, cost about 0.49 percent per year. There are no additional charges or fees to sell at any time.[22]

The people at Goldman Sachs wouldn't just get out of bed if they could charge annual investment fees of 4.5 percent. Their heads would hit the roof.

Masters of the Insured Death Benefit Illusion

Those flogging offshore pensions, however, may point to the insured death benefit. It's often craftily worded. Hong Kong-based educator Steve Batchelor owned a Friends Provident investment scheme. This is how the death benefit in his scheme's prospectus was described:

In the event of the death of the Life Assured (or the last surviving Life Assured if the policy is written on more than one life) while the policy is in force, 101 percent of the cash-in value of your plan will be payable.

The literature accompanying the policy offered no other reference or explanation of what this meant. So I wondered: Did it mean the deceased earned a 101 percent bonus on top of the investment portfolio's actual value?

I had to call four separate advisors flogging Friends Provident pensions before one of them even attempted to explain the insurance policy. He said that if the policy holder (the investor) dies, then his or her heirs would receive the account's proceeds, or if the account were valued less than what was deposited into it, the surviving members (spouse, brother, sister, whoever was on the policy) would earn an amount equal to 101 percent of what the deceased had invested.

Manipulation with numbers is an art. The contract claims the descendant receives "101 percent of the cash-in value." But consider this. If I loaned you $5 and you gave the $5 back, you would have returned 100 percent of what I had loaned you. By offering 101 percent of the "cash-in value," Friends Provident offers to pay back 1 percent more than what was invested: not 1 percent per year, but 1 percent overall. There's no upward adjustment to cover inflation. If inflation averaged 3.5 percent per year, the insurance guarantee equals a real (inflation-adjusted) loss exceeding 40 percent for the decade, if the investor died while the portfolio was worth less than what he or she had deposited.

Free Fund Switching Isn't a Perk

Sales reps also promote the idea that clients dissatisfied with their fund performances can switch into other funds for free. Costs to switch into different funds are called sales loads. In a 2012 Bloomberg.com article titled "The Worst Deal in Mutual Funds Faces a Reckoning," Ben Steverman writes, "Those paying loads are the poorest and least sophisticated of investors."[23] Only the naïve would believe that free fund switching is a perk. Load fees are as easy to avoid as a 10-foot-wide drainage ditch.

Such costs are even banned in Australia and the United Kingdom.[24]

Expatriate workplaces, however, aren't the only feeding grounds for commission-hungry sales reps; some do almost anything to build a client base. Random cold calls aren't beneath them. A sales representative from Austen Morris Associates cold-called Icelander Lawrence Graham just three to four months after he became an expatriate.

"I have no idea how he found my number," Graham says. "The rep explained the expected returns over the next few decades and made it all sound fairly good: low expected returns for the first few years with exponential growth in the later years of the plan due to the larger amount of money that would have been invested by that point. But there's a lot they didn't tell me. I had no idea how much the fees would eat into my profits. The money I gave them during the first 18 months has to stay with the firm for 30 years. I can't take it out earlier without paying a hefty penalty. They didn't tell me that when I signed up."[25]

Making Millions off the General Public

With such massive commissions paid to brokers, sales of these products won't likely abate any time soon. When BBC Panorama investigated one of the largest offshore pension sellers, deVere Group, the investigators revealed that the company's top sales brokers earned on average more than £220,000 in the first three months of 2010. The top broker was on track to exceed £1 million for the year.

Penny Haslam reported such findings in the BBC Panorama documentary *Who Took My Pension?* After asking pension providers to supply data on charges, she revealed the most expensive pensions in Great Britain.

Here's how they stacked up if investors had contributed £120,000 over 40 years. Legal and General's Co-Funds Portfolio Pension would have taken £61,000 in fees, the Co-operative Bank's Personal Pension would have absconded with £95,900 in fees, and HSBC's World Selection Personal Pension would have lifted £99,900 in total fees.[26]

The documentary included costs of management fees in these calculations, but didn't include costs of actively managed funds within the pensions themselves. Doing so would have doubled total fees, aligning them closely with offshore pension costs.

Fooling the Masses with Numbers

While the offshore pension providers have subtle differences, most seduce investors with the promise of loyalty bonuses. But it's a smoke and mirrors show.

To dramatize an example, I'll introduce you to a hypothetical bonus platform that's far more generous than anything offered by an offshore pension. It's going to look amazing. But don't be fooled.

Hallam's offshore pension guarantees a 50 percent bonus on unlimited cash deposits. If you invest $10,000 each year, we'll chip in an extra 50 percent, ramping your invested proceeds to $15,000 per year.

Annual management charges are just 1.5 percent per year. How can you lose when receiving a 50 percent annual bonus?

In this fantasy broker scenario, I haven't included costs of the actively managed funds. If the fund expenses added another 2 percent per year, total costs for the account would run 3.5 percent per year

Table 4.3 Bonuses Don't Offset Costs

Investors Has $10,000 Per Year To Invest	Fantasy Offshore 50% Bonus Pension	Low–Cost Indexed Portfolio
Amount annually invested	$10,000	$10,000
Annual fantasy bonus paid on deposits	50%	0%
Total annual amount invested after bonus	$15,000	$10,000
Assumed global market's average return	10%	10%
Annual fees paid on total portfolio value	3.5%	0.2%
Annual returns after fees	6.5%	9.8%
Total portfolio value after 30 years	$1,379,838	$1,739,129

(1.5 percent for the management fee plus 2 percent for the mutual funds).

Still, that 50 percent bonus *appears* to trump the comparatively small 3.5 percent annual account charge. Or does it?

Keep in mind that no offshore pension firm offers a 50 percent bonus every year on annual deposits. But even if one did, investors could still get fleeced. Deception with numbers is an art. Not receiving a bonus but paying just 0.2 percent in annual fees would reap far greater rewards.

Table 4.3 lists the fantasy bonus pension alongside an indexed portfolio.

No offshore pension provider offers a 50 percent annual bonus on unlimited deposits every year. But even if one did, the investor could still end up hundreds of thousands of dollars poorer.

When High Fees Meet Gunslingers

Unfortunately, high costs aren't the only problem with offshore pensions. Many advisors selling them fail to build diversified portfolios. Diversification increases safety. Stuffing too many eggs into the same basket increases risk. And when the basket tips (all baskets tip at some point), the investment portfolio cracks.

Most offshore pension sellers aren't Certified Financial Planners (CFP) or Chartered Financial Planners. The CFP designation ensures that advisors have been trained to diversify their clients' money, spreading it across multiple asset classes and geographic regions. Instead, many offshore pension sellers obtain impressive-sounding three-letter credentials that require fewer than three weeks to obtain.

Former broker Shawn Wong says,

"People wanting to sell ILAS products [offshore pensions] don't require strict financial training. The firm I worked at often sold Friends Provident, Zurich, and Standard Life products because they offered high commissions and low-level entry points. Someone directly out of high school could pass the required licensing tests in a couple of weeks. The tests are easy, with minimal focus on multi-asset-class portfolio allocation and rebalancing. Not surprisingly, many client portfolios get built without adequate diversification. The focus on sales and commissions outweighs the need for a responsible portfolio."[27]

Odds are that those investing with a CFP or a Chartered Financial Planner won't suffer from a lack of diversification. But CFPs aren't all saints. Such an advisor looking for fat commissions *could* still push your money into an offshore pension. However, CFPs are more likely to diversify their clients' accounts across global stock and bond markets—instead of gambling everything on a few pet sectors.

Expatriates and their employers need to take responsibility. Some investment products are bona fide rip-offs. Others are solid. But when investors and employers don't know the difference, a lot of pain follows. In the following chapters, I'll explain what products you should buy instead.

Chapter Take-Away and Tips

1. Expats are golden targets for some of the world's worst financial investment schemes. If you wonder whether you own one, see if you can sell everything without the financial company penalizing

you (this wouldn't be a tax penalty, but a penalty levied by the investment firm). If you can't sell everything without paying a penalty, you are likely invested in an investment linked assurance scheme.

2. If you own one of these products, it typically makes sense to sell, pay the penalty, and invest the proceeds in a diversified portfolio of low-cost ETFs. When doing so, the odds of mathematics are strongly in your favor.

3. Don't be fooled by slick-talking salespeople or the promises of bonuses. People earn massive commissions to sell such products, and they'll do almost anything to earn such commissions.

4. If you are in a leadership position at your workplace, do not allow any financial salespeople through your doors. Don't make exceptions or excuses.

Notes

1. Interview with Daniel Rix. Email interview by author, February 2, 2021.
2. Interview with Sam Instone. Email interview by author, March 15, 2021.
3. "Zurich Collection Guide (Mirror, Managed and Money funds): For use with Vista, InvestPlus and Lifelong, https://www.zurichinternational.com/letsgo/uploads/msp13565-zurich-collection-guide-mirror-funds-(02-18).pdf
4. Interview with Daniel Rix. Email interview by author, February 2, 2021.
5. Interview with Farai Patrick Dunduru. Email interview by author, February 15, 2021.
6. Interview with Mark Gray. Email interview by author, April 3, 2021.
7. Katie Morley, "Exposed: The Rip-Off Investment 'Advisors' Who Cost British Expats Billions," *The Telegraph,* August 9, 2015. Accessed August 11, 2021. https://www.telegraph.co.uk/finance/personalfinance/investing/11726158/Exposed-the-rip-off-investment-advisers-who-cost-British-expats-billions.html
8. Ibid.
9. Interview with Tuan Phan. E-mail interview by author, April 26, 2017.
10. Zeke Faux, Benjamin Robertson, Matt Robinson, "Firm Targeting Nest Eggs of UK Expats Faces SEC Probe," Bloomberg, May 24, 2017. Accessed May

28, 2017. www.bloomberg.com/news/articles/2017-05-24/firm-targeting-nest-eggs-of-u-k-expats-said-to-face-sec-probe

11. Katie Morley, "Exposed: The Rip-Off Investment 'Advisors' Who Cost British Expats Billions," *The Telegraph,* August 9, 2015. Accessed August 11, 2021. https://www.telegraph.co.uk/finance/personalfinance/investing/11726158/Exposed-the-rip-off-investment-advisers-who-cost-British-expats-billions.html

12. Interview with Ben Sherwood. Email interview with author, March 9, 2017.

13. Interview with Simon Glazier. Email interview with author, March 22, 2017.

14. Policy paper. "Qualifying Recognised Overseas Pension Schemes: Charge on Transfers," Gov.UK, March 8, 2017. Accessed May 28, 2017. www.gov.uk/government/publications/qualifying-recognised-overseas-pension-schemes-charge-on-transfers/qualifying-recognised-overseas-pension-schemes-charge-on-transfers

15. Frank Furness, "The 10 Habits of Successful Financial Advisors," YouTube, December 19, 2013. Accessed May 6, 2014. www.youtube.com/watch?v=jOgIMDdAwdg

16. "Frank Furness and Steve Young," YouTube, December 19, 2013. Accessed May 6, 2014. www.youtube.com/watch?v=kEQVV2B9hGw

17. Simon Danaher, "Want to Be a Sales Commando?" International Adviser, April 10, 2014. Accessed May 6, 2014. http://www.international-adviser.com/news/sales-commando-a-former-devere-adviser

18. Interview with Chip Kimball. E-mail interview by author, April 20, 2014.

19. Interview with Jon Williams. E-mail interview by author, April 15, 2013.

20. Interview with Matthew Backus. E-mail interview by author, April 30, 2017.

21. Alice Haine and Gillian Duncan, "Do long term savings products serve their customers or their sellers?" *The National,* February 6, 2016. Accessed May 28, 2017. http://www.thenational.ae/business/personal-finance/the-money-roundtable-do-long-term-savings-products-serve-their-customers-or-their-sellers

22. All Goldman Sachs Funds, Morningstar.com. Accessed May 28, 2017. http://quicktake.morningstar.com/fundfamily/goldmansachs/0C00001YRF/fund-list.aspx

23. Ben Steverman, "The Worst Deal in Mutual Funds Faces a Reckoning," Bloomberg.com, May 1, 2012. Accessed May 6, 2014. www.bloomberg.com/news/2012-04-30/the-worst-deal-in-mutual-funds-faces-a-reckoning.html

24. Rudy Luukko, "Embedded Mutual Fund Commissions Hurt Investors," Thestar.com, June 15, 2013. Accessed May 6, 2014. www.thestar.com/business/personal_finance/investing/2013/06/15/embedded_mutual_fund_commissions_hurt_investors.html

25. Interview with Lawrence Graham. E-mail interview by author, November 21, 2013.

26. "Pension Plans & Hidden Charges": "BBC *Panorama* P1—Who Took My Pension?" YouTube, October 11, 2010. Accessed July 1, 2014. www .youtube.com/watch?v=rS36OlVCY5s; "BBC *Panorama* P2—Who Took My Pension?" YouTube, November 3, 2010. Accessed May 6, 2014. www .youtube.com/ watch?v=gajTHiHW8iA

27. Interview with Shawn Wong. E-mail interview by author, May 20, 2014.

Chapter 5

Self-Appointed Gurus and Neanderthal Brains

Thousands of years ago, a couple of your ancestors pushed their way through jungle foliage looking for their next meal. A tiger attacked from behind and ate one for lunch. The survivor told other villagers. One woman shared a similar story. So the villagers realized a pattern. Giant cats eat people. Better avoid them.

Another time, your ancestors discovered which berries were poisonous, which caused diarrhea, and which they could safely eat and enjoy. To survive and propagate, they learned patterns: which berries would kill, which would woo, and which could ruin a perfect picnic.

Humans are hardwired to seek such patterns. But while good for survival, these same pattern-seeking tendencies make us lousy investors. We figure if something is rising in price, it will keep rising.

And if something drops in price, it will keep falling. But the stock market isn't a tiger or a jungle berry.

Still, our Neanderthal brains seek patterns and we justify those patterns with modern story telling. For example, when investors first learn that index funds beat actively managed funds, they often scour historical track records to find the best performing index. In 2007, that represented an emerging market index. Over the previous eight years, emerging markets trounced the returns of US stocks and other developed markets. For example, from January 2000 to December 31, 2007, a $10,000 investment in an emerging market index fund would have averaged a compound annual return of 15.07 percent. That would have turned $10,000 into $30,734 over just eight years. In contrast, a US stock market index averaged just 2.32 percent over the same time period. The same $10,000 investment would have grown to just $12,011.[1]

Eight years is a long time for a Golden Retriever...and for investors seeking patterns. An eight-year pattern tells plenty of investors, "Yes, this will go on forever." That's why, from 2005–2007, plenty of investors (especially new investors) stacked their portfolios with emerging market funds. And why wouldn't they? Emerging markets were destroying the returns of developed market stocks. Countries like India and China represented (as they still do today) the fastest growing consumer markets in the world. Average wages were rising and GDP soared. And the narrative at the time (typically coming from analysts at the biggest banks) said this pattern would persist.

That's why so many investors from 2005–2007 built lopsided portfolios that focused on emerging market funds. But then pattern-seekers got spanked. Over the next ten years, from January 2007 to December 31, 2016, emerging markets stumbled. They averaged a compound annual return of just 1.72 percent. Meanwhile, over the same time period, US stocks averaged 7.11 percent per year.[2]

Sadly, most investors in emerging markets loaded up on them after they had risen...just in time for their money to dive and roll.

One of the first rules of effective investing is this: nobody can predict the future. That's why smart investors build globally diversified portfolios of stock and bond market index funds. They don't tweak their portfolios based on predictions. And they don't chase hot stocks or hot economic sectors.

While I was writing this, halfway through 2021, leagues of (mostly new) investors emailed me to ask, "What's the best index or ETF I can buy to track the S&P 500 index?" They wanted the S&P 500 index for the same reason investors were pining for emerging market shares a dozen years previous. They looked at past patterns. Over the period from January 2010 to May 31, 2021, US stocks averaged 14.58 percent per year. That trounced the returns of other developed market stocks, which averaged 6.89 percent per year. US stocks also destroyed the returns of emerging market stocks, which averaged 4.78 percent annually over the same time period.

So, pattern seekers wanted to load up on US shares. They then told stories to support their decisions:

US stocks have the best 100-year track record.
US stocks are filled with innovative companies.

As is always the case, after a sector has had a really strong run, investors load up on that sector. They see it as a prologue to the future. Such pattern seeking helped our ancestors survive, but it's not particularly useful for investors.

One of history's top performing funds was Fidelity's Magellan fund, run by Peter Lynch. From 1977 to 1990, the fund averaged an eye-popping 29 percent per year. But investors would have only earned that return if they bought it before it became famous, and held it for the full 13 years. Most people didn't do that...because they couldn't see the future. So what did they do? They loaded up on Fidelity's Magellan fund after it had posted a really strong run. They sought a pattern, and they rationalized that with a story: "Peter Lynch is the best fund manager in the world!"

But referencing a Fidelity study, IAG Wealth Management, reports the average investor in Peter Lynch's Fidelity Magellan fund actually lost money. They bought high, based on the fund's strong past returns, and when the fund fell hard, they either sold or they ceased to add new money.[3]

Cathie Wood might be today's Peter Lynch. Her ARK's Next Generation Internet ETF (ARKW) gained 157.46 percent in 2020. ARK's Fintech Innovation ETF (ARKF) soared 152.82 percent. The firm's Genomic Revolution ETF (ARKG) ballooned 180.56 percent. The ARK Innovation ETF (ARKK) gained 152.52 percent and the firm's Autonomous Technology & Robotics ETF (ARKQ) rose 107.22 percent. For the first few months of 2021, each fund continued to earn double-digit gains. Cathie Wood promoted her funds with great stories about innovation.

Wood's spectacular returns in 2020 (and the beginning of 2021) boosted her funds' average returns since inception. Since their launch date on September 30, 2014, they averaged compound annual returns of 39.77 percent (ARKW); 25.87 percent (ARKG) per year; 33.97 percent (ARKK) and 25.87 percent (ARKQ) Her fifth fund (ARKF) averaged a compound annual return of 55.28 percent since its inception on February 4, 2019. These were the posted annual returns on the ARK website, on May 14, 2021.[4]

But by mid-May 2021, these funds had fallen hard. *The Wall Street Journal*, referencing analysis from Bespoke Investment Group, says the average investor in Cathie Wood's five funds only earned about 5.24 percent per year from the funds' September 2014 inception dates to Monday, May 10, 2021.[5] You might wonder, "How can this be?" As with investors in emerging market shares in 2007, and with Peter Lynch's Fidelity Magellan fund in the late 1980s, they bought after the fund had a big, profitable run. They then justified their purchase with stories supporting why their funds would continue to fly.

I'm not saying Cathie Wood's funds won't recover and soar. But one thing's for sure. Investors will pine for them after they've had a strong run and they'll shun them after they post lousy years. That's why, even if Cathie Wood's funds post strong returns going forward, most of the investors in these funds won't do well.

Why Most Investors Should Hope for Falling Markets

Do you freak out when the stock market drops? If you're employed and in a position to buy stock market investments for at least the next five years, you should celebrate falling markets.

The stock market is like a grocery store filled with nonperishable items. When prices fall, stock up on those products. Prices will inevitably rise again. If you like canned beans, and the store is selling them this week at a 20 percent discount, you have a choice. You can sit on your haunches and wonder whether they'll be even cheaper the following week, or you can stop being silly and just buy the beans. If the price drops further the following month, you can buy more of them. But if you sit on your butt and miss out on the sale (because you're speculating that beans will get even cheaper), well, you miss out on the sale.

A stock market drop is much the same. But most investors shun stock market discounts. Amateurs and professionals alike often dive out of stock investments when they forecast rough times ahead. Stock markets, however, are extremely unpredictable. If you (or an advisor) move money based on forecasts, your wealth will eventually suffer.

Are You Cheering for the Right Team?

My brother-in-law loves the Toronto Maple Leafs. It's one of Canada's most iconic ice hockey teams. When his kids were younger, he used to put them in his favorite team's sweaters every time the Leafs played.

He celebrates when the Maple Leafs win. But if you love the Boston Bruins, the Montreal Canadiens, or the Chicago Blackhawks, you would rather see your team give the Maple Leafs a beating.

Not everybody cheers for the same team. That should go for the stock market too. In fact, most people should cheer when the stock market falls. Headlines shouldn't say, "Investors Win as Stocks Rise!" Only retirees (and near-retirees) should be thrilled to see stocks rise.

Let's look at a Canadian example, while keeping in mind that these statistics would likely be similar for other countries too. Statistics Canada says the majority of Canadians are between the ages of 20 and 60.[6]

Most of these people should be adding money to the stock market every month. They should hope that stocks don't rise for several years in a row. That's because, long term, stock market growth tracks corporate earnings' growth. On aggregate, business earnings grow almost every year. When stocks don't follow, investors get to buy an increasingly higher percentage of corporate earnings with their savings and enjoy higher dividend yields.

This is great for workers who are adding money to the market. It's like piling projectiles onto an ancient catapult. The more money that they add, while the catapult is low, the more money they'll make when the catapult launches. That's why Warren Buffett says those who have at least five more years to work and invest should prefer to see stocks sink. About 28.4 million Canadians are over the age of 20. Of that number, about 71 percent are below the age of 60.[7] That means most working Canadians should prefer to see stocks sputter.

Statistics Canada says the average retirement age in 2020 was 64 years of age. Just 18 percent of Canadians are 65 years of age or older. This minority should be cheering when stock markets rise. But it's bat-poop crazy for anyone else to cheer when the stock market rises.[8]

If you're employed, you should be buying. If you're retired, you should be selling. That's why workers and retirees should cheer for different teams.

If You're Just Starting Out, Pray for Stocks to Sputter

Plenty of people, understandably, want their investments to gain ground as soon as they begin investing. But despite what our guts might say, this is often counterproductive over a long time period.

Imagine this. You just invested your first $10,000 in a portfolio of index funds or ETFs. Would you prefer to see the stock market average 6.5 percent per year over the next 20 years or 9.33 percent for the next 20 years?

When I ask young people this they say, "I would definitely like to see the stock market gain 9.33 percent over the next 20 years, not 6.5 percent."

I then follow up with a second question:

> "Would you prefer that stocks have three horrible years in a row, starting this year, or would you like to see stocks soar over the next three years?"

Obviously, people say they would like to see big gains right away. It's normal to think that. But if you want to do well in the stock market, you can't think like a normal person. Look at the two scenarios below:

20-Year Investment Durations

Scenario 1	Scenario 2
Stocks average 9.33% for 20 years	Stocks average 6.5% for 20 years
Stocks soar for the first 3 years	Stocks drop for the first 3 years

Most young investors would prefer scenario one. But they could make far more money with scenario two.

The first scenario represented the 20 years from 1995–2015. The S&P 500 averaged a compound annual return of 9.33 percent. That period also started off with three big years. US stocks gained 37.58 percent in 1995, 22.96 percent in 1996 and 33.36 percent in 1997.

The second scenario represents the 20 years from 2000–2020. The S&P 500 averaged a compound annual return of 6.5 percent. And during the first three years, 2000, 2001 and 2002, US stocks plunged 9.1 percent, 11.89 percent and 22.10 percent respectively."

But if the person invested $10,000 and then continued to add $1000 a month, scenario 2 would have made them much more money over the next 20 years.

In scenario 1, despite the markets averaging 9.33 percent over 20 years, the money would have grown to $645,288, and in scenario 2, when the markets averaged just 6.5 percent per year, the money would have grown to $871,223.

When stocks crash, you're able to buy more stock market units at lower prices. It might take years for your money to recover, but when stocks soar, so will your money. As a result, as shown in Table 5.1, the investors' money-weighted return is higher in scenario two.

William Bernstein, the former neurologist turned financial advisor, says much the same thing: Young investors should *"pray for a long, awful [down] market."* In his booklet, *If You Can*, he says that when stocks drop, investors pay less money for a greater number of shares. When people invest consistent sums every month (dollar cost averaging) they can stockpile assets when they're cheap. When the markets recover, those asset values soar.

Warren Buffett says the same thing in his 1997 letter to Berkshire Hathaway shareholders:

"If you will be a net saver over the next five years, should you hope for a higher or lower stock market during that time period? Many investors get this one wrong. Even though they are going to be net buyers of stocks for many years to come, they are elated when stock prices rise and depressed when they fall . . . This reaction makes no sense. Only those who will be sellers of equities [stock market investments] in the near future should be happy at seeing stocks rise. Prospective purchasers should much prefer sinking prices."[9]

Based on this logic, you might ask yourself, "Why not just wait for stocks to crash before I invest?" But trying to time the market is

Table 5.1 $10,000 Initial Investment + $1000 a Month Based on returns of the S&P 500

	Scenario 1		Scenario 2
Year	Year-end Value	Year	Year-end Value
1995	$27,515	2000	$20,337
1996	$47,161	2001	$29,638
1997	$76,312	2002	$33,964
1998	$111,878	2003	$57,647
1999	$148,810	2004	$76,772
2000	$146,577	2005	$92,947
2001	$140,699	2006	$120,524
2002	$120,431	2007	$139,051
2003	$168,759	2008	$96,827
2004	$199,817	2009	$136,971
2005	$221,867	2010	$170,908
2006	$269,609	2011	$186,192
2007	$296,167	2012	$228,139
2008	$195,778	2013	$315,149
2009	$262,129	2014	$370,566
2010	$314,732	2015	$387,268
2011	$332,843	2016	$445,940
2012	$397,998	2017	$555,723
2013	$539,660	2018	$541,680
2014	$625,406	2019	$724,719
2015	**$645,288**	**2020**	**$871,223**
Average annual return of the market	9.33%	**Average Annual Return of The Market**	6.5%
Money-weighted return for the investor	7.62%	**Money-weighted return for the investor**	9.95%

SOURCE: portfoliovisualizer.com.

one of the worst things an investor can do. Almost nobody gets it right. And if they get lucky once, they try again, much like someone winning during a trip to the casino. That person will almost certainly come back and give up most, if not all, of their winnings.

Should You Worry When Stocks Hit All-Time Highs?

I wish I could control part of your brain. I know that sounds evil, but my motives are pure. I want to help you make money with your index funds.

Here's how I would do it. When stocks hit all-time highs, you wouldn't know. When experts on TV predict the next market crash, you would fall into a trance and hear a soothing Celtic song. Many people are addicted to looking at their investment performance. But don't bother looking more than once a year. In my mind-control world, if you looked more often, I would flick a mental switch to make you scratch your crotch in public.

Here's the reason behind my quirky mind-control desire. The less you think about the market, the more money you will make.

In 2014, *Business Insider*'s Myles Udland wrote the following awkwardly titled story: "Fidelity Reviewed Which Investors Did Best and What They Found Was Hilarious." He reported that Fidelity (a mutual fund company) wanted to find out "who are our best investors?" Amazingly, they were the people who had forgotten that they had an account with Fidelity.[10]

When we worry about the markets, Donald Trump, Brexit, the European Union, a pandemic or a global banking crisis, we do silly things. We might juggle our investments "to adjust to market conditions." But doing so is foolish.

The Only Thing That Matters

With a diversified portfolio of low-cost index funds, you will beat 90 percent of investment professionals over your investment lifetime if you don't do anything silly. In other words, just stay the course with a globally diversified portfolio of index funds or ETFs, no matter what's happening with the economy or the stock market.

Stocks will crash, from time to time. But they will also keep hitting new highs. Don't be afraid of all-time highs. After all, despite what the media might want you to believe, all-time highs are normal.

I'm 51 years old. Over my lifetime, the S&P 500 (with dividends reinvested) has hit all-time highs during 33 different calendar years. I've listed them in Table 5.2.

As shown in Table 5.3 the global stock market hit all-time highs during 35 calendar years since 1970. As a reminder, the global stock market index is a compilation of the world's markets, including the USA.

During years when stocks hit all-time highs, what did the headlines say? Many said stocks were going to crash. Most of them were wrong. Forecasters who got lucky were almost always wrong the next time. Nobody can predict when stocks will rise or fall.

I started to invest in 1989. The stock market hit an all-time high that year. I'm glad I didn't worry. Stocks hit another high in 1991.

Table 5.2 Years US Stocks (with Dividends Reinvested) Hit All-Time Highs, 1970–2021

1970	1980	1986	1993	1998	2013	2019
1971	1982	1988	1994	1999	2014	2020
1972	1983	1989	1995	2006	2015	2021*
1976	1984	1991	1996	2007	2016	
1979	1985	1992	1997	2012	2017	

*2021 data to August
SOURCE: NYU Stern School of Business and portfoliovisualizer.com.

Table 5.3 Years Global Stocks (with Dividends Reinvested) Hit All-Time Highs, 1970–2021

1971	1977	1983	1988	1995	2005	2016
1972	1978	1984	1989	1996	2006	2017
1973	1979	1985	1991	1997	2007	2019
1975	1980	1986	1993	1998	2013	2020
1976	1982	1987	1994	1999	2014	2021*

*2021 data to August
SOURCE: Morningstar Direct.

Once again, I'm glad I didn't sell. US stocks hit a new all-time high in 1992, 1993, and 1994. I think you get the picture. If I had sold, I would have been a victim of my own speculation.

But what if I had guessed correctly? That would have been worse. Next time, the stock market gods would have knocked me on my butt.

It's Not Timing the Market That Matters; It's Time in the Market

There are smart people (and people who aren't so smart) who think they can jump in and out of the stock market at opportune moments. It seems simple. Get in before the market rises and get out before it drops. This is referred to as "market timing." But most experts have a better chance of beating Usain Bolt in a footrace than effectively timing the market over an investment lifetime.

Vanguard founder John Bogle, named by *Fortune* magazine as one of the four investment giants of the twentieth century, says this about market timing:

After nearly 50 years in this business, I do not know of anybody who has done it successfully and consistently. I don't even know anybody who knows anybody who has done it successfully and consistently.[11]

Warren Buffett, the world's greatest investor, stated in a 1992 Berkshire Hathaway annual report, "We've long felt that the only value of stock forecasters is to make fortune tellers look good."[12] Pundits try forecasting, of course. And they all sound logical spewing their theories in the *Wall Street Journal* or on CNBC. But predictions rarely jibe with future realities. Consider unemployment figures. If you've watched a bit of market-based TV, you've probably heard experts predicting rough times for stocks when unemployment figures rise. And it makes perfect sense, right? Wrong. Unfortunately, short-term market movements make no sense at all.

High Unemployment and High Stock Returns

What if a creepy, toothless fortune teller could tell you, six months in advance, when unemployment would peak? She would send you a warning text. And no, she wouldn't be one of those carnival clowns or a Wall Street analyst. This woman would be the real deal–fully capable of seeing the future. Would you sell stocks after getting that text? She would laugh if you did.

In his excellent book *Markets Never Forget*, money manager Ken Fisher pokes our Neanderthal brains. He explains that, historically, high unemployment has been followed by high future stock returns.[13] No, I'm not suggesting keeping money out of the stock market until soup kitchens outnumber Starbucks coffee shops. Nor was Fisher. This is a random phenomenon, as likely to be repeated as not. But can you imagine the headline? *Stocks will surge next year because unemployment is getting close to hitting a new peak!*

Note the correlation between high unemployment and future, short-term stock returns in Table 5.4. I listed dates representing six months before every unemployment peak since 1932 and the 12-month stock market returns that followed. Always remember, however, that correlation and causation is not the same thing. High unemployment, for example, is not the cause of strong market performance. This is just crazy random stuff. It should also make you think twice when an analyst or journalist predicts poor stock market performance based on projected unemployment figures.

If Table 5.4 inspires you to try predicting when we're six months from an unemployment peak, then you're missing the point. You can't predict such a thing any more than you can forecast the next zit on your nose. And the pattern won't likely perpetuate. Predicting a tiger would eat you in a one-on-one cage match is a pretty safe bet. But forecasting stock markets and zits is next to impossible.

But come on, surely experts can predict the stock market. Many would like you to think so. Yet five-year-old kids and house pets can make them look foolish. In 2012, the British paper *The Observer* pitted

Table 5.4 Do Economic Unemployment Numbers
Predict a Stock Market Drop?

Six Months Before Unemployment Peaks	S&P 500 Returns 12 Months Later
November 30, 1932	+57.7%
December 31, 1937	+33.2%
July 30, 1946	-3.4%
April 30, 1949	+31.3%
March 31, 1954	+42.3%
January 31, 1958	+37.9%
November 30, 1960	+32.3%
February 26, 1971	+13.6%
November 29, 1974	+36.2%
January 31, 1980	+19.5%
June 30, 1982	+61.2%
December 31, 1991	+7.6%
December 31, 2002	+28.7%
April 30, 2009	+38.8%
October 30, 2019	+11.39%

SOURCE: Kenneth Fisher's, *Markets Never Forget*, referencing data from The Bureau of Labor Statistics; Global Financial Data Inc., S&P 500 total returns updated unemployment figures (post 2012) came from The Bureau of Labor Statistics: https://ourworldindata.org/time-use#:~:text=We%20spend%20the%20most%20time,Consider%20sleeping%2C%20for%20example.

selected professional stock pickers against a group of children and a cat named Orlando in a one-year stock-picking competition. The feline purred to the top, gaining 10.8 percent, compared to a 3.5 percent gain for the professionals and a 2.9 percent loss for the kids. (Orlando made his picks by throwing a toy mouse at a grid of numbers allocated to different companies.)[14] How did Vanguard's British stock market index measure up? It beat them all, gaining 17.4 percent.[15]

In 2002, the *Financial Times* reported a stock-picking battle between a five-year-old kid, an astrologer, and a professional portfolio analyst. The child won, beating the professional analyst by 52 percent.[16]

Ah, I can hear what you're thinking. Hallam is cherry-picking anomalies. Data-crunching firm CXO Advisory proves otherwise after putting dozens of the world's highest-profile financial forecasters to the test. When these so-called experts publicize their stock market predictions, the company tracks their accuracy. If you believe the talking heads on CNBC or the experts profiled in the *Wall Street Journal* are worth listening to, I'm sorry to disappoint you. Between 2005 and 2012, CXO Advisory collected 6,584 forecasts by 68 experts. When predicting the direction of the stock market, they were right just 46.9 percent of the time. Coin flippers would rival them.[17]

On March 5, 2009, comedian Jon Stewart, of US television's *The Daily Show*, humiliated some of CNBC's highest-profile stock market forecasters. His list of suffering victims included Jim Cramer, host of CNBC's *Mad Money* program.

Footage of Cramer's failed predictions gave plenty of video fodder for the clever Jon Stewart.[18]

What Stewart didn't realize (and it would have made great viewing) is that CXO Advisory has tracked Cramer's long-term forecasting performance. He has been correct just 46.8 percent of the time.[19]

Instead of following a guru's recommendation (or asking your house cat) whether to buy US stocks, British stocks, or Asian stocks, consider owning them all. By doing so with index funds, you'll beat most professional investors.

What Can You Miss by Guessing Wrong?

Predicting stock market movements, even with the benefit of hindsight, is next to impossible. Jeremy Siegel agrees. Author of *Stocks for the Long Run* and professor of business at the University of Pennsylvania's Wharton School, Siegel looked back at the biggest stock market moves since 1885 (focusing on trading sessions where the markets moved by 5 percent or more in a single day) and tried connecting each of them to a world event.[20]

Seventy-five percent of the time, he couldn't find logical explanations. Yet he had the luxury of looking back in time and trying to match the market's behavior with historical world news. If a world- renowned finance professor like Siegel can't make connections between world events and the stock market's movements with the benefit of hindsight, then how is someone supposed to predict future movements based on economic events—or the prediction of events to come?

If anyone tries convincing you to act on their short-term stock market predictions, ignore them. Doing otherwise could cost you plenty. For example, let's look at the US stock market from 1982 through December 2005.

During this time, the stock market averaged 10.6 percent annually. But if you didn't have money in the stock market during the 10 best trading days, your average return would have dropped to 8.1 percent. If you missed the best 50 trading days, your average return would have been just 1.8 percent.[21] Markets can move so unpredictably, and so quickly. If you take money out of the stock market for a day, a week, a month, or a year, you could miss the best trading days of the decade. Neither you nor your broker can predict them.

A lucky guess or two (as exhibited by Orlando the cat) may be a curse. Like winning a few thousand dollars on your first trip to the casino, it could take plenty of beatings before realizing your skill was just luck.

Morningstar's research shows that most investors underperform the funds they own (as previously explained with Fidelity Magellan fund and Cathie Wood's ARK ETFs). This is especially true when a fund jumps around a lot. When it falls, a mad voice inside us says, "Sell this sucker! After a fund has risen a lot, that same crazy voice says, "Buy this winner, now!"

If this behavior weren't common, we would call it a disorder and name it after some dead Teutonic psychologist.

Here's another example, this time with Fidelity's Emerging Market Fund (FEMK). Over the 15-year period ending April 30, 2017, it averaged a compound annual return of 8.9 percent after fees. But according to Morningstar, the average investor in that fund, over that same time period, averaged a compound annual return of just 4.12 percent.[22]

Investors felt good about the fund after it had risen, so they added more money. Their sentiments turned negative after the fund had dropped—so they either sold, or they ceased to add fresh money.

If somebody had invested $10,000 in that fund on April 30, 2002 (and if they had just left it alone!), it would have grown to $35,926 fifteen years later. Instead, the average investor in that fund turned $10,000 into just $18,323.

Should You Invest a Windfall All at Once?

You've inherited a windfall. Should you invest it all at once? Or should you add the money to the markets, month by month, dollar-cost averaging? Nobody knows for sure. But earlier lump-sum investments usually win. In other words, it's usually best to invest as soon as you have the money.

A Vanguard case study found that investing a lump sum, as soon as you have it, usually beats dollar-cost averaging. Vanguard compared a series of historical scenarios. They assumed that someone had invested a $1 million lump sum. They wanted to find out if, 10 years later, that investment would have grown higher than if the deposits were spaced out over 6, 12, 18, 24, 30, or 36 months.

Vanguard compared rolling 10-year periods for the US market between 1926 and 2011. They analyzed the same scenario for the UK market (1976–2011) and for the Australian market (1984–2011). Lump sum investing won 67 percent of the time. It's usually best to invest as soon as you have the money.[23]

When Investors and Advisors Sabotage Their Rides

Most people don't add consistent sums to the same funds. They prefer to chase what's rising and shun what's falling. Such performance gaps between what funds earn and what investors make are prevalent across every major asset group. People jump onto bandwagons—with Neanderthal brains in the driving seat.

If a financial advisor ever suggests an investment product because "it's performing really well right now," don't walk from the bozo—run! Recent past results rarely indicate a strong future. In most cases, the opposite holds true. Most mutual funds earning top ratings as superb performers eventually fall from their mantels, underperforming the typical fund in the years ahead. Winning geographic sector funds often do likewise.

Are Women Better Investors Than Men?

When I ask married couples, "Who is in charge of your investments?" most say it's the man. But couples should work together. After all, women appear to be better investors.

I first suspected this after giving several financial seminars about investing in low-cost index funds or ETFs. I often returned to speak to the same people years later. When I asked specific couples, "How are things going?" some said they had managed to stay on track. But plenty didn't. Those who deviated from the plan often started chasing hot stocks, jumping into cryptocurrencies, or trying to time the market. More often than not, the results were disastrous. When I asked heterosexual couples, "Whose idea was it to stray from the plan?" I learned that most of the time it was the man's.

Every study I can find reveals that women investors perform much better than men, whether the markets are moving up, down or sideways. They include research by Vanguard, Berkley University's Brad Barber and Terrance Odean, Fidelity and Wells Fargo.[24]

A 36-month-long UK-based study by Warwick Business School came to the same conclusion after examining 2,800 investment accounts. Women beat men.

It's mostly a result of men's overconfidence and their tendency to speculate.[25]

Men's higher testosterone might be their undoing. Finance researchers Yan Lu and Melvyn Teo published fascinating findings via the University of Central Florida and Singapore Management University. They looked at 3,228 male hedge fund managers between January 1994 and December 2015.

But saying that they "looked at them" is a serious understatement. The researchers literally measured the widths of their faces. Men with wider faces tend to have higher testosterone levels. The researchers found that the hedge fund managers with narrower faces beat their higher-testosterone, wider-faced counterparts by 5.8 percent per year on a risk-adjusted basis.

Lu and Teo wrote, "In the context of the ultra-competitive and male-dominated hedge fund industry, where masculine traits such as aggression, competitiveness, and drive, are encouraged, expected, and even celebrated, our results on the underperformance of high-testosterone fund managers are indeed surprising. Investors will do well to go against conventional wisdom and eschew masculine fund managers."[26]

This brings me back to married heterosexual couples. Most often, men take the investment reins, leaving the women on the sidelines. But couples should establish a solid plan, stick to it, and not let fear, greed, or machismo send them off track.

Collar Your Inner Neanderthal

If you're a carbon-based life form, you will be tempted to time the market, chase hot stocks, hot ETFs or scorching actively managed funds. Even if you have a globally diversified portfolio of index funds or ETFs, you will be tempted to alter your allocation. If you receive a lump sum, you will wonder whether it's the "right time" to invest it. You will feel pulled by people on Facebook groups who claim to be making big, speculative gains (these same people are surprisingly quiet when they lose).

Everything will tempt your Neanderthal brain. But remember, investing isn't a sprint. It's a marathon. To do well in this race, you have to ignore the people who are sprinting during the first few miles. After all, you will beat most of them (perhaps all of them) over your lifetime if you have the emotional mettle to stick with a globally diversified portfolio of low-cost index funds or ETFs.

Below, I've listed the golden rules for investors who want to give themselves the highest lifetime odds of beating at least 90 percent of the world's investment pros.

Chapter Take-Away and Tips

1. **Do not buy a fund "because it is doing well."** Whether that's an actively managed fund or a passive index fund or ETF. That's one of the worst things an investor can do. Sadly almost everybody does it (including most financial advisors, see Chapter 3). Such funds will always, also, come with a story suggesting why they'll keep going up. Ignore such stories.
2. **If you have at least five more years before retirement, be happy when markets fall.** But never try to wait for stocks to fall before you invest. Neither you, nor anyone, can predict the market with any useful degree of consistency.
3. **Invest as soon as you have the money.** Then ignore the value of your account and keep adding money when you have it.
4. **Do not worry when stocks hit all-time highs.** Most years, they will (see Tables 5.2 and 5.3).
5. **Do not worry when stocks drop.** Keep buying when you have the money. You'll be getting a discount, compared to the prices you paid before.
6. **Ignore all stock market and economic forecasts.** As Warren Buffett says, stock market forecasters exist to make fortunetellers look good.
7. **Build a globally diversified portfolio of low cost index funds or ETFs.** Then stay the course.

Notes

1. portfoliovisualizer.com
2. Ibid.
3. Kirk Chisholm, "Why are individual investors so bad at investing?" IAG Wealth management. Accessed August 12, 2021. https://innovativewealth.com/wall-street-wisdom/individual-investors-bad-investing/
4. ARK Invest. Accessed May 14, 2021. https://ark-funds.com/
5. Spencer Jakab, "Cathie Wood's ARK wasn't built for a flood," *The Wall Street Journal,* May 11, 2021. Accessed August 12, 2021. https://www.wsj.com/articles/ark-wasnt-built-for-a-flood-1620749548
6. Statistics Canada. Accessed October 1, 2021. https://www150.statcan.gc.ca/t1/tbl1/en/tv.action?pid=1710000501
7. Ibid.
8. Ibid.
9. Warren E. Buffett, "Chairman's Letter—1992," Berkshirehathaway.com. Accessed May 6, 2014. www.berkshirehathaway.com/letters/1992.html
10. Myles Udland, "Fidelity Reviewed Which Investors Did Best and What They Found Was Hilarious." Business Insider, Sept 4, 2014. Accessed September 27, 2021. https://www.businessinsider.com/forgetful-investors-performed-best-2014-9
11. John C. Bogle, *Common Sense on Mutual Funds: New Imperatives for the Intelligent Investor* (Hoboken, NJ: John Wiley & Sons, 2010), 28.
12. Warren E. Buffett, "Chairman's Letter—1992," Berkshirehathaway.com. Accessed May 6, 2014. www.berkshirehathaway.com/letters/1992.html
13. Kenneth L. Fisher and Lara Hoffmans, *Markets Never Forget (but People Do)* (Hoboken, NJ: John Wiley & Sons, 2012).
14. Mark King, "Investments: Orlando Is the Cat's Whiskers of Stock Picking," *The Observer,* January 13, 2013. Accessed October 1, 2021. https://www.theguardian.com/money/2013/jan/13/investments-stock-picking.
15. "Vanguard UK Equity Index," Vanguard UK. Accessed May 7, 2014. www.vanguard.co.uk%2Fuk%2Fmvc%2FloadPDF%3FdocId%3D2034.
16. Daniel R. Solin, *Does Your Broker Owe You Money?* (Bonita Springs, FL: Silver Cloud, 2004), 141.
17. "Guru Grades," CXO Advisory RSS. Accessed May 7, 2014. www.cxoadvisory.com/gurus/
18. Jon Stewart, "CNBC Financial Advice," *Daily Show.* Accessed May 7, 2014. www.thedailyshow.com/watch/wed-march-4-2009/cnbc-financial-advice
19. "Guru Grades," CXO Advisory RSS. Accessed July 1, 2014. www.cxoadvisory.com/gurus/

20. Jeremy J. Siegel, *Stocks for the Long Run: The Definitive Guide to Financial Market Returns and Long-Term Investment Strategies* (New York: McGraw-Hill, 2008), 217–218.
21. Kenneth L. Fisher, Jennifer Chou, and Lara Hoffmans, *The Only Three Questions That Count* (Hoboken, NJ: John Wiley & Sons, 2007), 279.
22. Morningstar.com
23. "Dollar-cost Averaging Just Means Taking Risk Later," Vanguard Research, July 2012. Accessed October 1, 2021. https://static.twentyoverten.com/5980d 16bbfb1c93238ad9c24/rJpQmY8o7/Dollar-Cost-Averaging-Just-Means-Tak ing-Risk-Later-Vanguard.pdf
24. Andrew Hallam, "Is Your Family's Best Investment Player Sitting On the Bench?" AssetBuilder, February 18, 2018. Accessed August 12, 2021. https:// assetbuilder.com/knowledge-center/articles/is-your-familys-best-investment-player-sitting-on-the-bench
25. "Are women better investors than men?" Warwick Business School, June 28, 2018. Accessed August 12, 2021. https://www.wbs.ac.uk/news/are-women-better-investors-than-men/
26. "Do Alpha-Males Deliver Alpha?" *Journal of Financial and Quantitative Analysis*, December 15, 2020. Accessed August 12, 2021. https://www.wbs.ac.uk/news/are-women-better-investors-than-men/

Chapter 6

Investment Advisors with a Conscience

C ome on, admit it—you're better looking than the average person, right? If you drive a car, you probably think you drive better than most behind the wheel. Chances are you also think you're smarter than average. Unfortunately, peer-assessed reviews of your desirability, car-driving ability, or intelligence could burst your bubble.

Likewise, many people overestimate their ability to manage a portfolio of index funds or ETFs. Don't get me wrong. It's a simple thing to do. But most people can't do it effectively.

When the world is high on a profitable asset class, most mortals have a tough time selling portions when it's time to rebalance. Equally difficult is embracing a reeking asset class when the rest of the world is shunning it. I'm not going to lie. Controlling emotional reactions to a gyrating portfolio is an investor's greatest test.

Do You Have a Ninja's Discipline?

If you're emotionally wired like a ninja warrior, you shouldn't have any problem managing your own portfolio of indexes. But consider the following questions:

Do you ever overeat?
Did you binge drink in college because your friends did?
Have you ever tried a cigarette?
Do you eat foods you know aren't healthy?
Do you worry about stock market crashes?
Do you ever consider acting on financial predictions?

If you answered yes to any of those questions, congratulations—you're normal. But investors capable of rebalancing a portfolio of index funds or ETFs are anything but. Don't feel misled. The process is simple. But when markets gyrate or plunge, it's a tough challenge.

Qualities of a Good Financial Advisor

For this reason, scrupulous advisors building and managing a client's indexed portfolio can easily be worth the fees they charge. Unfortunately, such advisors are a bit like ninjas themselves. They exist, according to legend, but you've probably never seen one. They won't stomp into your place of employment or cold-call you looking for business. Most don't advertise. They're stealth-like. I can hear what you're thinking. Why would any financial advisor bypass massive commissions or mutual fund kickbacks to do the right thing? We shouldn't have to ask. Not every financial advisor succumbs to the dark side. Some scrupulous advisors charge consultation fees, providing direction for a one-time cost. Others charge a low percentage of the portfolio's assets each year.

The Advisor Shouldn't be Compensated by Commission

Advisors charging commissions contend with a conflict of interest. Instead of providing the best products for clients, they may climb into bed with firms that satisfy their own needs.

The Advisor Shouldn't Purchase Individual Stocks for Your Portfolio

Some advisors shun actively managed mutual funds, but claim they can pick individual stocks to beat the market. Don't fall for that. Most stock pickers underperform indexes over time.

Not only do stock-picking brokers underperform, but most fail to adequately diversify. Full diversification, of course, isn't just limited to stocks of different sizes. It also includes international exposure. Unless your broker is going to add hundreds of foreign stocks, you won't receive a broad representation of the global markets. And because your advisor can't predict the movements of hundreds of different stocks from multiple countries, you're better off with indexes.

The Advisor Should Charge No More than 1.25 Percent Each Year

Ensure that your prospective advisor charges 1.25 percent (or less) each year to manage your indexed portfolio. If an advisor charges as much as 1.25 percent, you should demand exceptional ongoing service. This would be a $1,250 annual charge on a $100,000 portfolio. As you've seen, costs add up. Paying 1.5 percent instead of 1.25 percent could cost tens of thousands of extra dollars over time when calculating the effects of compounding interest.

The Advisor Shouldn't Gamble

Speak to prospective advisors about their investment philosophy. Avoid advisors who alter portfolios based on economic predictions. They may sound sophisticated while referencing soothsaying economists, but don't fall for it. If forecasting (whether the advisor's or the firm's) is the order of operation, plug your ears and walk. Most economic predictions are wrong—making them very costly indeed.

The Advisor Shouldn't Buy High-Cost Indexes

Advisors can choose from a variety of index fund providers from which to build your portfolio. But insist they do so from Vanguard, Fidelity, Schwab, Dimensional Fund Advisors (DFA), or T. Rowe Price only. If they're using exchange-traded index funds (ETFs), insist on Vanguard, Schwab, iShares, Horizon, BetaShares, or Power-Shares. A few other low-cost providers exist, but if your advisor can't build a portfolio with the ones I've named, you're dealing with a charlatan.

Investment Professionals Worth Considering

I'm not going to endorse any financial advisory firms. As an investor, you must make your own decisions. But here are a few advisory firms that meet all of the aforementioned standards. It's a short list. If you research further, you might find others. The levels of service differ. All of these firms will build (or help you build) a portfolio of low-cost index funds. But many offer more. They provide full financial planning. They help clients set savings and retirement goals. They assist with tax planning, estate planning, inheritance planning, children's education costs, and how to deal with tax differences relating to couples of different nationalities.

Many other firms say they offer full-service financial planning. But most are just asset gatherers. They want to sell you investments so their firm can make money. If they do offer financial services, it's usually watered down.

I've done my best to describe the levels of services and costs for firms that might be worth checking out. I've categorized them under specific nationalities. But some of them, such as Creveling & Creveling and PlanVision, service all nationalities, so please read through the profiles to see which firms might be best for you.

Index Advisors for American Expats

Company Name: Noto Financial Planning
Minimum Account Size: US$1,000,000
Website: notofp.com

Years ago, the Campbell Soup Company stuck a boy's face on each of its cans. He represented wholesome goodness, and even today I can't get his image out of my mind when tucking into a bowl of mushroom soup.

Spend 10 minutes with Tony Noto and you might think you've found the adult manifestation of Campbell's wholesome image (the Campbell soup kid now sometimes sports a beard).

Tony Noto is a Certified Financial Planner (CFP) and Chartered Financial Analyst (CFA). "When I began advising expats in Shanghai on their finances in 2008," says Tony, "all of the companies were focused on selling offshore pensions. I started Noto Financial Planning to provide expatriates with an alternative: financial advice free from commission bias."

After living in China for eight years, he relocated to Hawaii, where he continues to specialize in expatriate financial planning. He accepts clients with a minimum of US$1,000,000, charging 1 percent of assets under management, with lower rates for larger balances. He sometimes charges a retainer: a set annual fee. All portfolios utilize an index fund approach.

Unlike most financial advisors, he keeps his client base small. Doing so allows him to provide the highest level of personal attention. He meets with clients in person or via teleconferencing two to six times each year. His annual fee covers all aspects of financial planning: insurance, investment needs, US tax planning, goal setting, and tuition for children's education.

Tony doesn't receive compensation from offshore pension firms, insurance companies, or mutual funds. With his expatriate experience, integrity, and credentials, he's a very sought-after advisor.

Company Name: Creveling & Creveling Private Wealth
   Advisory
Servicing: All nationalities
Suggested Minimum Account Size: US$750,000
Website: crevelingandcreveling.com

Creveling & Creveling's clients often refer to the firm as the Gold Standard for financial planning. Based in Bangkok, it's run by the husband-and-wife team of Chad and Peggy Creveling. Both carry the Certified Financial Planner designation. They're also Chartered Financial Analysts and previously worked as equity research analysts. They work with clients of all nationalities, including many mixed-nationality couples.

Instead of building a large client base, Creveling & Creveling focus on a high level of continuing service.

Many expats also require advice in order to save enough money. Creveling & Creveling offers comprehensive planning. They help their clients monitor their income, expenditures, tax planning, and future retirement needs. Rather than selling financial products, they work with clients in an advisory capacity.

The firm charges for its services based on a declining fee structure applied to assets under advisement. A fee of 1.2 percent is applied to the first $1 million and the percentage fee declines above that threshold. C&C's services typically make sense for those clients with at least $750,000 in investible assets.

Creveling & Creveling has been a Registered Investment Advisor (RIA) with the US Securities and Exchange Commission (SEC), and a licensed Investment Advisor with the Thai SEC since the firm's inception in 2006. They also provide general expat financial advice in their monthly newsletter.

Company Name: MASECO Private Wealth
Minimum Account Size: US$1,000,000
Website: masecoprivatewealth.com
Limitation: For American expats in Great Britain and British
   expats living in the US

Americans living in Europe sometimes languish in a tax vice. Those in the United Kingdom, for example, must pay British and US taxes on their American investments once they've lived abroad for seven years or longer. UK-based Americans often marry spouses of different nationalities, complicating tax matters. MASECO specializes in such issues as it builds investment portfolios and provides full-service financial planning for American expats in Great Britain and British expats in the United States.

It's a niche market, for sure, but one with massive followings. Cofounder Josh Matthews explains: "We started the business in 2008, figuring demand would be high. In [the first] six years we've accumulated $870 million under management." Most of the firm's clients have between $1 million and $10 million invested. As of 2021, MASECO's assets under management had grown to $2.4 billion.

The complicated tax structures involved when coupling the regulations of the United States and Great Britain have drawn a huge client following for the employees at MASECO. Josh explains that many larger US-based investment firms came to the United Kingdom to do much the same thing. But they soon abandoned that idea after recognizing the tax complexities. "It's a great marketplace, but very complicated. It's a disaster [for clients] if you don't get it right."

MASECO charges a maximum 1.25 percent on assets for the first $500,000 invested, dropping its fees for subsequently larger sums. Those hoping to use the firm require a minimum $1 million investment.

Company Name: Buckingham Strategic Wealth
Minimum Account Size: None
Website: buckinghamstrategicwealth.com

Buckingham Strategic Wealth is a huge US-based firm that builds portfolios of low-cost index funds. Located in over 40 US cities, they manage about $21 billion. To open an account, American expats would need to submit a US taxpayer's ID and a US address.

The firm accepts investment accounts of any size, but there's a $1,000 minimum annual charge. As such, investors would pay 2 percent in fees with a $50,000 account. They would pay 1.25 percent in annual fees with a $100,000 account. With a $1 million account, they would pay annual fees of 1.09 percent. They would pay 0.89 percent per year with a $2 million account; 0.76 percent for a $3 million account; 0.67 percent for a $4 million account and 0.62 percent for a $5 million account. Fees, as a percentage, continue to drop from there. For example, investors with $10 million would pay 0.48 percent per year.

Company: Index Fund Advisors, Inc. (IFA)
Minimum Account Size: US$100,000
Website: www.ifa.com

Index Fund Advisors (IFA) has been advising clients and building index portfolios since 1999. The company, which can service American expats, had $3.69 billion in assets under management as of September 2020. Mark Hebner is the firm's founder and president. He says, "Investors should always seek fiduciaries that avoid conflicts of interest. As such, we recommend that members of your financial team should be independent of each other: a registered investment advisor (like IFA), an independent estate planning attorney, an independent CPA, and an independent insurance advisor."

The firm's philosophy makes sense. Plenty of investment advisors also act as insurance salespeople. Mark says such advisors "can be tempted to sell various financial products that pay them the most—while their clients get the shaft."

Mark Hebner and the 40 employees at IFA service their clients and provide unique and robust investor education. They have created a documentary film (Index Funds), 375 videos, 1,550 articles, 2,800 charts and an online financial book library. IFA says they have designed a series of portfolios providing 89 years of simulated returns, which the firm demonstrates with calculators, tables, and dynamic charts.

IFA's investment strategy is based on academic research, including the work of Eugene Fama (2013 Nobel Prize in economics), Harry Markowitz (1990 Nobel Prize in economics), and highly respected academic Kenneth French. Its advisory fee starts at 0.9 percent annually for the first $500,000, with lower fees charged for larger accounts.

Index Advisors for Canadian Expats

Company Name: CI Direct Investing (formerly **WealthBar**)
Servicing: Canadians only
Minimum Account Size: CAD$25,000
Website: cidirectinvesting.com

Unofficially, CI Direct Investing is called a Robo-Advisor. No, the firm isn't run by robots. That's a media-created name that rings well with science fiction. I prefer to call it an Intelligent Investment Firm. Such firms are growing in popularity and it's easy to see why. These firms have said, "People are getting smarter. Let's offer something better!"

Unlike most Canadian-based investment companies, CI Direct Investing offers services to expat Canadians. Such investors would be registered as nonresident account holders. That should keep them free and clear of Canadian capital gains taxes.

CI Direct Investing offers several portfolio options for investors. They help clients determine their risk tolerance before they select a ready-made, diversified portfolio of ETFs. CI Direct Investing does all the lifting. They offer full financial planning for those whose financial circumstances aren't too complicated. They also build and rebalance client portfolios. All investors need to do is add money to their accounts.

The firm charges between 0.35 percent and 0.60 percent per year, depending on each account's size. That's CI Direct Investing take. Investors pay a further 0.20 percent (approximately) to the separate ETF provider. Investors with accounts valued below $150,000 pay total fees of about 0.80 percent per year. Investors with account sizes between $150,000 and $500,000 pay 0.60 percent in total fees. Those with more than $500,000 pay just 0.40 percent.

To get started, new clients create a login password at https://www.cidirectinvesting.com/signup and they get assigned an advisor. The advisors look at each client's long-term financial needs, based on their goals, savings rates, investment time horizons, and insurance needs, as well as different tax-deferred account opportunities.

Investors can request a plan to be reviewed at any time, either online or over the phone. Before doing so, investors fill in some easy-to-follow online questionnaires. They ask for information such as current savings rates, investment assets, types of accounts owned (if any), risk tolerances, and salary. Based on client-entered responses, they show a model of a suitable portfolio. Investors with questions can speak to an advisor.

Plenty of expat Canadians rave about CI Direct Investing. Such online investment firms, I believe, are the way of the future. It won't be long before other online firms take the expat market by storm, much as they have for Americans and Canadians who live in North America. Unfortunately, however, based on new European regulations, Canadians living in Europe cannot use CI Direct Investing. See Chapter 10 for a work-around solution.

Company Name: Objective Financial Partners Inc.
Certified Financial Planner: Jason Heath
Website: objectivefinancialpartners.com

Jason Heath is in a tough business. He provides objective financial planning but doesn't receive a dime in commissions. The Markham, Ontario–based CFP and income tax specialist doesn't earn annual fees based on his client account sizes, either. So how does the guy make money?

Jason charges consultation fees for broad financial planning: everything from estate planning to budgeting to retirement goals and investment allocation. Because he doesn't benefit from investment purchases or client account sizes, he advises with no strings attached. His firm has an in-house accountant and an estate lawyer. And Jason isn't too proud to use external resources when it makes sense to do so.

"I was disillusioned by the mainstream financial industry," he says, "so I wanted to do something different." Few investment advisors could survive such a lean, transparent compensation structure. But Heath builds a client base through heaps of credibility. He writes a column devoted to financial planning for the *National Post,* one of Canada's two national papers. Such a platform gives him plenty of exposure.

"I have clients in Canada, Brazil, Europe, the United States, and Africa," he says. Jason's services are perfect for Canadian expats building portfolios of low-cost index funds. "If they open accounts with an offshore discount brokerage [like Swissquote, Interactive Brokers or Saxo Capital Markets] I can assist them with portfolio allocation after providing comprehensive short-term and long-term retirement, children's education, and asset allocation strategies."

Heath spends plenty of time constructing financial planning goals with clients. He charges anywhere from $1,500 to $4,500 for a plan. "Some of my clients have relatively simple goals and asset distributions," he says. "But other individuals might have assets all over the place: a home in London, investment accounts in Asia, RRSPs [registered retirement savings plans] in Canada, college funds in an RESP [registered education savings plan]. My job is to negotiate strategies to best utilize these resources with tax efficiency, while aligning with the clients' goals. And as they invest each month, they can call me up and I'll ensure they stick to a logical investment allocation."

Jason's services might be worth the money. Consider someone with a $100,000 portfolio paying 2.5 percent in Canadian actively managed mutual fund fees. That person would pay $2,500 each year ($2,500 is 2.5 percent of $100,000). Those with $500,000 portfolios would pay $10,000 a year in hidden expenses. Advisors stuffing client accounts with such products aren't objective. Canadian actively managed mutual funds are the world's most expensive. Those selling them benefit nicely. With Jason, however, investors could pay as little as $1,500 once, before getting on track with their plan and their ultra-low-cost portfolio of index funds.

Index Advisors for British Expats

Company Name: Satis Asset Management
Minimum Account Size: £500,000
Website: satisuk.com

Many expatriates feel betrayed by those selling them expensive off-shore pension schemes. They may wonder whether there truly are firms that shun commissions, embrace low-cost index funds, and provide high levels of personal financial planning. Fortunately, a few exist, such as Satis Asset Management.

Based in London, the firm was established by the chartered accountant and tax advisory firm Hillier Hopkins LLP in 2012. Today, Satis Asset Management provides investment and taxation advice to a modest number of wealthy families. As director Ben Sherwood explains, "We have a number of expatriate British clients [and] business growth has exceeded our expectations. We are also one of only a handful of firms that have experience and competence to advise Americans residing in the UK."

Sherwood is a Certified Financial Planner and Chartered Financial Analyst. He also coauthored the book *The 7 Secrets of Money: The Insider's Guide to Personal Investment Success* (2nd ed., SRA Books, 2013). In it, he emphasizes the importance of low-cost investing and diversifying investments across a variety of asset classes. One of the key messages of the book is that investors should concentrate on factors within their control, such as taxes and fees.

For bond allocations, Satis Asset Management usually buys a combination of gilts (individual bonds) and bond funds for clients.

For client equity allocations, the firm currently uses Vanguard and Dimensional Fund Advisors' indexes.

Clients wishing to open accounts with Satis must do so with a minimum £500,000.

Investment consultancy and wealth management charges are 0.9 percent per year for the first million pounds, dropping to 0.75 percent for the next £4 million, down to 0.6 percent for the next £5 million.

Company Name: AES International
Servicing: All nationalities (except Americans)
Recommended Account Size: US$250,000
Website: aesinternational.com

AES International focuses on high net worth clients, most of whom open accounts with at least $250,000 USD. Such clients can receive additional services that include investment counseling or comprehensive financial planning services.

All investment portfolios use Dimensional Fund Advisors (a form of index fund) or they use individual Vanguard or iShares ETFs. The funds cost between 0.2 and 0.4 percent per year. Those are the fund expense ratio charges. AES International charges an additional 1.25 percent per year for investment advice and ongoing financial management.

Clients who want a comprehensive financial planning service pay an additional fee, depending on the nature of their requirement. This might cost between 1 and 3 percent of the amount invested. Depending on the circumstances, it could also be a fixed fee or an hourly rate. AES International discloses all fees during client consultations.

They also offer an offshore private banking option for investors through Nedbank. AES charges an additional 0.1 percent per year for this service, based on the client's portfolio's size. A South African company based on the Isle of Man, Nedbank offers multi-currency accounts, and lending and tax structuring services, among a variety of other options. Nedbank has its own schedule of fees and charges.

Not only does Nedbank offer favorable mortgage rates, but investors using this private bank don't have to worry about their adopted home country freezing their financial assets.

As such, ongoing charges with AES International could be as low as 1.45 percent per year or as high as 2 percent per year (if it includes the Nedbank service or the more expensive fund options).

Company Name: Sarwa
Servicing: All nationalities (except Americans)
Minimum Account Size: US$5
Website: sarwa.co

If you have as little as $5USD, you can invest with Sarwa. The firm is part of the fin-tech (financial technology) revolution. Similar to Canadian firms such as CI Direct Investing and WealthSimple, or American firms like Betterment and AssetBuilder, Sarwa builds globally diversified portfolios of ETFs.

They're based in the UAE, but they can also open accounts for non-Americans living outside the UAE. Sarwa doesn't penalize investors for pulling money out at any time, and they charge a modest 0.85 percent per year. When a client's account grows, they charge lower fees. They charge 0.70 percent for accounts valued between $50,000 and $100,000. And they charge just 0.50 percent for accounts valued above $100,000.

Sarwa (which means wealth in Arabic) uses Interactive Brokers' platform. The firm doesn't offer time-intensive wealth management and comprehensive financial planning services. But with more than 40,000 clients (at the time of writing) Sarwa has found a niche.

Company Name: Marc Ikels Consulting
Servicing: All nationalities (except Americans)
Minimum Account Size: $500,000 USD
Website: marcikelsconsulting.com

"I had a choice between the in-flight entertainment system and the live entertainment," says German-born financial advisor Marc Ikels. "I chose the live entertainment." It was 2004. Marc was flying from Singapore to run the New York City Marathon. His "live entertain- ment" became Marc's future wife. He married the Singapore Airlines flight attendant in 2006.

On Singapore's National Day, four years later, the couple's twin boys were born.

That's when Marc decided to quit his job with American Express to become a financial advisor. "The American Express job involved far too much travel, and it was a challenge to align the business life with the personal life with newborn twin boys," he says.

A few years earlier in 2003, he had earned his MBA through INSEAD. He specialized in finance. And like a driven student, once he decided to become a financial advisor, he wanted to be one of the best.

He builds portfolios of low cost index funds. Marc cooperates with a firm called Dimensional Fund Advisors. Based in Texas, it has the best client loyalty ratings in the world. They don't pay commissions to advisors that use their products. And they're a picky firm. To build portfolios of DFA index funds, financial advisors must undergo heavy scrutiny. Most have to fly to the United States for extra training.

Those wanting a top quality investment portfolio might fit Marc Ikels' requirements. "It has to be a good fit," he says. "I won't invest people's money if they want me picking individual stocks or chasing hot trends. That's not how to make solid, long-term gains. I strictly follow an evidence-based approach based on the ideas of Nobel laureates and substantiated with data going as far back as 1926."

Because Marc doesn't earn commissions, he accepts clients with a minimum $500,000 to invest. "Otherwise," he says, "the business model doesn't make sense."

He charges a minimum of $7,000 a year. That's 1.4 percent per year for investors with $500,000 invested. The fee percentage drops to 0.85 percent for portfolios valued between $2 million and $5 million. He charges 0.75 percent for portfolios valued between $5 million and $7 million; 0.6 percent for portfolios valued between $7 million and $10 million; and 0.45 percent for portfolios valued above $10 million. All figures are in US dollars.

Marc is a fully licensed CFP, and he offers holistic financial planning that goes beyond portfolio construction. His services include investment planning, risk planning, and estate planning.

Company Name: Providend Ltd
Servicing: All nationalities (except Americans)
Minimum Account Size: $1,000,000 SGD
Contact E-mail: max_keeling@providend.com
Website: providend.com/max-keeling/

Max Keeling is Head of Expat Advisory at Providend Ltd. Providend's wealth management advisors exclusively build portfolios with low-cost index funds, including those offered by Dimensional Fund Advisors (DFA). "We charge SGD$5,000 for initial financial planning work, which typically takes 4–6 meetings," says Max. These meetings focus on goal-setting, with respect to lifestyle and plans relating to future repatriation. They include a review of any current investments and a savings trajectory analysis to see if the client is on track. Within the first three or four meetings, Providend also reviews approaches to any company stock options and formulates plans for the client to cover children's education costs. They review insurance needs and also help with wills and estate planning.

"We charge ongoing fees on assets we manage which starts at 1 percent, which would be scaled down for accounts over SGD$2m," says Max. "We also charge an implementation fee on initial funds invested."

Why Many Global Expats are Naming Their Newborns Mark

PlanVision's Mark Zoril might be one of the most popular people among expats worldwide. He helps investors of every nationality set up portfolios of low-cost index funds. Unlike most financial advisors, he doesn't invest his clients' money. Instead, he instructs them how to do it on their own.

The father of two daughters has been in the financial services industry since 1994. He has worked with plenty of smaller employers on their company-sponsored retirement plans. Forming PlanVision in 2012 was a groundbreaking decision.

"My philosophy in forming PlanVision was that most people massively overpay for investment guidance," he says. "I had grown weary of the sales tactics and convoluted payment and commission systems throughout the industry." He knew that low-cost index funds (and ETFs) gave investors the best odds of success. That's why he coaches investors to build portfolios with such funds.

Mark says, "The best strategy for people is to create a broadly diversified portfolio, save as much as possible, ignore investments up and downs, and keep the financial services industry away from your money."

PlanVision charges $189 a year. "Getting to know and helping people of so many different nationalities and residences is the most satisfying part of the work we do," he says, "We help our clients use platforms such as Vanguard, Interactive Brokers, Saxo Capital Markets and Swissquote, among others." Mark shows clients how to build a portfolio of index funds through a screen sharing process. Investors can ask for his advice as often as they want. His firm helps with financial planning, too. It's all included in the total cost of $189 a year, which is renewable after the first year, at $8 a month.

It's easy to see why so many expats are naming their children Mark.

Table 6.1 Firms Building Index Fund Portfolios for Expatriates

Advisory Firm	Nationality Serviced	Maximum Management Costs	Minimum Account Size	Contact Information
Noto Financial Planning	Americans	1.0%	$1,000,000	notofp.com
Creveling & Creveling	All nationalities	1.2%	$750,000	crevelingandcreveling.com
MASECO Private Wealth	US expats in the UK and UK expats in the US	1.25%	$1,000,000	masecoprivatewealth.com
Index Fund Advisors	Americans	0.9%	$100,000	ifa.com
Buckingham Strategic Wealth	Americans	$1000 minimum	No minimum	buckinghamstrategicwealth.com
Jason Heath at Objective Financial Partners Inc.	Canadians	Consultation charges	No minimum	objectivefinancialpartners.com
CI Direct Investing (formerly WealthBar)	Canadians	0.35%–0.60%	$25,000 CAD	cidirectinvesting.com
Satis Asset Management	British Investors	0.9%	£500,000	satisuk.com
AES International	All nationalities (except Americans)	1.25%	$250,000 USD	aesinternational.com
Sarwa	All nationalities (except Americans)	0.85%	$5 USD	sarwa.co
Marc Ikels Consulting	All nationalities (except Americans)	$7000 minimum (fees drop as a percentage of assets)	$500,000 USD	marcikelsconsulting.com
Max Keeling at Providend Ltd	All nationalities (except Americans)	1% (fees drop as a percentage of assets)	$1,000,000 SGD	max_keeling@providend.com providend.com/max-keeling/
PlanVision	All nationalities	$189 per year (renewable at $8 per month)	None	planvisionmn.com

Why are the Entry Points Often High?

Table 6.1 lists some investment firms that offer services for expats. You'll notice that some of the required account minimums are high. Such firms aren't greedy; they're practical. Many provide time-intensive customer service multiple times each year. For this reason, they can service only a small number of clients. Because they don't earn commissions or mutual fund kickbacks, their profit margins are also slim. As a result, many require large-dollar entry points just to survive.

Expats who wish to fly solo, however, can build lower-cost portfolios of indexed mutual funds or ETFs. In the chapters ahead, I'll explain how to do that.

Chapter 7

Thirty-four Questions Do-It-Yourself Investors Ask

1. How do I Purchase ETFs or Indexed Mutual Funds Through a Brokerage?

If you haven't done this before, you could hire PlanVision to show you how to open an account and purchase your funds. As mentioned in the previous chapter, PlanVision uses a screen share concept to hold your hand through the process with a live human being. They charge $189 a year, and it might be the best $189 you'll ever spend. It can save a lot of time and hassle. What's more, your annual subscription entitles you to ask as many questions as you want for a 12-month period, and you can renew their services for $8 a month.

2. What's the Best Brokerage To Use?

For Americans

Most American expats invest with Vanguard, Interactive Brokers or Schwab. But in most cases, if Americans don't already have an account before they move overseas, they will need to put a US address on the application to open their new account.

Other Nationalities

Several reputable brokerages allow non-American expats to build portfolios of ETFs (or indexed mutual funds) without jeopardizing their non-residency tax status. This means, depending where you live, you won't have to pay capital gains taxes. Some of the popular brokerages include Interactive Brokers, Swissquote, Swissquote Bank Europe and Saxo Capital Markets. Each brokerage charges different commission rates per trade, but Interactive Brokers is the lowest cost and a favorite among expats.

That, however, doesn't mean Interactive Brokers is the best brokerage for everyone. After all, it's a US brokerage. The US government can charge deceased heirs of expats an American estate tax if their holdings exceed $60,000 USD. That risk *might* drop to zero if expats purchase off non-US exchanges (which all non-American expats should do, regardless of the brokerage they use). Some people, however, prefer to pay higher commissions with other firms (such as Swissquote or Saxo Capital Markets) to keep their money away from any US-based firm.

Marc Ikels is one of them. The financial advisor (profiled in the previous chapter) says, "I don't use Interactive Brokers for my clients' accounts or my own. Brokerages like Swissquote Bank Europe and Saxo Capital Markets charge higher commissions. However, I view those higher charges as if they were cheap insurance policies against US tax rules that could change anytime and then hit expats' heirs with a big tax bill."

No matter which brokerage you choose, the differences in commission fees won't make or break your retirement. Internal fund costs (expense ratio fees) matter more, so we need to keep those fees low. Commissions, in contrast, are relatively small, one-time charges for each purchase or sale.

3. What's the Difference Between an Exchange-Traded Index Fund (ETF) and an Index Fund?

An ETF and an index fund (also known as a tracker fund or indexed mutual fund) are much the same. If they track the same market and charge equivalent expense ratios, they should perform identically. For example, Vanguard's S&P 500 index fund holds the same 500 stocks that the iShares S&P 500 ETF holds. But the manner of purchasing an index fund and ETF differ. You buy index funds directly from a fund company. Doing so rarely incurs commission costs, and investors can often reinvest dividends for free.

In contrast, investors purchase ETFs directly from a stock exchange through a brokerage that usually charges commissions. All of the ETFs I list in my model portfolios pay dividends. But with some of those ETFs, dividends get invested automatically. These are called *accumulating units ETFs*. Non-accumulating units ETFs (known as *distributing units* ETFs) don't reinvest dividends automatically. In such cases, the dividends get pushed into the cash portion of the brokerage account. You can use such cash to purchase an ETF holding, combining the money you deposited from your savings.

Non-expatriate investors in some countries can purchase commission-free index funds from a few select brokerages. But opportunities for expats to do likewise are limited. It's tempting for Canadian, Australian, or British expats to purchase index funds from their home-country financial institutions. But doing so may generate higher taxable consequences.

Many expatriates (with Americans being an exception) can avoid paying capital gains taxes on investment profits if they invest with firms situated where they won't be charged capital gains taxes and if their resident country won't tax them on foreign earned investment gains. Legal tax havens for investments include locations such as Luxembourg, Singapore, and Hong Kong.

4. Do Non-Americans Have to Pay US Estate Taxes upon Death if They Own US Index Shares?

The US Internal Revenue Service (IRS) is crafty. Non-Americans buying ETFs off a US stock market could end up paying estate taxes to the US government at death if the investment holdings exceed US $60,000.[1] Some people living *la vida loca* might enjoy sticking their heirs with an American estate tax, but most expats would prefer to bequeath money to their family, not the US government.

Table 7.1 shows four identical US index funds that non-Americans could buy shares in through an offshore brokerage. The only differences are the expense ratio costs and where each product is

Table 7.1 S&P 500 Indexes Available on Different Global Exchanges

ETF	Purchasing Symbol/Quote/Ticker and Available Exchange	Expense ratio	Would US Estate Taxes Apply?
State Street Global Advisors S&P 500 ETF	SPY: New York Stock Exchange	0.09%	Yes
Vanguard Canada S&P 500 ETF	VFV: Toronto Stock Exchange	0.08%	No
Vanguard S&P 500 UCITS ETF	VUSA: London Stock Exchange	0.07%	No
iShares Australia S&P 500 ETF	IVV: Australian Stock Exchange	0.04%	No

Costs as of June 2021.
SOURCES: Vanguard USA; Vanguard Canada; Vanguard UK; iShares Australia.

domiciled. Non-American expats should not purchase the State Street Global Advisors S&P 500 ETF because it trades on the New York Stock Exchange. Doing so might ensure that an expat's heirs pay US estate taxes when the expat dies.

5. What's a Sector-Specific ETF?

Hundreds of different ETF products exist, many of which are sector specific. That means you can buy ETFs tracking almost anything: small company stocks, mining stocks, health care stocks, retail company stocks. Some of the ETFs flooding the markets are just plain wacky. An ETF focusing on the fishing industry is one.

Most exist to excite gamblers. Those thinking that mining stocks will surge this month may purchase a mining stock ETF, perhaps trading their health care ETFs to do so. Meanwhile, an even more backward stock market junkie might choose (and yes, it exists) an ETF specifically designed for its gut-wrenching volatility. The ETF market is a bit like Bangkok. Anything goes.

Some investors (usually those who don't know what they're doing) buy sector-based ETFs with the best recent performance record. For example, as I write this in June 2021, the iShares Nasdaq Biotechnology ETF (IBB) reports a 10-year compound annual return of 15.93 percent per year. The iShares US Medical Devices ETF (IHI) has a 10-year compound return of 18.34 percent per year.[2] Both outperformed the US stock market index. But chasing yesterday's winners is an expensive game to play. A hot-performing sector during one time period often stinks like a turd over the next measured time period.

Stick to ETFs providing global exposure and exposure to your home-country market (if you're from a large, first world country). The chapters that follow will show how to build responsible, diversified portfolios.

6. Should I Buy an Index that's Currency Hedged?

If it's a stock market ETF, that answer should be no. Some funds are hedged to a specific currency. When British investors buy, for example, a US stock market index, the fund is subjected to US dollar movements. When a fund company creates a currency-hedged version, it attempts to limit the foreign currency's influence on the fund.

But currency fluctuations are natural. If we accept that, we'll be better off than if we try engineering fixes for the problem.

To understand the problems with currency-hedged funds, it's important to recognize that currency fluctuations aren't always bad. If, for example, the British pound falls against most foreign currencies, then investors could profit from a nonhedged international index, as the growing strength of foreign currencies against the pound juices the returns of a foreign stock index in British pounds.

Buying products that try to smooth these ups and downs through currency hedging involves an extra layer of costs—and those costs can hurt your returns.

In Dan Bortolotti's book *MoneySense Guide to the Perfect Portfolio,* he outlines the true cost of hedging using two US S&P 500 indexes trading on the Canadian market. One was hedged to the Canadian dollar; the other was not. In theory, their returns in local currencies should be the same, but they're not even close. The currency hedging adds an extra cost of 1 percent to 3.5 percent per year.[3]

According to Raymond Kerzérho, a director of research at PWL Capital, currency-hedged funds get burdened with high internal costs, dragging down results. In a PWL Capital research paper, he examined the returns of hedged S&P 500 indexes between 2006 and 2009. Even though the funds were meant to track the index, they underperformed it by an average of 1.49 percentage points per year. Although less dramatic, he also estimated that between 1980 and 2005, when currencies were less volatile, the tracking errors caused by hedging would have cost 0.23 percentage points per year.[4]

The more cross-currency transactions that a fund makes, the higher its expenses—because even financial institutions pay fees to have money moved around. Consider the example of a currency exchange booth at an airport. Take a $10 Canadian bill and convert it into euros. Then take the euros they give you, and ask for $10 Canadian back. You'll get turned down. The spreads you pay between the buy and sell rates will ensure that you come away with less than $10.

Large institutions don't pay such high spreads, but they still pay spreads.

With indexes, it's best to go with a naturally unhedged product. Accepting currency volatility (instead of trying to hedge against it) will increase your odds of higher returns.

If an ETF is currency-hedged, it will say so. For example, here are two S&P 500 ETFs that trade on the Canadian stock market. Here's how they look on the iShares Canada website:

XSP iShares S&P 500 Index ETF (CAD-Hedged)
XUS iShares Core S&P 500 Index ETF

If bond ETFs are currency-hedged, they don't tend to have the same long-term performance drags that occur with currency-hedged stock market ETFs, when compared to their non-hedged alternatives.

7. What's the Scoop on Withholding Taxes? (For Non-Americans)

Most stocks pay dividends, which are cash proceeds to shareholders. Indexes and exchange-traded funds do likewise because they comprise individual stocks. Regardless of whether your money is situated in a capital-gains-free zone, most investors are liable for dividend taxes.

I'll show a Canadian stock market ETF to demonstrate how much an investor would pay in dividend withholding taxes.

If you averaged a pretax return of 10 percent per year, roughly 8 percent of that growth would come from capital appreciation. Such growth reflects the rising value of the stocks within the index. Most stocks pay shareholder dividends as well, and ETF investors are entitled to their share. If dividends were 2 percent per year, then you would pay 15 percent tax on your 2 percent dividend. In this case, your 2 percent dividend would be reduced to 1.7 percent. As a result, if the pretax return on your ETF were 10 percent, your posttax return would be 9.7 percent.

How Withholding Taxes Affect Returns on a Canadian ETF or Stock

8% from capital gains
+2% from dividends
=10% pretax return
15% tax on dividends ($2 \times 0.15 = 0.3$)
=10% pretax return − 0.3% dividend tax
Net return: 9.7%

Non–American expats choosing to own individual US stocks (Google, Microsoft, Coca-Cola, etc.) must fill out a W-8BEN form. It's officially known as a "Certificate of Foreign Status of Beneficial Owner for United States Tax Withholding." Brokerages mail the forms to investors every couple of years. Investors fill them out before mailing them back to the brokerages. The brokerage then sends them to the IRS.

ETF investors trading on non-US stock exchanges don't have to fill out such forms. But there's one thing to remember. In most cases, they're still charged withholding taxes. The rate may differ, depending on the country's respective tax treaty, but if there are US stocks within the index (for example), the US government has a way of siphoning off money. You probably won't see it, so consider it a ghost tax.

★ ★ ★

Investors in offshore pension schemes also pay dividend withholding taxes. Unknowledgeable sales reps won't disclose this, but the company must. Here's an example on the Friends Provident International website, under "Investment Benefits":

"Virtually tax free accumulation of your savings (some dividends may be received net of withholding tax, deducted at source in the country of origin)".[5]

When investing offshore using ETFs, you can see the tax machinery under the hood. Other costs of the financial industry also become apparent. Many can't be avoided, but it's good to know what they are.

8. Will You Have to Pay Currency Conversions?

If an investor earning a salary in Malaysian ringgit buys a mutual fund of Southeast Asian stocks, she'll get dinged on a currency conversion. Investors earning Australian dollars and buying a global stock market mutual fund will pay likewise. There's no way around this. You might not see the cost of such a transaction, but that doesn't mean it doesn't exist.

For instance, if your salary is in Indian rupees and you buy an Indian stock or shares in an Indian stock market mutual fund, you won't pay a currency conversion fee. However, if the same Indian-based investor bought an Indian-based mutual fund focusing on US stocks, some kind of currency spread would take a nibble from the fund's returns. The Indian fund manager would need to convert Indian rupees to purchase the fund's US stocks.

You'll never see such costs on your statement, of course, but they're an unavoidable cost of doing business.

When investing in ETFs from a brokerage, you'll likely see such nibbling fees. It's much like driving a car with a transparent hood. If your salary is in Singapore dollars and you buy a global ETF off the Canadian stock market, your money must be converted to Canadian dollars. Like a money exchange at an international airport, the banks are going to take a bite. Don't let anyone convince you otherwise.

Such hidden banking costs occur only during transactions. And they're negligible, compared to high ongoing mutual fund costs or account fees.

9. Should I Be Concerned about Currency Risks?

Many investors think that if they buy an ETF priced in a foreign currency, their money is subject to that foreign currency's movement. This isn't the case. For example, assume a Spanish expatriate buys an ETF tracking the Spanish market. If he buys it off a British stock exchange, the investor might see the price quoted in British pounds. However, the movement of the British currency has no bearing on the Spanish ETF.

Imagine the following scenario:

- An investor buys a Spanish ETF trading at 20 pounds per unit on the British market.
- Spanish stocks slide sideways for one year after the investor purchases the ETF.
- The British pound falls 50 percent against the euro during that year.

The British pound's movement wouldn't affect the investment itself. In this case, despite the fact that the Spanish market didn't make money, the ETF purchased at 20 pounds per unit would now be priced at 40 pounds per unit. The British currency crash would affect the ETF's listed price in pounds, but its overall value in euros would be entirely dependent on the movement of the Spanish stock market.

Likewise, a New Zealander buying a global stock market ETF off the Australian market wouldn't be pegged to the value of the Aussie dollar. While the ETF may be priced in Australian dollars, its holdings reflect the currencies of the stock markets it tracks.

If the Australian dollar dropped 90 percent compared to a basket of global currencies, a global stock market index trading on the Aussie market would shoot skyward in price. Australian dollar currency movements wouldn't affect its true value.

New investors sometimes compare posted performance returns in different currencies. They might ask, "Why is the posted five-year return on the global stock market index in US dollars different to the posted five-year return on the global stock market in GBP?" The returns are actually identical if the gains are converted into a constant currency.

10. Do the Unit Prices of ETFs Show Which are Expensive or Cheap?

I often receive e-mails from investors asking me about the prices associated with certain exchange-traded funds. For instance, an American might see a Vanguard S&P 500 ETF trading at $90 per share, and an iShares S&P 500 ETF trading at $180 per share. Although Vanguard and iShares are different providers, their respective ETFs are still tracking the same 500 large American stocks. Their values are identical.

In the same vein, five $1 bills aren't worth less than one $5 bill. The quoted price difference between two ETFs tracking the same market is a mirage.

That said, one ETF is actually cheaper than another if its expense ratio is lower. If Vanguard's S&P 500 ETF has an expense ratio of 0.09 percent per year and the iShares S&P 500 ETF carries costs of just 0.07 percent, the iShares ETF would be cheaper, based on its lower annual fee (To be clear, nobody should ever sweat about such a minor cost difference).

11. If I Have a Lump Sum, Should I Invest It All at Once?

Most stock market investors add monthly or quarterly to their investments. Such a process is called dollar cost averaging. Doing so ensures that they pay less than an average cost over time. If they invest a constant, standard sum, they'll purchase more units when prices are low and fewer units when prices are high.

But what if you found $100,000 on the street? You report it to the local police, nobody claims it, and you become the happy (or paranoid) recipient of a drug dealer's spoils. Should you invest it all at once, or divide your purchases over many months or quarters?

Much depends on your psychology. If you invest the entire amount and the markets crash 20 percent the following day, how would you feel? If it wouldn't bother you, consider the lump-sum investment. This is based on findings by University of Connecticut finance professors John R. Knight and Lewis Mandell. In a 1993 study spanning a variety of time periods, they found that investing a windfall up front beat dollar cost averaging most of the time.[6]

Vanguard agrees. They published a similar study in 2012. It came to the same conclusion.[7]

Odds will be in your favor if you invest the money as soon as you have it.

12. I'm in Some Expensive Products, but They're Currently Down in Value. Should I Sell Now or Wait?

Selling investments at a loss is like a kick to the groin. But if your money is languishing in a high-cost account, making a switch is usually best. Don't wait until the account recovers. Here's why:

Rising and falling markets influence most investment portfolios. If a well-allocated, actively managed portfolio gets hammered in a given year, a well-allocated index portfolio would have done likewise. The opposite applies during years when the markets roar: a rising tide raises all boats. This is one of the reasons you can't congratulate yourself (or your advisor) for gaining 15 percent, 20 percent, even 25 percent in a single year. The big question should be: How did an equally allocated portfolio of index funds perform in comparison?

Here's another example that puts the same concept in perspective.

Imagine you bought a house for $100,000. It drops in value to $80,000. You're interested in buying the house next door, but you would need to sell your own house in order to do so. Should you wait for your house to rise in value, back to the $100,000 you paid, before buying the house next door? If you do, you're nuts. The same factors increasing the price of your home would do likewise for the house next door.

The same premise applies with the stock and bond markets. If you're trading one diversified portfolio for another, you'll make a market-to-market switch. If stock markets are on a low and you sell your high-cost account to build an index portfolio, you'll likely be selling and buying on a low as well. If markets are on a high, you'll be selling high to buy high. Whatever you do, don't time your sales or purchases based on where you or someone else thinks the markets are headed. That's a fool's mistake.

13. What If I Find a Higher-Performing Bond Index?

Some people might find better-performing bond indexes than what they originally started with. But always remember that the past is rarely repeated in the future. If a bond ETF pays a 4 percent yield today and a different bond ETF pays 2 percent, don't consider the yields to be carved in stone. Prices of the bonds themselves, as well as the ever-changing average yields (while new bonds replace old) can influence bond ETF returns. Rather than obsessing over past returns and current interest yields, here are the three most important considerations:

- Ensure that your bond ETF comprises just first-world government or AAA-rated corporate bonds.
- When possible, make sure it comprises short-term bonds (maturing in three or fewer years) or buy a broad bond market index (never a long-term bond index).
- Ensure that the expense ratio charge is 0.4 percent or less.

14. What If I Find a Cheaper ETF?

New ETFs keep getting launched. Be wary of trading. Moving from one ETF to another will cost a commission fee, and it might not be worth it. An ETF charging 0.15 percent per year costs just $15 for every $10,000 invested. Another ETF charging 0.12 percent would cost $12. Is it really worth saving $3 per year when it might cost as much as $50 to make a trade? Besides, the ETF that charges 0.15 percent this year might charge 0.09 percent next year. Over time, ETFs often reduce their expense ratio fees.

Brokerages want you to trade. But don't. Rapid trading equals more money for the brokerage, less for the trader. Many brokerages offer discounted commissions to frequent traders. But don't get sucked into the bank's web.

15. Should I Be Most Concerned about Commissions, Annual Account Fees, Fund Costs, or Exchange Rate Fees?

Hands down, ongoing fund costs and annual account fees are far more detrimental than commissions and exchange rate fees. Here are two scenarios. Joe pays 3 percent commissions on each of his purchases.

Table 7.2 Joe's and Julie's Profits

	Joe	Julie
Invests per year	$10,000	$10,000
Commission paid on purchases	3%	0%
Amount annually invested after commissions	$9,700	$10,000
Annual return made before fees	8%	8%
Annual fund/account costs	0.3%	2.5%
Annual returns after fees	7.7%	5.5%
Investment duration	25 years	25 years
Money grows to	$731,066.88	$539,659.81

Joe then pays 0.3 percent in hidden ETF expense ratio charges, with no additional account fees.

Julie doesn't pay any commissions to purchase her investments, but her mutual fund expense ratios average 1.5 percent per year, and her account carries an additional 1 percent annual cost. As you'll see, annual costs on the account's total value are a far bigger drag on profits than commissions are.

If Joe and Julie each invested $10,000 per year, earning 8 percent per year before fees, Table 7.2 shows how their profits would compare.

Sure, purchase commissions and exchange rate costs are a pain. I liken them to doing a bike race, where once in a while your opponent leans over and flicks at your brake. But ongoing account fees and high fund charges are worse. They're like another rider holding your seat for the duration of the race.

16. How Little Can I Invest Each Month?

Some brokerages, such as Vanguard for Americans, allow people to invest as little as $100 a month without charging them commission. But those using a discount brokerage (and paying commissions on each purchase) should consider only larger monthly sums.

Let's assume you're a non-American using a brokerage where minimum commissions are 28 euros per trade. If you invest 100 euros, you would be giving away 28 percent in commissions. To keep costs low, think of the 1 percent rule. Never pay more than 1 percent of your total invested proceeds in commissions.

You can't exactly strong-arm your brokerage into providing a better deal. But think strategically about how much you'll invest at any one time. Assume minimum commissions are 28 euros. By following the 1 percent rule, you would never invest less than 2,800 euros. If you don't have 2,800 euros a month, save for the investing occasion.

Perhaps you can save 500 euros monthly. In this case, keep the money in a savings account until you've accumulated 2,800 euros. Then make your purchase.

Don't be afraid to buy one index at a time. The first time you save 2,800 euros, perhaps you could buy an international stock index. A few months later, buy a bond index. Build your portfolio slowly, one index at a time. Don't worry about rebalancing until your portfolio hits roughly 50,000 euros. From that point, just make purchases that will align your portfolio with its goal allocation.

In the case of all-in-one portfolio ETFs, which I'll describe in later chapters, you won't even have to rebalance or worry about which ETF to buy in any given month or quarter.

17. Stock Markets Are High. Should I Really Start Investing?

Finance writers and news media love writing headlines such as these: "US Markets Hit Their Highest Point Ever!" "Are Stocks Ready for a Crash?" "Bonds Are Ready to Fall!"

Let me cut through the murk and give you the market certainties. Ready?

Stocks will continue to hit new heights.

Stocks will crash.

Bonds will decline in value.

Bonds will rise in value.

These four scenarios will occur over and over during your investment lifetime. Those trying to time their purchases and sales will almost certainly underperform a disciplined, rebalanced portfolio of stock and bond indexes. Sure, you might make a lucky prediction once or twice. But that would be a travesty. Much like the guy who wins big during his first trip to the casino, he's going to go back. And eventually the house will win.

When building your investment portfolio, forget about predictions. If you're adding a lump sum (because you happen to have the money), diversify it properly. Don't try to guess whether you should buy bonds, buy stocks, or sit on your rump waiting for a better deal. Investing isn't a sprint; it's an ultramarathon. You're not trying to race somebody else to the next telephone pole. The real finish line is many years ahead.

Always remember how the average investor performs. Fear, greed, and general speculation cause investors to buy high, sell low, and miss opportunities. Instead, put your calculating brain toward something more constructive: how to best wash the car, shave your face or legs, or get a whole pizza down your gullet in less than five minutes. Speculating with the stock market is a loser's game. If you can't restrain yourself, hire an advisor.

18. Should I Buy ETFs from Vanguard, iShares, Schwab or Another Low-Cost Provider?

This is a bit like asking, "Should I buy my bananas from WalMart or Safeway?" If two ETFs track the same market, you're buying the same bananas. Fund companies post expense ratios on their websites. It matters little, for example, whether you choose Vanguard, iShares, or Schwab. These are three of the biggest names in the world of ETFs. As such, they're good at tracking stock market returns and their costs are competitive. If all other things are equal, choose the ETF with the lowest expense ratio.

19. Can Muslims Build a Portfolio of Shariah-Compliant Funds?

Muslims want to respect Shariah law. That's why they shouldn't invest in companies that sell or produce alcohol, tobacco, pork products, conventional financial services (banking, insurance, etc.), weapons, defense products, and entertainment. Shariah compliance also means Muslims should shun government and corporate bonds. The Koran states that interest payments are considered usury. This makes it tougher to create a diversified portfolio.

But it's not impossible.

The London Stock Exchange offers several Shariah-compliant index funds (ETFs). The most diversified is the iShares World Islamic ETF (ISWD). Over the 10-year period ending May 31, 2021, it averaged a compound annual return of 10.52 percent. By comparison, its non Shariah-compliant equivalent, the iShares Core MSCI World Index (SWDA) gained an average of 14.31 percent.

But don't assume Shariah-compliant index funds won't perform as well. Sometimes, they'll beat plain vanilla index funds. Other times, they won't. For example, during the 2008–2009 financial crisis, Shariah-compliant funds trounced the returns of traditional index funds because the stocks of financial companies led that decline. Shariah-compliant funds didn't own such stocks.

Some decades the Shariah-compliant ETF will beat its non Shariah-compliant equivalent. Other decades it won't. But over an investment lifetime, their results will be similar.

When constructing diversified portfolios, most investors use stocks and bonds. But Muslims shouldn't invest in traditional bonds because bonds pay interest. That's against Shariah law. As a result, financial institutions have created Sukuks. They're known as Shariah-compliant bonds, but they aren't really bonds at all. Many have complex internal frameworks. For that reason, gold ETFs (which are also Shariah-compliant) might be a better option. Like bonds, a gold ETF serves to stabilize a portfolio when stocks fall hard.

Table 7.3 Shariah-compliant Portfolio Samples

Fund Name	Conservative	Cautious	Balanced	Assertive	Aggressive
iShares MSCI World Islamic ETF (ISWD)	25%	40%	45%	60%	85%
iShares MSCI Emerging Markets Islamic ETF (ISEM)	5%	5%	10%	15%	15%
iShares Physical Gold (SGLN)	70%	55%	45%	25%	0%

In fact, from 1972–2021, a portfolio comprising 60 percent US stocks and 40 percent gold recorded just 10 down years. That compares similarly to 60 percent US stocks and 40 percent bonds, which recorded 9 down years over the same time period. Each portfolio would have also earned similar long-term returns: the portfolio with 60 percent US stocks and 40 percent gold averaged 10.81 percent compared to the portfolio with 60 percent US stocks and 40 percent US bonds, which averaged 9.67 percent.[8]

Table 7.3 shows my recommendations for Shariah-compliant portfolios that represent different tolerances for risk. Gold, in isolation, is more volatile than stocks, which surprises a lot of people. From 1972–2020, gold recorded 19 losing years. Eight of those years saw drops that were worse than 10 percent. In contrast, US stocks had just 11 losing years over the same 49 calendar years. Six of those drops were worse than 10 percent.[9] But during big calendar year declines for stocks, gold doesn't fall as far. Sometimes, it even rises. That's why gold can help to stabilize a portfolio when stocks hit the skids.

20. What Percentage Should You Have In Stocks and Bonds?

This is an important investment decision because it could affect whether you're able to stay the course when stocks crash. Not everyone, for example, is emotionally wired to see their hard-earned money sink. Yet most people don't know that. They overestimate their tolerance for risk.

Imagine you were just diagnosed with cancer. I know it's horrible to think about that. But for many people, it's a frightening reality. You look up the odds of survival and find that, with the right treatment, your odds of dying within 5 years are 30 percent. How would you respond emotionally to that news over the following week, month or two year period? If you haven't had cancer, let me help with the answer. You won't know. That's right. You might think you know, but you don't. Some of the bravest people fall apart. Others, with a quiet internal resolve, remain surprisingly upbeat.

Stock market crashes aren't as scary as the dreaded C. But they have something in common. Unless you began investing before 2007 (and lived through the crash of 2008/2009) you have no clue how you would respond to a stock market dump. You can read all you want about market history. You could meditate and do your best to block out the media's noise. But if you overestimate your personal tolerance for risk, you might eventually capitulate and sell at a low. I can guarantee that several of your friends will do so. Several media experts will also claim (as they always do) that the markets will get worse before they get better.

If you began investing after 2009, you still don't know how you would respond to calls for financial Armageddon. After all, from 2009 until the time of this writing (June 2021) stocks had an easy ride. A couple of short blips occurred along the way (yes, the mid-year 2020 COVID drop was a blip). But there weren't any multi-year declines. In fact, the period from 2009 to 2021 saw only one calendar year drop for the world's largest stock market. US stocks fell about 4.52 percent in 2018.

Most financial advisors show their clients a variety of scenarios to determine the investors' tolerance for risk. They ask clients if they could handle seeing their money drop 10 percent, or 15 percent, or 40 percent in a given year. Clients that claim they could emotionally withstand large drops are deemed, "high risk" investors. Advisors build such clients' portfolios with high stock allocations and low bond allocations. In other words, they might be portfolios comprising 100 percent stocks, or 80 percent stocks and 20 percent bonds. Such portfolios, historically, have earned higher returns than portfolios with higher bond allocations. But such portfolios fall harder when stocks drop, so such investors would require strong stomachs.

Table 7.4 shows historical returns for US stocks and bonds, based on different allocations.

But investors also require a broader sense of market history. After all, higher risk portfolios of 100 percent stocks, or 80 percent stocks and 20 percent bonds don't win every decade. If high-risk investors don't know that, they might give up if their portfolio underperforms a lower risk allocation. They might sell on a low, sealing in losses. Or, they might cease to add fresh money, or add less money every month.

For example, according to portfoliovisualizer.com, a lump sum comprising 100 percent to a global stock market index would have gained 6.09 percent annually from January 2000 to May 31, 2021. That would have turned $10,000 into $35,447.

Table 7.4 Historical Investment Returns Depending on the Mix (1926–2020)

	100% Stocks	80% Stocks/ 20% Bonds	70% Stocks/ 30% Bonds	60% Stocks/ 40% Bonds	50% Stocks/ 50% Bonds
Average Annual Return	10.1%	9.4%	9.1%	8.6%	8.2%
Calendar Years with a Loss	26/93	24/93	23/93	22/93	18/93
Calendar Years with a Gain	67/93	69/93	70/93	71/93	75/93
Worst Year	−43.1% (1931)	−34.9% (1931)	−30.7% (1931)	−26.6% (1931)	−22.5% (1931)
Best Year	+54.2% (1933)	+45.4% (1933)	+41.1% (1933)	+36.7% (1933)	32.3% (1933)

Source: Vanguard.com (using US stocks and US intermediate government bonds).

But over the same 21 years and five months, a lower-risk portfolio comprising 60 percent in a global stock index and 40 percent in a global bond index would have averaged 6.41 percent. That would have turned $10,000 into $37,808.

Portfolios with higher stock allocations should beat portfolios with lower stock allocations over a long time period. But investors with higher risk allocations might require a surprising amount of patience and mental strength.

For example, assume three neighbors selected different allocations in January 2000. They each started with $10,000 and they added a further $1000 a month. Tom wanted to earn the best possible returns, so he chose to put 100 percent of his money in a global stock index.

Dick selected a portfolio with 80 percent in a global stock index and 20 percent in a global bond index.

Harry, the most risk-averse of the three, chose a portfolio with 60 percent in a global stock index and 40 percent in a global bond index.

Three years later, on December 31, 2002, the three neighbors are chatting over beers. They had each invested a total of $46,000 ($10,000 as their initial investment, plus a further $1000 a month). Tom, who invested 100 percent in a global stock index, now has $34,185. Dick, who invested 80 percent in global stocks and 20 percent in global bonds has $37,742. And Harry, the most conservative investor, with 60 percent global stocks and 40 percent global bonds, has $41,569.

Tom asks, "How can this be? I have more in stocks than you guys, so I should have earned better returns." Harry replies, "Tom, we've only been investing for three years. Give it time. You probably will earn the highest long-term returns. But you might have to be really patient."

Ten years after they began their investment journey, on December 31, 2009, Tom, Dick and Harry get together at a neighborhood barbecue. By then, they had each invested a total of $130,000 ($10,000 as their initial investment plus $1000 a month).

At this point, Tom (the highest risk investor) has $159,600. But Dick and Harry both have more. Dick has $167,575 and Harry has $173,109. The previous year, Tom had to fight every urge not to give up. In 2008, his portfolio of 100 percent global stocks dropped a whopping 40.36 percent. Dick's portfolio (80 percent global stocks, 20 percent global bonds) fell 32.78 percent. And Harry's portfolio (60 percent global stocks, 40 percent global bonds) fell 25.14 percent.

Fifteen years after they began investing, Harry (the lower risk investor) still had more money. On December 31, 2014, Tom had $340,602. Dick had $344,786. And Harry had $345,381. In fact, it wasn't until their 17th year of investing that Tom's higher risk portfolio actually pulled away (possibly for good). But during those 17 years, would Tom have had the mettle to stay the course? Would Dick, with 80 percent global stocks and 20 percent global bonds have had enough emotional fortitude not to sabotage his ride? After all, he also had a high-risk portfolio that took 17 years before it caught the lower-risk portfolio with 60 percent stocks and 40 percent bonds.

Table 7.5 shows the portfolios side by side. As a reminder, they each began with $10,000 in January 2000. Then they added $1000 a month for almost 22 years.

Odds are, investors who stay the course will be rewarded for added risk. But how many people know their tolerance for risk? When I ask new investors whether they could emotionally handle a portfolio with 100 percent stocks or 80 percent stocks and 20 percent bonds, most say, "Yes." But most of them are wrong.

After speaking to dozens of financial advisors over the years, I've learned that no matter how many scenarios they show their clients, few investors are capable of knowing how they will respond when stocks hit the skids. There are a couple of reasons for this. First, we aren't good at projecting how we will feel during given circumstances (whether we get cancer or whether we experience a multiple year stock market drop). And when stocks fall hard, stories flood the media suggesting that stocks won't recover for several years. Financial experts who (supposedly) predicted a past stock market crash will be given

Table 7.5 Do You Have The Patience and the Mettle for a Higher Risk Portfolio? Starting with $10,000 and adding $1000 a month January 1, 2000 to May 31, 2021

Year End Portfolio Value	Total Sums Added	Tom 100% Global Stocks	Dick 80% Global Stocks, 20% Global Bonds	Harry 60% Global Stocks, 40% Global Bonds
2000	$22,000	$17,798	$20,551	$21,299
2001	$34,000	$28,357	$30,240	$32,221
2002	$46,000	$34,185	$37,742	$41,569
2003	$58,000	$61,004	$62,954	$64,741
2004	$70,000	$84,415	$85,212	$85,684
2005	$82,000	$106,235	$106,064	$105,436
2006	$94,000	$141,458	$137,343	$132,593
2007	$106,000	$168,149	$162,267	$155,646
2008	$118,000	$109,320	$118,701	$126,720
2009	$130,000	$159,600	$167,575	$173,109
2010	$142,000	$196,007	$202,848	$206,885
2011	$154,000	$194,873	$207,456	$217,987
2012	$166,000	$241,030	$252,582	$261,364
2013	$178,000	$314,037	$315,090	$312,253
2014	$190,000	$340,602	$344,786	$345,381
2015	$202,000	$345,775	$351,175	$353,227
2016	$214,000	$389,021	$392,803	$393,206
2017	$226,000	$495,693	$484,814	$469,456
2018	$238,000	$459,092	$458,128	$453,001
2019	$250,000	$593,066	$573,590	$549,675
2020	$262,000	$704,334	$670,694	$633,326
2021 (to May 31, 2021)	$267,000	$789,449	$736,914	$682,039

SOURCE: portfoliovisualizer.com.

plenty of airtime on TV. They'll say things will get worse before they get better. As you watch your portfolio decline, you'll feel like someone kicked you in the gut. The further the market drops, the more tempted you'll be to sell.

Plenty of your friends will sell on the way down. You'll wish you had, too. And at some point, you might capitulate.

Bonds earn paltry interest. But they prevent portfolios from falling as hard when stocks crash. This is especially important during multiple year stock market declines. You might have picked a portfolio with 100 percent stocks or 80 percent stocks and 20 percent bonds, but if you sell during the next supposed financial Armageddon (which I promise, will be scary) you'll hurt your long-term gains.

So, if you haven't experienced multiple year stock market declines you don't know your tolerance for risk. That's why you should go easy on yourself. If you think you can tolerate a portfolio of 100 percent stocks, choose a portfolio with 80 percent stocks and 20 percent bonds. If you think you can tolerate a portfolio with 80 percent stocks and 20 percent bonds, pick a portfolio with 70 percent stocks and 30 percent stocks. If you think you can handle a portfolio of 70 percent stocks and 30 percent bonds, pick a portfolio with 60 percent stocks and 40 percent bonds. It takes wisdom, after all, to admit what you don't know.

21. Could You Build a Portfolio of Socially Responsible Index Funds?

I once met an expat who refused to invest. He didn't want to support businesses that supported building missiles, hooking kids on cigarettes, or extracting air-polluting fossil fuels. He met a financial salesperson who offered a solution. "Buy this socially responsible fund," he said. But its fees were higher than a looped-out guy at a Burning Man event.

Fortunately, low-cost socially responsible (SRI) index funds do exist.

Most SRI funds don't invest in industries that manufacture tobacco, alcoholic beverages, weapons, or nuclear power. But SRI investors face a few challenges. They might not find a fund that aligns with their beliefs. For example, Charles H. Hennekens and Felicita Andreotti reported in the *American Journal of Medicine* that obesity may soon overcome smoking as the leading cause of preventative death in the United States. Unfortunately, SRI funds don't discriminate against manufacturers of fast food, soft drinks, and processed foods.[10]

Still, SRI index funds have screened out many of Mother Earth's foes. As with Shariah-compliant funds, sometimes they'll beat traditional index funds. Sometimes they won't. But over long periods of time, they should provide similar returns to traditional index funds. Many people believe that SRI funds don't perform as well. But that isn't true.

A research paper by *RBC Global Asset Management* proves it. The FTSE KLD 400 Index tracks the performance of socially responsible US stocks. From April 1990 to April 2012, it beat the S&P 500.[11]

In the United States, Vanguard's oldest SRI index of US stocks has also performed similarly to the S&P 500 Index since its inception in 2000. And over the ten-year period ending November 30, 2020 (the date Vanguard gave me this information), it beat the S&P 500, averaging 15.35 percent per year compared to 14.05 percent for the broader index. That doesn't mean it will continue to win. But over long time periods it should put up a respectable fight.

In the chapters ahead, I've provided sample portfolios with SRI funds.

22. Why Doesn't My Brokerage Offer the Funds I Want?

Plenty of brokerages list a series of funds or available ETFs. Investors often mistake these lists for their respective brokerage's entire universe of offerings. But it isn't. When a brokerage offers access to the Toronto Stock Exchange, for example, investors have access to every stock or ETF that trades on that exchange. Don't get confused by a brokerage's list of selected funds. They simply can't list everything—so they don't. But if the brokerage provides access to a given market exchange, investors can buy anything that trades on that exchange.

For example, more than 6,000 stocks trade on US stock exchanges. Almost 1,600 trade on the Toronto Stock Exchange. The London Stock Exchange lists about 2,500 companies from around Europe. No brokerage would be crazy enough to list all these companies on a convenient home page.

The same goes for all the ETFs that trade on each respective market. If you try to order an ETF that you see in this book, and the brokerage declines the order, get on the phone and call them. They'll make sure you can buy it. They can't afford not to.

23. Why Hasn't My Bond ETF Risen in Value?

Bond index funds rise and fall in price. But over the long term, they aren't meant to gain elevation (unless it's an accumulating units bond ETF where interest gets automatically reinvested). Long term, profits are derived from bond interest payments. Some investors think they've lost money on their bond index, if the unit price has dropped. But with short-term or broad bond market index funds (or ETFs), that rarely happens over a period of two or more years. If it does occur, it will eventually revert to the mean.

For example, we could look at the iShares Core Canadian Short-Term Bond Market Index.

As of this writing (June 2021), it traded at $27.90 per share. Investors who own this index might think it lost money over the previous eight years if they're simply looking at the ETF's unit price on their brokerage statement. After all, on July 1, 2013, it was priced at $28.58.

But this bond index made a profit. It paid regular interest. This went into the cash portion of the brokerage account. If you look at the website at iShares.ca, you'll see this bond ETF's performance, including all interest. According to iShares, this bond index gained a total of 17.9 percent from July 1, 2013. No, it isn't great. But despite what many investors think, it didn't lose money.

From now until 2055 (I made up that year) this ETF's price will float slightly above and slightly below $27.90. Investors don't gain or lose money (at least, not long-term) based on gains from bond ETF unit prices. They just float up and down while the bonds within the ETF keep dishing out interest. The only exception would be an accumulating unit bond ETF. With such products, the interest gets added internally, thus raising the price of the ETF.

24. What If My Bond ETF Is Priced in a Different Currency?

Some investors own international bond ETFs that are priced in US dollars. If the US dollar rises against other currencies, the price of such a bond ETF will show an exaggerated loss. For an American investor, that loss could be real. After all, if they plan to retire in the United States, they'll pay future bills in US dollars. As such, if they buy an international bond market index, they would be taking a currency risk.

But for a non-American investor, that loss isn't real. Always remember that the listed currency of an ETF is irrelevant. For example, if a French investor buys a European bond ETF listed in US dollars, he isn't making a US dollar investment. Instead, he's buying bonds that are valued in euros.

If the US dollar rises against the euro, his bond ETF's price will fall. But if he sold the bonds (seemingly at a loss) and converted the proceeds into euros, he'll likely find that he didn't lose money if he measures his success in euros . . . including interest.

25. Are Cryptocurrencies, like Bitcoin, Good Investments?

These are the four most dangerous words for any investor: This. Time. It's. Different.

If you're reading this after Bitcoin or another cryptocurrency has made a big gain, you'll think, "Hell yeah, these are great investments!" If, on the other hand, cryptocurrencies have taken a recent dump, you're likely thinking, "These things are horrible. They're not real investments."

Bitcoin was the first cryptocurrency. It's also the most widely accepted. Satoshi Nakamoto (who isn't a real guy) is the pseudonym of the person who created it in 2008. It's a peer-to-peer electronic cash system.

Drug dealers were among the first to use Bitcoin. That's because it's tough for authorities to track digital currencies. Since its introduction, however, Bitcoin has yoyoed like a junkie on speed. If you had invested $1,000 in Bitcoin in November 2013, it would have been worth just $150 two months later.

This kind of drop could leave its users or investors with a really big headache. *Business Insider UK* interviewed a drug dealer in 2015. He was burned by Bitcoin's then-recent crash. "It's pretty damn sad," he said. "We have worked so hard over the past 3 months, and for profits to get halved? It's hard to swallow, simple as that, but what can you do. It's a gamble, whether you hold or sell."[12]

I don't feel sorry for a guy who pushes drugs. But there's truth to what he says. Bitcoin and other cryptocurrencies aren't businesses, bonds, or real estate. They don't create cash. They rely, instead, on the greater fool theory. They're only worth as much as the market wants to pay.

Short term, that's also the case with stocks. But if they produce cash—from reinvested earnings or dividends—their prices *can* keep rising. If they don't create profits, their prices won't increase. Assume a pharmaceutical company finds a cure for cancer. Its stock would soar. But if business profits didn't follow, it would eventually crash back to Earth.

Each generation has to learn the same lesson. In the early 1700s, Sir Issac Newton fell for a company that promised to shake the business world. He bought South Sea Company stock. It was meant to facilitate trade with the Americas. Back then, that was like a promise to bring riches from the moon. The stock rose on hope. But it was a fast-talking boxer who couldn't throw a punch. The business didn't earn profits, so the stock price soon collapsed. Newton lost a small fortune. In a way of mocking everyone involved (including himself), he said, "I can calculate the movement of stars, but not the madness of men."[13]

"This time it's different." These words were whispered during The South Sea Bubble. They were uttered during the 1600s Dutch Tulip Craze when multicolored tulips were as expensive as some houses. They were shouted from the rooftops during the 1990s dot-com charade. Tech stocks had soared high on hot air, until sobriety (and the stocks' lack of business profits) brought them crashing back to Earth.

Bitcoin and its contemporaries don't make profits either. As a medium of exchange, they're like new-age checks or fancy money orders. As for investing in Bitcoin or other cryptocurrencies, it might be best to turn an ear to Warren Buffett.

In an interview with CNBC, he said, "Stay away. Bitcoin is a mirage. It's a method of transmitting money... The idea that it has some huge intrinsic value is just a joke in my view."[14]

26. Should I Buy a Real Estate Investment Trust (REIT) Index?

You're getting comfortable in bed. Then the phone rings. Your tenants have an emergency. A pipe broke in their bathroom and the place is starting to stink. Forget that early night. You have work to do.

Many people enjoy the business of renting out a home. Others don't. But if you own a home already (whether you're renting it out or not), you're a real estate investor. It might even comprise a large part of your net worth.

Some people, however, don't own real estate. They wish they could do it without the added hassle that might come with crazy tenants. Such investors might add a REIT to their portfolios.

REITs are real estate companies that buy income-producing properties. Some focus on hospitals. Others focus on office buildings, shopping malls, or warehouses. They collect rents from tenants, as you would with a second home. But nobody bugs you—ever.

REITs trade on the stock market. You could buy a collection all at once with a REIT index or REIT ETF.

Dividend payouts tend to be higher than they are with common stocks. Historically, REITs and traditional stocks battle like Roger Federer and Rafael Nadal. Sometimes REITs win. Other times, traditional stocks knock them out.

Between 1996 and 1999, US stocks pounded American REITs into a corner. Between 1999 and 2002, REITs reigned supreme. REITs then outclassed stocks for the next five years. But when the financial crisis arrived in 2008, both hit the canvas. It didn't take long, however, before they both recovered well.[15]

By adding real estate to a portfolio of stocks and bonds, investors might enhance returns while decreasing volatility. Using data from Standard & Poor's, Barclays, and Gerstein Fisher Research, *Forbes* contributor Gregg S. Fisher gave two historical portfolio scenarios. By investing 60 percent in US stocks and 40 percent in US bonds, he found a portfolio would have averaged a compounding return of 8.72 percent between January 1990 and October 2014.

If, however, investors had added a 10 percent overall allocation to global REITs, compounding returns would have improved to 8.83 percent per year. The portfolio, with REITs, would have also been less volatile.

Fisher also checked different rolling 10-year periods. For example, how did they stack up between 1990 and 2000? How did they compare between 1991 and 2001? Did he find different results between 1992 and 2012? Fisher writes, "In about 80 percent of rolling 10-year periods, the portfolio with [10 percent real estate added] . . . achieved a higher return; volatility was lower in about 65 percent of the same periods."[16]

Having said this, I don't own an individual REIT ETF. After all, REITs are already included in a total stock market index. If you own a separate REIT ETF, it can make the investment process a bit more complicated. You might wonder whether you should add fresh money to your REIT ETF, to your bonds, or to your stock market ETF. In a real-world scenario, investors in simpler portfolios beat investors who juggle more products. After all, how a portfolio allocation performs is not as relevant as how the investor performs with a specific allocation. I delve into this behavioral gap more thoroughly later in the book.

27. Should I Buy a Smart Beta ETF?

Marketers are smart. They know that plenty of investors like low-cost index funds. But those who smell opportunity have sprinkled fairy dust. Many firms have created smart beta funds, also known as factor-based funds.

Smart beta firms use back-tests. They claim that index funds weighted differently produce better returns. For example, take a traditional index fund. Its stock weightings will emphasize the largest stocks. If Apple is the largest company in the S&P 500, then Apple's fortunes (good or bad) would have the greatest influence on the S&P 500. Smart beta indexes promise something different. Sometimes, they build higher emphasis on stocks that are quickly moving up in price.

Other times, they build equal weighted indexes. In this case, larger stocks don't move the index fund's needle any more than smaller stocks do.

Back-tests often dazzle. They prove that such index fund strategies would have triumphed in the past. But the past isn't the future. Often, the newly emphasized stocks in these index funds become more expensive. This can hurt returns.

Research Affiliates' Rob Arnott, Noah Beck, Vitali Kalesnik, and John West say that smart beta or factor-based funds could disappoint investors. They published the paper "How Can 'Smart Beta' Go Horribly Wrong?"[17] In it, they show that much of the past decade's market-beating gains from such funds have come from rising valuations. Investors rushed into such funds because they had performed well. That raised the price-to-earnings (PE) ratios of certain stocks to higher than normal levels.

Higher-than-normal valuation levels could bring poor returns in the future. Here are some factor-based (smart beta) styles so you'll know them when you see them: Momentum, Value, Growth, Small-Cap, Equal-Weighted, Quality, and Minimum Volatility.

Smart beta index funds are cheap, compared to actively managed funds. But they cost a lot more than most standard index funds. Strategies based on a cherry-picked past might sell new Wall Street products. But they aren't always better for investors. That's why I suggest that you keep things simple.

28. Should I Invest in Gold?

Here's a cool trick that you should try on the street. Find some educated people. Ask them to imagine that one of their forefathers bought $1 worth of gold in 1801. Then ask what it would have been worth in 2021.

Their eyes might widen at the thought of the great things they could buy if they sold that gold. They might imagine buying a yacht or a personal jet. Unfortunately, they couldn't afford either. With the proceeds, they couldn't treat five friends to beer and burgers at a pub. One dollar invested in gold in 1801 was only worth about $84 by 2021.

How about $1 invested in the US stock market? Now you can start thinking about your yacht. One dollar invested in the US stock market in 1801 would have been worth about $34.5 million by 2021.[18]

Gold isn't an investment that can expect to beat inflation. From time to time, it jumps around a lot. But in a long-term game, it comes up short. When I wrote this book's first edition, I included gold in something called the Permanent Portfolio. Rebalanced annually, such a portfolio has done well—but not because of gold's long-term growth. If you're curious, and you haven't read my book's first edition, check out my online story, "The World's Best Investment Strategy That Nobody Seems to Like" at AssetBuilder.com.[19]

29. Don't Small-Company Stocks Beat Larger-Company Stocks?

Whenever possible, I recommend total stock market index funds (especially all-in-one portfolio funds) instead of breaking down investment allocations into different sized indexes. For example, investors can buy large-company indexes, medium-sized company indexes, or small-sized company indexes.

But I prefer to keep things simple. It's true that, historically, there's evidence to suggest small-company stocks beat large-company stocks. But there's also evidence against that.

Economic Nobel Prize winner Eugene Fama and his colleague Kenneth French determined that between July 1926 and February 2012, small-cap stocks cumulatively beat large stocks by 253 percent.[20] But in 1999, Tyler Shumway and Vincent Warther argued otherwise. They published a paper in the *Journal of Finance*, "The Delisting Bias in CRSPs NASDAQ Data and Its Implications for the Size Effect." They should have called it "Size Doesn't Matter."[21]

They said small stocks often have shakier financial foundations. They have a tougher time weathering storms. Many can't, so they get dropped (or delisted) from the stock market. Shumway and Warther say that when we measure small-cap returns, the data is rose colored. We only see the results of the survivors.

Ted Aronson manages institutional money through AJO Partners. He manages two small-cap funds. They have each earned strong returns. So does Aronson believe in the small-cap premium? Nope. Interviewed in 1999 by Jason Zweig, Aronson said, "Small-caps don't outperform over time . . . Sure, the long-run numbers show small stocks returning roughly 1.2 percentage points more than large stocks . . . [But] the extra trading costs easily eat up the entire extra return—and then some!"[22]

Some people might argue that their small cap index has out-performed the market. But Ken Fisher says no. Sometimes smaller-company stocks outperform. Other times, they don't. Small stocks usually do well early in a bull market (when stocks are starting a period of high growth). But they often disappoint when the bull is running on fumes.[23]

Does It Really Work Like That?

The firm Research Affiliates is always looking for a performance edge. They created the Fundamental Index in hopes of beating traditional cap-weighted index funds. Their researchers Jason Hsu and Vitali Kalesnik researched the apparent small-cap premium to see if small stocks really outperform. Based on their research, it appears that they don't.

Following Fama and French's research method, they split stocks into two groups for a variety of different countries. The largest 90 percent were put in one group. The smallest 10 percent were put in the other. They examined performances from 1926 to 2014.

After adjusting for extra transaction costs and delisting bias, Research Affiliates' Vitali Kalesnik and Noah Beck say small stocks don't beat large stocks at all. "If the size premium were discovered today, rather than in the 1980s, it would be challenging to even publish a paper documenting that small stocks outperform large ones."[24]

I checked five-year periods for US stocks back to January 1977. Using Morningstar, I compared Vanguard's Small Capitalization Index Fund (NAESX), comparing it to Vanguard's S&P 500 Index

Table 7.6 Do Small Stocks Really Beat Large Stocks?

*Time Periods	Large Stocks (VFINX) Five-Year Average Returns	Small Stocks (NAESX) Five-Year Average Returns	Winner
1977–1982	8.1%	16.4%	Small stocks
1982–1986	15.8%	9.7%	Large stocks
1986–1991	13%	0.6%	Large stocks
1991–1996	16.5%	21.4%	Small stocks
1996–2001	18.3%	11.4%	Large stocks
2001–2006	0.5%	9.1%	Small stocks
2006–2011	2.2%	5.5%	Small stocks
2011–2016	12.4	10.28%	Large stocks
2016–2021	15.07%	13.47%	Large stocks
1977–2021	**11.34%**	**11.0%**	**Large stocks**

*Beginning January 1 of each year and ending January 1 of each listed second year.
NOTE: Vanguard's small cap index was an actively managed small cap fund until 1989.
SOURCE: Morningstar.com.

(VFINX). The S&P 500 is a large-stock index. As shown in Table 7.6, over the nine different periods, the small-stock index won four times. The large-cap index won five times. When I measured the total 44-year time period, it was close to a dead heat.[25]

Based on actual fund returns, it's tough to argue that small stocks have any long-term advantage.

30. What If You and Your Spouse Represent Different Nationalities?

The following chapters provide sample portfolios for DIY investors based on different nationalities. Couples who represent different nationalities have choices:

1. Build two portfolios. Each could represent the couple's relevant nationalities. This is what my wife and I chose to do. She's American. I'm Canadian. Each portfolio is taxed differently. Having two portfolios also provides easy access to immediate money when one of us dies.

2. Build a single portfolio that blends the components of each respective portfolio. Plenty of couples (when one is American) choose to do this, with the account in the non-American's name. Americans are taxed on worldwide income and must pay capital gains taxes on non-tax-deferred accounts. They aren't eligible to open accounts with non-American brokerages located in capital gains–free jurisdictions. But when the couple represents different (non-American) nationalities, they could create a joint account.

3. Build a single portfolio that focuses on the country that the couple might choose to retire in. For example, if an Australian and a Canadian plan to retire in Canada, they could build a portfolio that represents a Canadian bias, such as what you'll find in Chapter 10. If they wanted to retire in Australia, they could build a portfolio with an Australian bias, such as what you'll find in Chapter 12.

4. Build a single, globally diversified portfolio that has no home-country bias. Out of convenience, I've chosen to call these Global Nomad portfolios. Such portfolios would work well for couples that don't know where they want to retire. They would also suit couples retiring in an emerging-market country. Emerging-market countries have small, volatile markets. Retirees who choose to invest with a "home-country" emerging-market bias would be taking unnecessary risk. Instead, they could spread their risk across a multitude of global economic regions. I've provided samples of such portfolios later in the book.

31. Why Should I Rebalance My Portfolio?

In the following chapters, I'll provide portfolio samples for people of different nationalities. Each portfolio represents a different tolerance for risk. For example, a Canadian investor might have 30 percent in Canadian bonds, 50 percent on global stocks and 20 percent in Canadian stocks. This could constitute several individual ETFs or an all-in-one ETF combining everything into one.

Each year, these markets will perform differently. Some years, Canadian stocks will soar above the global stock market. Other years, both Canadian and global stocks will fall hard while the bond index drops slightly or rises. It's important that investors maintain a consistent allocation. That means investors should do one of two things. Once a year, rebalance their portfolio back to its original allocation. That might mean selling some of the proceeds of the better performing ETF (or the one that fell the least!) and adding those proceeds to the lagging ETF.Such rebalancing reduces risk, and sometimes it can even juice returns.

Investors can also work at maintaining a consistent allocation by purchasing the lagging ETF each month. In other words, they could see which ETF requires more money to bring the portfolio closer to the desired goal allocation. By doing so, investors might not need to manually rebalance once a year, especially during the early years, when their account values are low.

32. What Are The Best ETFs To Buy?

Your choice of ETFs will not make or break your retirement. If you read one of this book's earlier editions, you might notice some changes to the portfolio models in my next chapters. This doesn't mean you should switch to these ETFs, from those I listed before. New ETFs get launched every year. In most cases, they are neither better nor worse than the ETFs I listed in this book's first edition, back in 2014.

If you notice changes to the portfolio models, it was simply for ease. When all-in-one portfolio ETFs were first launched in 2018, for example, I viewed those as the simplest solution. Investors don't have to rebalance because the investment provider maintains a consistent allocation. That also means the investor never needs to ask, "Which ETF should I add money to this month?" Investors would own a complete portfolio in a single fund. Best of all, according to Morningstar's research, investors in all-in-one funds also behave much better. In other words, if you're a normal carbon-based life form, you should earn better returns with an all-in-one fund, versus buying individual ETFs. Research suggests we end up speculating less with all-in-one funds and we don't tend to second-guess our monthly purchases.[26]

Having said that, not everybody is "normal." Some have the discipline to stick to a plan of individual ETFs and maintain a consistent allocation. Whatever you do, stay the course. Pick an allocation of ETFs (or an all-in-one ETF) and simply stick to it.

33. What's the Difference Between an Accumulating ETF and a Distributing ETF?

Broad stock market ETFs pay dividends. But with an accumulating ETF, those dividends get reinvested automatically. When doing so, it increases the price level of the ETF. ETFs that distribute dividends don't reinvest the cash. Instead, they deposit those dividends into the cash portion of your brokerage account. When you add new money to your account, this money goes into your cash portion, too. In other words, it would get combined with the dividend payouts you received. From that point, you could invest the cash into an ETF of your choice (not necessarily the ETF that paid the dividend). This can help you maintain a consistent allocation. Whether you own an accumulating ETF or a distributing ETF, you will still pay dividend withholding taxes. With the accumulating ETF, however, you just might not see it. The taxes come off at source. In contrast, with the distributing ETF, most brokerages will show you the dividend taxes you have paid. Which are better? That depends on you. The after-tax returns will be about the same.

34. Should I Buy An ETF or Index That Pays High Dividends?

Would you like a high-dividend stock or ETF that pays 4 percent or more a year? You can find them. But you won't make more money with them.

When a company pays a dividend, it reduces the value of that company in direct proportion to the cash it pays. In other words, if a business paid shareholders a total of $500 million in dividends, the company's book value lowers by exactly $500 million. That $500 million "corporate loss" cannot be reinvested back into the company. As a result, the business can't use that money for future growth. Long-term, this hampers share price growth.

This is why Warren Buffett's company, Berkshire Hathaway doesn't pay a dividend. The company's chairman, Warren Buffett, has successfully retained and reinvested all net corporate earnings. As a result, Berkshire's share price has experienced higher long-term growth than any high-dividend paying stock. Retirees that own this stock simply sell shares if they want income. Authors Larry Swedroe and Andrew L. Berkin explain this well in their book, *The Incredible Shrinking Alpha (2nd edition)*.

They write:

> *"What is particularly puzzling about the preference for dividends is that taxable investors should favor the self-dividend (by selling shares) if cash flow is required. Unlike with dividends, where taxes are paid on the distribution amount, when shares are sold, taxes are due only on the portion of the sale representing a gain. And if there are losses on the sale, the investors gains the benefit of a tax deduction."*

Swedroe and Berkin also say investors seeking high dividend funds won't be as diversified. For example, a broad US stock market index holds more than 3000 stocks. But a high-dividend paying ETF might hold fewer than 100.[27]

Notes

1. "Some nonresidents with US assets must file estate tax returns," IRS. Accessed August 13, 2021. https://www.irs.gov/individuals/international-taxpayers/some-nonresidents-with-us-assets-must-file-estate-tax-returns
2. Morningstar.com.

3. Dan Bortolotti, *MoneySense Guide to the Perfect Portfolio*, *MoneySense*, November 29, 2011. Accessed July 2, 2014. http://www.moneysense.ca/uncategorized/moneysense-guide-to-the-perfect-portfolio-2

4. Raymond Kerzerho, "Currency-Hedged S&P 500 Funds: The Unsuspected Challenges," PWL Capital White Paper, September 1, 2010. www.pwlcapital.com/pwl/media/pwl-media/PDF-files/Articles/Currency-Hedged-S-P500-Funds_The-Unsuspected-Challenges_2010_10_21.pdf?ext=.pdf

5. "Friends Provident International Key Features," Accessed September 29, 2021. https://www.fpinternational.com/documents/ge-r-kf-crp.pdf

6. John R. Knight and Lewis Mandell, "Nobody Gains from Dollar Cost Averaging: Analytical, Numerical and Empirical Results," *Financial Services Review* 2, no. 1 (1993): 51–61. Accessed September 21, 2021. https://citeseerx.ist.psu.edu/viewdoc/download?doi=10.1.1.320.2252&rep=rep1&type=pdf

7. "Dollar-Cost Averaging Just Means Taking Risk Later," Vanguard.com, July 2012. Accessed June 15, 2017. www.bloomberg.com/news/articles/2017-05-24/firm-targeting-nest-eggs-of-u-k-expats-said-to-face-sec-probe

8. Portfoliovisualizer.com

9. Ibid.

10. Charles H. Hennekens and Felicita Andreotti, "Leading Avoidable Cause of Premature Deaths Worldwide: Case for Obesity," *American Journal of Medicine*, February 2013. Accessed September 29, 2021. https://www.amjmed.com/article/S0002-9343(12)00547-5/fulltext

11. "Does Socially Responsible Investing Hurt Investment Return?" *RBC Global Asset Management*, September 2012. Accessed June 15, 2017. http://funds.rbcgam.com/_assets-ustom/pdf/RBC-GAM-does-SRI-hurt-investment-returns.pdf

12. Rob Price, "Deep Web Drug Dealers Are Freaking Out about the Bitcoin Crash," *Business Insider UK*, January 16, 2015. Accessed June 15, 2017. http://uk.businessinsider.com/bitcoin-crash-drug-dealers-2015-1

13. Isaac Newton Quotes, BrainyQuote.com. Accessed June 15, 2017. www.brainyquote.com/quotes/quotes/i/isaacnewto384639.html

14. Alex Crippen, "Buffett Blasts Bitcoin as 'Mirage': 'Stay Away!' CNBC. Accessed June 15, 2017. www.cnbc.com/2014/03/14/buffett-blasts-bitcoin-as-mirage-stay-away.html

15. Portfoliovisualizer.com

16. Gregg S. Fisher, "Why We Believe Your Portfolio Needs Global REITs," *Forbes*, December 1, 2014. Accessed June 15, 2017. www.forbes.com/sites/greggfisher/2014/12/01/why-we-believe-your-portfolio-needs-global-reits/

17. Rob Arnott, Noah Beck, Vitali Kalesnik, "How Can 'Smart Beta' Go Horribly Wrong?" *Research Affiliates*, February 2016. Accessed June 15, 2017. www.researchaffiliates.com/en_us/publications/articles/442_how_can_smart_beta_go_horribly_wrong.html

18. Calculated from 1801 to 2001 returns of US stocks and gold from Jeremy Siegel, *Stocks for the Long Run* (New York: McGraw-Hill, 2002), then extrapolated further using gold's 2021 price.

19. Andrew Hallam, "The World's Best Investment Strategy That Nobody Seems to Like," AssetBuilder.com, November 6, 2014. Accessed June 15, 2017. https://assetbuilder.com/knowledge-center/articles/the-worlds-best-investment-strategy-that-nobody-seems-to-like

20. John Davenport and Fred Meissner, "Exploiting the Relative Outperformance of Small-Cap Stocks," *American Association of Individual Investors (AAii) Journal,* January 2014. Accessed June 21, 2017. www.aaii.com/journal/article/exploiting-the-relative-outperformance-of-small-cap-stocks.touch

21. Tyler Shumway and Vincent Warther, "The Delisting Bias in CRSPs NASDAQ Data and Its Implications for the Size Effect," *Journal of Finance,* February 1999. Accessed June 21, 2017. www.researchgate.net/publication/4992527_The_Delisting_Bias_in_CRSP's_Nasdaq_Data_and_Its_Implications_for_the_Size_Effect

22. Jason Zweig, "He's Not Picky, He'll Take Whatever Is Wounded," *CNN Money,* January 15, 1999. Accessed June 21, 2017. http://money.cnn.com/1999/01/15/zweig_on_funds/zweig_on_funds/

23. "Nothing Is Better—Stocks Are Stocks. Even Small Caps." Fisher Investments Editorial Staff, September 25, 2014. Accessed June 21, 2017. www.marketminder.com/a/fisher-investments-ken-fisher-nothing-is-better-stocks-are-stocks-even-small-caps/5d5a3afc-e98d-455f-b90e-d31631d7fa65.aspx

24. Jason Hsu and Vitali Kalesnik, "Busting the Myth About Size," *Research Affiliates,* December 2014. Accessed June 21, 2017. www.researchaffiliates.com/en_us/publications/articles/284_busting_the_myth_about_size.html

25. Morningstar.com

26. Jeffrey Ptak, "Success Story: Target Date Fund Investors," Morningstar, February 19, 2018. Accessed August 18, 2021. https://www.morningstar.com/articles/850872/success-story-targetdate-fund-investors

27. Larry Swedroe and Andrew Berkin, The Incredible Shrinking Alpha (2nd edition) 164.

Chapter 8

Couch Potato Investing

Imagine a couch potato for a moment. A beer resting on his gut, he lies on the sofa watching football. The only time he perks up is when the home team scores or when a streaker (why are they always men?) races across the turf.

It might be hard to believe, but an investment strategy inspired by sloth runs circles around most professionally managed portfolios. Practitioners of the strategy spend less than an hour each year on their investments. They don't have to follow the economy, read the *Wall Street Journal*, subscribe to online investment publications, or hire an advisor. This champion slacker is called the Couch Potato portfolio.

Devised by former *Dallas Morning News* columnist Scott Burns, the original Couch Potato portfolio is an even split between a stock and a bond market index. It's easier to manage than a crew cut. If you invest $1,000 per month, you would put $500 into the stock index and $500 into the bond index. After one year, you would see whether you had more money in stocks or more in bonds. If you had more in stocks, you would sell some of the stock index, using the proceeds to buy more of the bond index. Doing so realigns the portfolio with its original allocation: 50 percent stocks, 50 percent bonds. Scott Burns says anyone who can fog a mirror and divide by two can pull this off.

Don't Bonds Tie You Down?

Many investment cowboys think bonds are boring and unprofitable, and have no place in a portfolio. It's a good thing such Wild West throwbacks (even if they're bull-riding studs) aren't running government pensions, corporate pensions, or university endowment funds. Responsible individual and professional investors understand the importance of bonds in a diversified portfolio.

By rebalancing back to the original allocation, they sell a bit of what's hot and buy a bit of what's not. They manage money much like disciplined government-held pension systems. Most other investors do the opposite: they buy high and sell low. With a Couch Potato portfolio and a bit of discipline, investors avoid such lunacy.

Because stocks beat bonds over time, having bonds in a portfolio reduces returns—but not by as much as you might think. And during time periods with multiple stock market crashes, re-balancing with bonds might even enhance returns.

According to portfoliovisualizer.com, if someone put $10,000 in a global stock market index on January 1, 2000, it would have grown to $35,235 by May 31, 2021.

But if $10,000 were invested 60 percent in global stocks and 40 percent global bonds, it would have grown to $37,808 over the same 21 year, five month period.

In contrast, as mentioned in Chapter 7, if someone invested a $10,000 lump sum on January 1, 2000 and they continued to add

Table 8.1 Bonds Can Add Stability At A Low-Cost To Returns January 1, 2000–May 31, 2021 Starting with $10,000 and adding $1000 a month

	100% Global Stock Index	60% Global Stock Index, 40% Global Bond Index
Compound Annual Average Money-Weighted Return	7.47%	7.05%
Worst Year	−40.43% (2008)	−25.14% (2008)

SOURCE: portfoliovisualizer.com.

a further $1,000 a month, the portfolio invested 100 percent in the global stock index would have beaten a portfolio comprising 60 percent global stocks and 40 percent global bonds. But as shown in Table 8.1 it didn't win by as much as you might think. And the higher risk allocation would have brought a lot more sleepless nights.

Are You Worried That Bond Interest Rates Are Low?

Bond interest rates are low. But bonds always deserve a role. Let me ask a couple of questions:

Will bond yields remain low over the next 1-, 3-, 5-, or 10-year periods?
Will stocks hit new highs over the next 5 to 10 years?

If you *know* the answers to those questions, congratulations. You can see the future. So stop reading this and go out and save some people.

Unfortunately, nobody can see the future. But here's what we know. Long-term, stocks beat bonds. That doesn't mean stocks always beat a diversified portfolio of stocks and bonds. Take the 17-year period from 1996 to 2012. The S&P 500 gained a compound annual return of 6.92 percent. A combination of stocks and bonds actually did better. A portfolio with 60 percent in an S&P 500 index and

40 percent in a broad US bond market index gained a compound annual return of 7.01 percent. Such an investor would have taken lower risk *and* earned higher returns over that 17-year period.

In 1996, nobody *knew* that a portfolio split between stocks and bonds would beat the S&P 500 for close to two decades. Likewise, nobody knows if a stock market index will beat a balanced portfolio over the next 17 years.

But I recommend portfolios that include bonds because they can collar your inner Neanderthal. That's important. Always remember that how a specific allocation performs isn't as relevant as how you perform with a specific allocation. If a higher risk portfolio makes you wet the bed when stocks go on a multiple year decline, then what would be the point of a higher risk portfolio? Bed wetting = selling or ceasing to add new money until "markets stabilize again."

Where Do You Plan to Retire?

Americans should have a nice chunk of US exposure if they plan to retire in the United States. Canadians, Australians, Brits, Europeans, or any other nationality with an established stock market should do likewise with their home-country market.

Keeping it simple, you could split your stock market money between your home-country index and a global index. By doing so, especially if investors own a bond index (or ETF) that represents their home currency, investors reduce currency risk.

For example, a 30-year-old British investor could have a portfolio consisting of 30 percent government bonds, 35 percent global stock index, and 35 percent British stock index.

An American's portfolio composition would be different: 30 percent bond index and 70 percent global stock index.

You may be wondering where the US stock market fits into the 30/70 portfolio. Global stock indexes contain roughly 53 percent US stocks. As a result, no separate US index would be required.

If you're making monthly investment purchases, you need to look at your home country stock index and your global stock index, and determine which one has done better over the previous month. You'll know by looking at your account statement and comparing it with the previous month's report. When you figure it out, add newly invested money to the index that hasn't done as well, to keep your account close to your desired allocation. Remember that if each stock index soared over the previous month, you would add fresh money to your bond index.

What do most people do? You guessed it. Metaphorically speaking, they sign long-term contracts to empty their wallets each morning into the trash bin—buying more of the high-performing index and less of the underperforming index. Over an investment lifetime, such behavior can cost hundreds of thousands of dollars.

Please note that I'm not talking about chasing individual stocks or individual foreign markets into the gutter. For example, just because the share price of company Random X has fallen, this doesn't mean investors should throw good money after bad, thinking it's a great deal just because it has dropped in value. Who knows what's going to happen to Random X?

Likewise, you take a large risk buying an index focusing on a single foreign country, such as Chile, Brazil, or China. Who really knows what's going to happen to those markets over the next 30 years? They might do really well. But it's better to spread your risk and go with a global stock market index (if you want foreign exposure). With it, you'll have exposure to older world economies such as the UK, France, and Germany, as well as younger, fast-growing economies like China, India, Brazil, and Thailand. Just remember to rebalance. If the global stock market index outperforms your domestic index, don't chase the global index with fresh money. If your domestic stock index and the global stock index both shoot skyward, add fresh money to your bond index.

Are You Retiring in an Emerging-Market Country?

Those retiring to an emerging-market country should remember a few things. Emerging markets tend to be volatile. Their stocks can fall dramatically. Inflation in such countries can run like a pack of Kenyans. Depending on economic stability, currencies can plummet. For this reason, if you plan to retire to a developing country, consider a global stock allocation without any added exposure to your new home country market.

The Magic Of All-in-One Portfolio ETFs and Index Funds

When I wrote the first two editions of this book, I suggested investors build portfolios with individual ETFs. For example, I said Canadians should build portfolios with a Canadian stock index, a global stock index and Canadian bond index. If you have done so, that's super. I continue to recommend those portfolios. But all-in-one portfolio fund options might be better because they promote better human behavior (which I'll soon explain). A handful of years ago, only Americans could buy them. But the concept has spread for investors of different nationalities. Such products combine globally diversified portfolios into single funds. They're low-cost products, charging similar fees to individual index funds or ETFs. But the fund companies rebalance the components annually, so investors don't have to. As French novelist George Sand once said, "Simplicity is the most difficult thing to secure in this world; it is the last limit of experience and the last effort of genius."[1]

Let me explain their magic.

For starters, if you select an all-in-one portfolio fund, it will be the only investment product you need to buy. That means, in any given month, you won't need to worry whether you should be adding money to your global stock index, your bond market index or your domestic stock index. However, I'm not recommending them just to save you time and thought. With an all-in-one portfolio fund, you should beat the pants, shirts and shoes off the performance of most investors who buy individual ETFs.

That's because many investors speculate, especially when stocks are soaring or when they're spinning down a toilet bowl. They might buy a specific ETF, only to trade it for another that they think will do better. Others make tactical choices: tweaking their portfolio allocations based on economic news. This might sound smart. But it's one of the silliest things an investor can do.

The fund rating company, Morningstar, publishes mutual fund and index funds returns. They also calculate how individual investors perform in each fund. If people were rational, the results would be about the same. But they aren't because humans are prideful, fearful, emotional and greedy.

Few investors mess things up when stocks are soaring. But when Morningstar measures periods that include fast, rising markets and big declines, they find that most investors fail their behavioral tests. As shown in Table 8.2, from June 30, 2004 to June 30, 2019 (a period of big ups and downs) the average investor dramatically underperformed their funds. They added more money when stocks were rising and they sold (or added less money) when stocks collapsed. As a result, they paid a higher-than-average price over this 15-year period.

For example, Vanguard's S&P 500 Index (VFINX) averaged a compound annual return of 8.62 percent over the 15 years ending June 30, 2019. Yet, the typical investor in this fund averaged just 6.34 percent.

It was different, however, for Americans who picked all-in-one funds. In 2018, Morningstar's Jeffrey Ptak published, Success Story: Target Date Fund Investors. The firm's research says those who buy all-in-one funds behave much better than those that pick individual funds. Individual index fund investors, as shown in Table 8.2, were no exception.

Table 8.2 How Did Investors Perform Compared To The Funds They Owned?
June 30, 2004–June 30, 2019

Fund	Fund's Average Annual Performance	Investors' Average Annual Performance	Annually, How Much Did Investors Underperform or Outperform Their Funds?
Vanguard's S&P 500 (VFINX)	8.62%	6.34%	−2.28%
Vanguard's Total Stock Market Index (VTSMX)	8.88%	9.33%	+0.45%
Vanguard's Extended Market Index (VEXMX)	9.33%	8.65%	−0.68%
Vanguard's International Stock Market Index (VGTSX)	5.67%	4.47%	−1.20%
Vanguard European Stock Market Index (VEURX)	5.52%	0.93%	−4.59%
Vanguard Pacific Stock Market Index (VPACX)	5.05%	0.34%	−4.71%
Vanguard's Total Bond Market Index (VBMFX)	4.12%	3.61%	−0.51%

SOURCE: Morningstar.com.

However, investors in all-in-one funds behaved far better. They speculated less. Most added consistent sums of money every month (known as dollar-cost averaging). As a result, they paid a lower than average price over these measured time periods. That helped them beat the posted returns of their funds. That won't happen every year, or during every decade. But behavioral studies suggest such products help harness our emotions.

For example, Vanguard's all-in-one Target Retirement 2045 fund (a product sold only to Americans) averaged 7.38 percent annually over the 15-year period ending June 30, 2019. But according to

Table 8.3 Investors In All-In-One Funds Appear To Behave Better June 30, 2004–June 30, 2019

Fund	Fund's Average Annual Performance	Investors' Average Annual Performance	Annually, How Much Did Investors Underperform or Outperform Their Funds?
Vanguard Target Retirement 2015 Fund	5.95%	5.63%	−0.22%*
Vanguard Target Retirement 2025 Fund	6.53%	6.73%	+0.20%
Vanguard Target Retirement 2035 Fund	7.02%	7.53%	+0.51%
Vanguard Target Retirement 2045 Fund	7.38%	8.07%	+0.69%

*Investors in Vanguard's Target Retirement 2015 fund were likely withdrawing money after 2015. That might be the reason such investors underperformed their fund. While markets soared from 2015–2019, they were selling to cover retirement costs.
SOURCE: Morningstar.com.

Morningstar, investors in the fund averaged 8.07 percent per year. As shown in Table 8.3, this wasn't an aberration.

In the following chapters, I recommended several model portfolios, with all-in-one portfolio funds typically taking center stage.

Note

1. George Sand, BrainyQuote. Accessed June 6, 2017. https://www.brainyquote.com/quotes/george_sand_390195

Chapter 9

Model Portfolios for American Expats

L et's say you're an emotional rock, think casinos and lotteries are for suckers, and would like to stick it to the Wall Street types. If so, you could make more money building your own indexed portfolio, rather than paying an advisor to do it for you.

It's simple. And if you're doing it right, you'll spend more time on the toilet in a week (especially if you read) than you'll spend managing your portfolio in an entire year.

But emotionally, it's tough. You'll need to stick to your game plan.

The world's largest index fund provider is Pennsylvania-based Vanguard. It has more assets under management than any fund company in the world. Vanguard doesn't charge annual account fees, nor does it charge fees to enter or exit the funds.

Unfortunately, Vanguard hasn't allowed expatriates to open accounts since 2006. Since then, the only American expats who have done so have lied about their residency. Instead of naming an employer on the online application form, they've listed "retired." They've provided a US address. They've also strategically failed to reveal their location when speaking on the phone to a Vanguard rep. They haven't broken any laws. But it's not exactly James Dean cool.

Vanguard isn't alone in its discrimination. In the *Wall Street Journal* on July 1, 2014, Laura Saunders wrote, "Fidelity Bans US Investors Overseas from Buying Mutual Funds." She reports that a growing number of American firms are closing doors to US expats.[1] Schwab has also closed doors to many American expats. For example when I wrote this book's first edition, Americans in Singapore could open accounts with Schwab. But Schwab now says no to Americans in Singapore. The firm has also added other countries to its can't-serve list.

If you already had an account with Vanguard before moving overseas, you're luckier than a gecko without a house cat. You can maintain the account as long as the firm has a US address on record. Otherwise, you might require a different investment brokerage (Interactive Brokers is another favorite).

Do You Currently Invest with Vanguard?

Vanguard's investors own the company.[2] No, I'm not blowing smoke up a dark crevice. If you own shares in a Vanguard mutual fund, whether it's an index fund or one of Vanguard's low-cost actively managed products, you're a company owner. It's much like a nonprofit. Owners are the people who purchase the funds. The same can't be said for folks owning funds with Fidelity, Goldman Sachs, T. Rowe Price, Wells Fargo, American Funds, or Morgan Stanley. In every other case (exceptions being nonprofits Teachers Insurance and Annuity Association–College Retirement Equities Fund [TIAA-CREF] for educators and the Thrift Savings Plan for federal employees), American mutual fund companies have a conflict of interest.

Couch Potato Investing with Vanguard

The simplest way to own a hands-free portfolio is with Vanguard's Target Retirement funds. They're cheap, costing roughly 0.15 percent per year. Each target fund is a fully diversified portfolio that gets automatically rebalanced. As fund investors' age, bond allocations (as a percentage of each fund) increase. Table 9.1 provides an example of what's under the hood of Vanguard's Target Retirement funds.

★ ★ ★

It comprises four indexes in a single fund: two stock indexes representing the US and international markets and two bond indexes representing both US and international government bonds. If US stocks soar and international stocks sink, the fund shifts some money from US to international stocks.

When both stock indexes fall, Vanguard takes money from the bond component, adding it to the stock indexes. Vanguard doesn't speculate. The firm simply rebalances the fund back to its original allocation.

Vanguard's Target Retirement 2035 Fund has about 26 percent allocated to bonds (18.1 percent US bonds, 7.8 percent international bonds) and about 74 percent allocated to stocks (44.2 percent US stocks, 29.9 percent international stocks). Despite its name, it may

Table 9.1   Vanguard's Target Retirement 2035 Fund: A Look under the Hood

Fund	Includes	Allocation
Vanguard Total Stock Market Index Fund	Broad exposure to US stocks	44.2%
Vanguard Total International Stock Index Fund	Broad exposure to international shares, including emerging markets	29.9%
Vanguard Total Bond Market II Index Fund	Broad exposure to US bonds	18.1%
Vanguard Total International Bond Index Fund	Broad exposure to international bonds	7.8%

SOURCE: Vanguard.com.

not necessarily be suitable for expats wanting to retire in 2035. Conservative investors or those who won't earn Social Security payments (nor any other form of retirement income) might prefer a more conservative portfolio, such as Vanguard's Target Retirement 2020 Fund.

Likewise, somebody who wants to retire in 2035 might choose Vanguard's Target Retirement 2045 fund if they want the possibility of higher returns, and they wouldn't mind the added volatility.

Don't be fooled by the year in the fund's name. It's not a carton of milk with an expiration date. In 2021, investors could still purchase a Vanguard Target Retirement 2020 fund. It's just a name, not a "best before" warning.

Table 9.2 lists seven of Vanguard's Target Retirement funds, along with their identifying ticker symbols and respective allocations to stocks and bonds. In 2021, investors required a minimum of $1000 to begin investing in these funds.

If you have a US bank account, you can also set up automatic deposits into your chosen Target Retirement Fund each month.

There are two criticisms, however, of Vanguard's Target Retirement Funds. For starters, some young investors might have a tough

Table 9.2 Vanguard's Target Retirement Funds

Fund	Ticker Symbol	Rough Percentage In Stocks (6/13/21)	Rough Percentage in Bonds (6/13/21)
Vanguard Target Retirement 2025	VTTVX	58%	42%
Vanguard Target Retirement 2030	VTHRX	65%	35%
Vanguard Target Retirement 2035	VTTHX	74%	26%
Vanguard Target Retirement 2040	VFORX	81%	19%
Vanguard Target Retirement 2045	VTIVX	89%	11%
Vanguard Target Retirement 2050	VFIFX	90%	10%

NOTE: The stock and bond allocations per fund will shift to more conservative allocations over time.
SOURCE: Vanguard.com.

time stomaching the high volatility associated with a fund that matches their retirement goal date. For example, Table 9.2 shows that in mid-2021, Vanguard's Target Retirement 2050 fund had just 10 percent allocated to bonds with the remaining 90 percent in stocks. This fund will face big drops when markets crash . . . plunges that some young investors might not be able to tolerate. The second criticism is that the allocation to bonds shifts too high for people in retirement. For example, Vanguard's Target Retirement 2020 fund had only 48 percent in stocks and 52 percent in bonds mid 2021. Investors who retire early (and will presumably spend many years in retirement) increase their odds of not running out of money if they can cap their bond allocation to just 40 percent of their portfolio.

For these reasons, some investors prefer Vanguard's LifeStrategy funds instead. They're similar to Vanguard's Target Retirement funds, but they maintain a consistent allocation (instead of increasing the bond allocation as investors age). For example, a 20-year old investor with a moderate tolerance for risk might choose Vanguard's LifeStrategy Moderate Growth fund (VSMGX). It has about 60 percent in stocks and about 40 percent in bonds. It would also maintain that allocation, year-after-year. Such funds charge about 0.12 percent per year and investors require a minimum of $3000 to get started.

Table 9.3 lists some of Vanguard's LifeStrategy Funds and their approximate allocations.

Table 9.3 Vanguard's LifeStrategy Funds

Fund	Ticker Symbol	Rough Percentage In Stocks	Rough Percentage in Bonds
Vanguard LifeStrategy Growth	VASGX	80%	20%
Vanguard LifeStrategy Moderate Growth	VSMGX	60%	40%
Vanguard LifeStrategy Conservative Growth	VSCGX	40%	60%

Source: Vanguard.com.

Simple Investing with a Vanguard Stick Shift

Investors who want to build a portfolio with individual funds (and not all-in one funds) can also do so. The upside is you can build the portfolio at an even lower cost, especially once you qualify for Vanguard's Admiral Shares (more on that later).

And when managed with discipline, taxable turnover can be lower. Take Vanguard's Target Retirement 2030 fund as an example. According to Morningstar, its taxable turnover is about 21 percent per year. When investing in taxable accounts, the lower the turnover, the better. Turnover is a percentage of the holdings traded within a fund during a given year. Each index within a target fund trades a very small number of its stocks annually. If an S&P 500 company goes bankrupt, for example, Standard & Poor's would likely give it the boot. In this case, a newly eligible stock would replace it. The low turnover of index funds makes them especially efficient in taxable accounts.

A Target Retirement fund generates turnover based on the trading occurring within each individual index coupled with the target fund's rebalancing. An investor purchasing his or her own indexes instead can buy the lagging index each month or quarter. By purchasing the lagging index, the investor might be able to keep the portfolio aligned within their goal allocation without selling anything. This decreases turnover. It might frustrate Uncle Sam's tax collectors. But it leaves you legally richer.

It's important to remember, however, that the biggest risk to a DIY investor isn't the percentages they choose to invest in stocks versus bonds. It's the tendency to speculate.

If, however, you have a steely resolve, you might do just as well (or even better, after taxes) in a portfolio of individual index funds or ETFs. Table 9.4 shows examples of portfolios with different tolerances for risk. To increase the investors' odds of success, I've listed portfolios

Table 9.4 Vanguard Global Couch Potato Portfolios

Fund Name	Fund Code	Expense Ratio	Conservative	Cautious	Balanced	Assertive	Aggressive
Vanguard Total World Stock Index	VTWAX	0.10%	30%	45%	60%	75%	100%
Vanguard Short-Term Treasury Index	VSBSX	0.07%	70%	55%	40%	25%	0%
Or							
Vanguard's Total Bond Market Index	VBTLX	0.05%					

with the lowest number of moving parts. For example, it's easier to rebalance a portfolio with just two funds than it is to rebalance a portfolio with six.

The portfolios below use Vanguard's Admiral Series index funds. They require a minimum of $3000 each to invest. However, if you only have $1000 to start for each fund, you could select the Investor Shares equivalents. The Investor Shares equivalents are slightly more expensive, and they automatically convert to the lower-cost Admiral Series when the investor has at least $10,000 invested in each fund.

The Investors Series include the symbol VTWSX for the global stock index, and VFISX and VBMFX for Vanguard's Short Term Treasury and Vanguard's Total Bond Market Index funds, respectively.

Vanguard's Admiral Series Global Two-Fund Portfolio Solutions Socially Responsible Investing

Vanguard doesn't have a full-line up of Socially Responsible (SRI) indexed mutual funds. But SRI investors could choose Vanguard's FTSE Social Index Fund Investors Shares (VFTSX). The fund's holdings are screened for social, human rights and environmental criteria. It excludes companies involved with weapons, tobacco, gambling, alcohol, adult entertainment, and nuclear power. It also has very low exposure to oil and gas companies.

But this fund only contains US stocks.

Vanguard doesn't yet have an international stock market index equivalent. But it does have an international stock market ETF that you could buy (see the difference between an indexed mutual fund and an ETF in Chapter 7). If you use Vanguard's brokerage, there will be no transaction fees to buy or sell any of Vanguard's ETFs. You can see model SRI portfolios in Table 9.5.

Table 9.5 Vanguard's Socially Responsible Portfolios

Fund Name	Fund Code	Expense Ratio	Conservative	Cautious	Balanced	Assertive	Aggressive
Vanguard's FTSE Social Index Fund Investors Shares	VFTSX	0.18%	15%	25%	30%	40%	50%
Vanguard ESG International Stock ETF	VSGX	0.15%	15%	20%	30%	35%	50%
Vanguard Short-Term Treasury Index	VFISX	0.20%	70%	55%	40%	25%	0%
Or							
Vanguard's Total Bond Market Index	VBMFX	0.15%					

SOURCE: Vanguard.com.

Americans Using Interactive Brokers

If you can't open an account with Vanguard, Interactive Brokers (IB) offers another option. Investors can open accounts online. Unlike Vanguard, IB doesn't have its in-house brand of commission-free index funds or ETFs. Investors would have to buy ETFs and pay commissions. Interactive Brokers aims for $10 to be generated in monthly trading commissions. The firm charges investors extra if they don't generate at least this sum.

For example, investors paying $5 in commissions for a given month would be charged an extra $5, providing the brokerage with a minimum $10 for the month. But such extra fees are waived for investors with more than $100,000 in their account.

ETF Portfolios with Interactive Brokers

Table 9.6 shows sample portfolios for an ETF investor using Interactive Brokers. Once again, I selected model portfolios with just two moving parts.

As always, investors with a higher risk tolerance might choose a lower bond allocation. Older investors, or those who are risk averse, may prefer a higher allocation to bonds.

Socially Responsible ETF Portfolios

As of this writing, Americans can't yet construct a globally diversified, low-cost two-fund portfolio of socially responsible ETFs. But I've listed several four-fund ETF models below.

Don't Contribute Illegally to Your IRA

In February 2014, my wife and I met an American expatriate who had been living in Spain for the past eight years. I'll call her Mary. In a casual conversation, she said she had been investing the maximum

Table 9.6 Global Two–Fund ETF Portfolios

Fund Name	Fund Code	Expense Ratio	Conservative	Cautious	Balanced	Assertive	Aggressive
Vanguard Total World Stock Index	VT	0.08%	30%	45%	60%	75%	100%
Schwab Short–Term US Treasury ETF	SCHO	0.05%	70%	55%	40%	25%	0%
Or							
Schwab's US Aggregate Bond ETF	SCHZ	0.04%					

SOURCE: Morningstar.com.

Table 9.7 Global Couch Potato Portfolios With Socially Responsible ETFs

Fund Name	Fund Code	Expense Ratio	Conservative	Cautious	Balanced	Assertive	Aggressive
iShares MSCI KLD 400 Social ETF (US Stocks)	DSI	0.25%	15%	25%	30%	40%	50%
iShares MSCI EAFE ESG Optimized ETF (Developed World International Stocks)	ESGD	0.20%	10%	15%	20%	25%	35%
iShares MSCI EM ESF (Emerging Market Stocks)	ESGE	0.25%	5%	5%	10%	10%	15%
Schwab Short-Term US Treasury ETF	SCHO	0.05%	70%	55%	40%	25%	0%
Or							
Schwab's US Aggregate Bond ETF	SCHZ	0.04%					

SOURCE: Morningstar.com.

allowable (it was \$5,500 per year) into her individual retirement account (IRA). Unfortunately, by doing so, she poked a sleeping giant.

The giant (also known as the US government) didn't allow expatriates in 2013 to invest in an IRA if they earned less than \$97,600 per year. Mary earned just \$50,000.

All of her income qualified for the IRS foreign earned income exclusion. This dull legal label simply means (in her case) she didn't have to pay US income taxes because her Spanish income wasn't high enough. If she earned more than \$97,600, things would have been different.[3]

What Exactly Is an IRA?

An IRA is a tax-sheltered investment account. It isn't a portfolio itself. Instead, it's like a special classification. Many Americans have two types of accounts: a tax-advantaged IRA account and a non-IRA taxable account.

If Mary were living in the United States, she could invest a maximum of \$6000 in an IRA and receive some kind of tax-associated benefit. By depositing into a Traditional IRA, the government says, "Good for you, Mary. We'll give you a discount on your taxes this year. You can watch your investment grow. And we won't tax you on its growth until you pull it out."

Mary could withdraw the money without penalty once she reaches 59½. And she must start withdrawing money by the time she's 70½. This would all be fine—if she were living in the United States or making more money as an expat.

The foreign earned income exclusion was \$99,200 in 2014. If Mary earned \$120,000 while living in Spain, she probably would be eligible to add money to a Traditional IRA. In 2014, allowable contribution limits were \$5,500 per year for investors under the age of 50, and \$6,500 for investors over the age of 50.[4]

If her foreign earned income above $99,200 were taxable (check online IRS updates) and Mary's earnings exceeded $120,000 for the year, she would have to pay US income taxes on the $20,800 difference. However, if she made a $5,500 Traditional IRA contribution, she could reduce her taxable income by $5,500, thus reducing her tax bill.

Once investors start withdrawing from their Traditional IRAs, withdrawals are taxed at ordinary income tax rates.

Could You Retire And Never Pay US Taxes Again?

While Americans might justifiably moan about paying US taxes on worldwide income, their expat plight isn't all doom and gloom. After all, employment income and capital gains aren't taxed the same way. For example, Americans who live off investment income (capital gains and dividends) pay far lower taxes than Americans who earn the same level of income from earned salaries. In fact, based on government standard deductions, some retired American couples can "earn" as much as $100,000 a year and not pay any taxes. One starting resource is the blog at Go Curry Cracker. Every year, from 2013–2018, bloggers Jeremy and Winnie posted their taxable income online while explaining US tax laws.[5]

But don't let a blog (or well-meaning people on Facebook) direct your tax-filing and lifestyle decisions. Everyone should have a great accountant. Always speak to your accountant and don't be afraid to ask about ideas you have learned.

Notes

1. Laura Saunders, "Fidelity Bans US Investors Overseas from Buying Mutual Funds," *Wall Street Journal*, July 1, 2014. Accessed September 29, 2021. https://www.wsj.com/articles/fidelity-bans-overseas-investors-from-buying-mutual-funds-1404246385

2. "What we do. How we do it. Why it matters,". Accessed September 21, 2021. https://about.vanguard.com/investment-stewardship/perspectives-and-commentary/what_how_why.pdf
3. "Foreign Earned Income Exclusion," Internal Revenue Service. Accessed July 3, 2014. https://www.irs.gov/individuals/international-taxpayers/foreign-earned-income-exclusion
4. "Historical IRA Contribution Limits," DQYDJ. Accessed September 29, 2021. https://dqydj.com/historical-ira-contribution-limit/
5. GoCurryCracker Blog, Accessed August 15, 2021. https://www.gocurrycracker.com/never-pay-taxes-again/

Chapter 10

Portfolio Models for Canadian Expats

Thirty-three year old Jonathan Ho lives in Abu Dhabi with his wife and 6-month old daughter. The Canadian works as an IT specialist in the financial sector. "I've been invested in the stock market since my senior year of university," he says. "At first, it was primarily single stock picks, but as my knowledge of the financial markets grew, I slowly moved away from stock picking and gradually moved into diversified products such as ETFs."[1]

In 2020, Jonathan had what he describes as "a light bulb moment" when he consolidated all of his investments into one of Vanguard's all-in-one portfolio ETFs. He likes how easy it is to buy just one fund, and he's happy that he doesn't have to worry about rebalancing his portfolio.

All-in-one portfolio ETFs, such as what Jonathan Ho bought, began trading on the Toronto Stock Exchange in 2018. Vanguard Canada was the first to launch them. But iShares, BMO and Horizons followed with their own products, after noting their popularity (see Table 10.1). These products all charge low fees, ranging from 0.17 percent to 0.25 percent per year. And their fees will likely keep dropping. What's more, each fund company rebalances the funds' internal holdings to maintain a consistent allocation. In other words, if you're regularly investing each month, you'll never have to worry about whether to buy a Canadian stock ETF, a US stock ETF, an emerging market ETF or a bond ETF. And based on research I mentioned in Chapter 8, investors in all-in-one funds should outperform investors who choose individual ETFs.

Horizons' all-in-one ETFs have similar allocations to those offered by Vanguard, iShares and BMO. But their international stock market components are hedged to the Canadian dollar. As I explained in Chapter 7, currency hedging tends to hurt long-term returns.

Table 10.1   All-In-One Portfolio ETFs Offer Ease and Behavioral Benefits

Conservative	Balanced	Assertive	Aggressive
40% Canadian and Global Stocks, 60% Bonds	**60% Canadian and Global Stocks, 40% Bonds**	**80% Canadian and Global Stocks, 20% Bonds**	**100% Canadian and Global Stocks**
BMO's Conservative ETF (ZCON)	BMO's Balanced ETF (ZBAL)	BMO's Growth ETF (ZGRO)	NA
Vanguard's Conservative ETF Portfolio (VCNS)	Vanguard's Balanced ETF Portfolio (VBAL)	Vanguard's Growth ETF Portfolio (VGRO)	Vanguard All Equity ETF Portfolio (VEQT)
iShares Core Conservative Balanced ETF (XCNS)	iShares Core Balanced ETF Portfolio (XBAL)	iShares Core Growth ETF Portfolio (XGRO)	iShares Core Equity ETF Portfolio (XEQT)

SOURCES: BMO, Vanguard Canada, iShares Canada.

I can guess what you might be thinking. You might want a specific allocation, say 60 percent stocks and 40 percent bonds. But you don't know whether to buy the Vanguard, iShares or BMO all-in-one fund that reflects this allocation. As a result, you might look up their past performance and pick based on that. Unfortunately, that's the wrong thing to do. Flip a coin instead. Each of these funds has similar (although not exact) allocations. That means one of them might beat the others over the next 2 years, before falling behind the others slightly over the next 2 years. Picking a fund, based on its past performance is natural, but wrongheaded. Over the next 30 years, each of these funds (as long as their allocation is similar) will perform about the same.

You might also be tempted to buy the fund with the lowest fees. That's thinking with your head. But these fund fees will continue to drop and the all-in-one funds with the lowest expense ratios today could be beaten to the bottom as other funds drop their fees. So take that coin and flip it. Then stick with your selection, through thick and thin.

Socially Responsible Investing for Canadians

In Chapter 7, I introduced socially responsible index funds (see question 21). In 2020, iShares Canada launched all-in-one socially responsible ETFs trading on the Toronto Stock Exchange. They, too, each represent complete portfolios wrapped up into single funds. Table 10.2 lists these funds. They each represent different tolerances for risk, and they're also cheap. As of this writing, their expenses are just 0.24 percent per year.

Each of the all-in-one ETFs I listed above are categorized as "physical." That means, when they pay dividends, Canadian expats (and Canadian residents investing outside of RRSPs, TFSAs and RESPs) will pay a 15 percent withholding tax on dividends. But you could sidestep that tax (which is taken, at source, by your

Table 10.2   All-In-One Socially Responsible ETF Portfolio Funds

Conservative	Balanced	Assertive	Aggressive
40% Canadian and Global Stocks, 60% Bonds	**60% Canadian and Global Stocks, 40% Bonds**	**80% Canadian and Global Stocks, 20% Bonds**	**100% Canadian and Global Stocks**
iShares ESG Conservative Balanced Portfolio (GCNS)	iShares ESG Balanced ETF Portfolio (GBAL)	iShares ESG Growth ETF Portfolio (GGRO)	iShares ESG Equity ETF Portfolio (GEQT)

SOURCE: iShares Canada.

brokerage) by building what might be the most tax-free portfolio in the world.

Swap-Based ETFs—The Ultimate Legal Tax Dodge

Horizons Canada offers several swap-based ETFs on the Canadian market. Most indexes physically hold stocks or bonds within them, but not these. Instead, they're like contracts backed by the National Bank of Canada, promising investors the full return of a given index as if all dividends or interest were reinvested. Because investors don't actually own the index's holdings directly, they aren't charged dividend taxes on the stock indexes or income taxes on the bond index.

Finance writer and money manager Dan Bortolotti describes how swap-based ETFs work in his *Canadian Couch Potato* blog post, "More Swap-Based ETFs on the Horizon."[2] They're popular in Canada, having amassed several billion dollars in assets because capital gains are taxed at a lower rate than dividends.

Canadian-based investors in these products pay capital gains taxes only. In expatriate accounts, however, benefits multiply. Those not liable for capital gains taxes can legally avoid capital gains and dividend withholding taxes, as well as tax on the bond interest.

But there's a higher degree of counterparty risk. If Canada's National Bank gets into trouble, there's always a chance it could default on its promise. In Table 10.3, I list diversified portfolios of

Table 10.3 The Most Tax-Efficient Portfolios For Canadians Overseas

Fund Name	Ticker Symbol	Expense ratio	Conservative	Cautious	Balanced	Assertive	Aggressive
Horizons S&P/TSX 60 index ETF	HXT	0.03%	10%	15%	20%	25%	30%
Horizons S&P 500 index ETF	HXS	0.10%	10%	15%	20%	25%	30%
Horizons International Developed Market Equity ETF	HXDM	0.22%	8%	10%	15%	15%	20%
Horizons Emerging Markets Equity ETF	HXEM	0.28%	2%	5%	5%	10%	10%
Horizons Canadian Select Bond Universe ETF	HBB	0.10%	70%	55%	40%	25%	10%

*Note: although Horizon's all-in-one portfolio ETFs include currency-hedging, the individual ETF selected above do not.
Sources: Vanguard Canada; Horizons Canada.

Horizon's swap-based portfolios representing different tolerances for risk. But be warned. These require much more discipline than investing in an all-in-one ETF, even if they are slightly more tax-efficient. After all, each portfolio has five moving parts. And because of that fact, even though these ETFs don't require investors to pay dividend withholding taxes, most people who invest in all-in-one portfolio ETFs will likely make more money. Human nature sees to that.

What About RRSPs, TFSAs and RESPs?

Expatriate Canadians aren't eligible to invest in a registered retirement savings plan (RRSP). Nor can they add money to a tax-free savings accounts (TFSA) or a registered education savings plan (RESP) while living offshore. Such tax-deferred accounts encourage residents to invest. If you already invested money in such an account, before moving overseas, you can keep it. But you can't contribute fresh funds to your accounts. In some cases, expatriate Canadians might even choose to sell their RRSPs, which is what I did with my portfolio in 2004.

When I had my RRSP, I was living in Canada and paying roughly 40 percent marginal income tax. If I had decided to moonlight as a cashier at 7-Eleven (for additional income), I would have paid 40 cents in tax for every dollar earned.

Because of my tax rate, I earned a 40 percent rebate from the federal government on contributions to my RRSP. The money could have compounded, tax free, until I was willing to withdraw it at retirement. At that point, everything I withdrew would have been taxed at my marginal income tax rate.

But I sold the investments in 2004. At the time, I was living in Singapore. I paid a 25 percent withholding tax to do so. I had earned a 40 percent cash rebate for adding the money in the first place, and paid just 25 percent tax to sell. If you're an expatriate Canadian with an RRSP, you might consider doing the same, especially if you consider staying outside Canada for several years. If you're an expat Canadian (depending on where you live) you won't have to pay capital gains taxes on your stock market investment products. That applies to investors living in several regions, including the United Arab Emirates (and most of the Middle East), Singapore, Luxembourg, Switzerland, The Cayman Islands, Monaco, Malaysia, New Zealand, Belize, Hong Kong, Jamaica and Sri Lanka.[3]

As a result, Canadians living in several countries can invest in an all-in-one ETF (see Chapter 6 for some brokerage options) and not have to pay capital gains taxes while living abroad. In fact, even after repatriating to Canada, Canadian expats are not required to pay Canadian capital gains taxes on gains they earned while living overseas. In other words, you could have invested a million dollars while living in a country like Malaysia, and after several years, it could have grown to $3 million. Revenue Canada wouldn't be entitled to tax on any of those gains if you were deemed a non-resident of Canada while you earned those profits.

Children's Education Savings Plans

As an expat, you won't be able to add money to a RESP. But you can still invest for your children's education. Some expats use different all-in-one ETFs for this purpose. For example, you might add your personal retirement money to Vanguard's Balanced ETF Portfolio (VBAL). Within the same brokerage account, you could buy separate all-in-one ETFs for each of your children.

Here's how not to lump your children's education money with your retirement funds and how not to mix up the money allocated for each child.

For example, assume you have triplets. When they are younger than five years old, you could designate a different all-in-one growth fund for each of them. These include 80 percent stocks and 20 percent bonds. One child could have the iShares Core Growth ETF Portfolio (XGRO). The second child could have iShares ESG Growth ETF Portfolio (GGRO) and the third child could have the BMO Growth ETF (ZGRO).

When they reach five years of age, you could sell those and buy their balanced counterparts for an allocation of 60 percent stocks and 40 percent bonds. These include iShares Core Balanced ETF Portfolio (XBAL); iShares ESG Balanced ETF Portfolio (GBAL); and the BMO Balanced ETF (ZBAL).

When the children reach 11 years of age, you could switch those funds to something more conservative: 40 percent stocks and 60 percent bonds. Such funds could include the iShares Core Conservative Balanced ETF (XCNS); the iShares ESG Conservative Balanced Portfolio (GCNS); and BMO's Conservative ETF (ZCON).

When the children reach 16 years of age, it's time to protect that money. After all, they will begin liquidating everything the following year. If stocks crash hard the year before they start college, or during their second, third or fourth years of college, they could be forced to sell at a loss. That's why, when the child is 16, you should protect that money in a short-term bond market ETF.

You could put one child's money into Vanguard's Canadian Short-Term Bond Index ETF (VBAL). The second child's money could go into the iShares Core Canadian Short Term Bond ETF (XSB) and the third child's money could go into BMO's Short Term Bond Index ETF (ZSB).

Table 10.4 shows my recommended breakdown of stocks and bonds for each child's education account, as they age.

Table 10.4 How Much Of Your Child's Education Money Should Be Invested In Stocks and Bonds?

	Stocks	Bonds
Below Age 5	80–90%	10–20%
Aged 5–10	60–70%	30–40%
Aged 11–15	40–50%	50–60%
Aged 16 to College Graduation	0–10%	90–100%

Canadians In Europe

In January 2018, a new European Union regulation rattled plenty of Canadian expats living in Europe. Many had built diversified portfolios of low-cost ETFs.

But EU regulators now say European Union residents can't buy ETFs from the Toronto or the New York Stock Exchanges. Here are a few important facts:

1. If you don't live in a EU country, this won't affect you.
2. If you already own ETFs that trade on the Toronto Stock Exchange you don't have to sell them.
3. You can continue to hold your current ETFs if they trade on the Toronto or the New York exchanges, but you can't add money to them.
4. All EU brokerages have complied with this rule, as has the US brokerage, Interactive Brokers, which enforced the rule in June 2019 for its EU-based clients.
5. Even Canadians using CI Direct Investing (a roboadvisor I mentioned in Chapter 6) are affected by this rule.

European Country Residents not Affected By This Rule

As of this writing, there are 27 member countries in the European Union and three EFTA states, which together form the European Economic Area (EEA). But Canadians living in European, non-EEA countries can still buy from the Toronto Stock Exchange. Such resident countries include Switzerland, Andorra, Armenia, Azerbaijan, Belarus, Georgia, Moldova, Monaco, Russia, San Marino, Ukraine and the UK. You can also purchase Canadian-listed ETFs from several countries with pending EU membership: Turkey, Serbia, North Macedonia, Albania, and Bosnia and Herzegovina.[4]

Some Canadians living in the European Economic Area countries can buy Canadian-listed ETFs if they obtain Elective Professional status. This reclassifies them from "retail" to "professional" investors. But it's not for everyone. The investor's portfolio needs to be worth at least $500,000 and they need to either be a financial sector professional or have significant investing experience. The client needs to apply for this status, which can be granted at the discretion of the brokerage.[5]

For Most Canadians Living In an EU Country

Canadians living in the EU can buy Vanguard's all-in-one portfolio ETFs that trade on the Italian or Frankfurt stock exchanges. Such funds represent globally diversified portfolios. But unlike the all-in-one portfolios listed above, they don't include much Canadian stock or Canadian bond market exposure. Still, that won't make or break anyone's retirement. These are fabulous products with diversified exposure to the world's stocks and bonds. Vanguard also rebalances each fund's internal holdings to ensure they maintain their original allocation (see Table 10.5).

Table 10.5   Vanguard's All-in One ETFs For Canadians Living In Europe

Fund	Symbol on Xetra**	Approximate % in Stocks	Approximate % in Bonds	Annual Expense Ratio
Vanguard Life Strategy 20% Equity UCITS ETF	V20A	20%	80%	0.25%
Vanguard Life Strategy 40% Equity UCITS ETF	V40A	40%	60%	0.25%
Vanguard Life Strategy 60% Equity UCITS ETF	V60A	60%	40%	0.25%
Vanguard Life Strategy 80% Equity UCITS ETF	V80A	80%	20%	0.25%

*The stock market portion of these funds is roughly 60% US stocks and 40% international stocks.
**Xetra represents a Frankfurt stock exchange and is the commonly used exchange for this ETF.
SOURCE: Global.Vanguard.com.

One Drawback To Non-Canadian Listed ETFs

Canadians living in most European countries can't buy ETFs that trade on the Toronto Stock Exchange. But if you don't live in one of these countries, there's no reason not to buy one of Canadian-listed ETFs that I listed in Tables 10.1, 10.2 or 10.3.

If a Canadian buys an ETF that trades on the UK market, for example, and if they then move back to Canada, they will have to sell their ETFs before repatriating. Stocks move up more often than they move down. On a $1 million portfolio, if the market moves up by 1 percent while you are out of the market it could cost you $10,000 in opportunity cost.

If you own UK-listed ETFs (which are typically priced in USD or GBP) you will also pay a currency spread when you sell and convert your money into Canadian dollars. On a $1 million portfolio, this could cost you $5000 with a currency bid/ask spread of just 0.5 percent.

However, if you own ETFs that trade on the Canadian exchange, you don't have to sell them when repatriating. You can simply transfer them to a Canadian brokerage. As such, you won't risk the opportunity cost of being out of the market, nor will you have to pay a currency spread to move your money from a non-Canadian priced ETF into Canadian dollars. After all, as a Canadian in Canada, you'll pay all of your bills in loonies and toonies, not greenbacks or pounds.

Here's something else to consider. If, for some reason, you own a UK listed ETF, and you end up coming back to Canada for more than 180 days in a calendar year (to deal with a family emergency, or you get trapped there, much as I was during the pandemic) you will likely be declared a resident for tax purposes—whether you want to be, or not. In such a case, if you own UK-listed ETFs, you will legally have to file a T1135 tax form for Foreign Income Verification Statement. To do this right requires a professional accountant. And it's one heck of an onerous job.

On such a form, Revenue Canada will want to know the date of every past purchase or sale, the exact price at the point of every transaction and the exchange rate when purchased or sold. Filing a T1135 tax form properly can cost people several thousand dollars in professional help.

You say this doesn't apply to you because you won't visit Canada or repatriate back home? Never say never. Unless you're living in Europe (where you wouldn't be eligible to buy off the Canadian stock market) it makes little sense for a Canadian not to buy ETFs from the Toronto Stock Exchange . . . unless you know, for sure, that you'll never come home.

Repatriation: If You Decide To Move Back

The first step for anyone who's planning to repatriate is to find a great accountant. Don't take this lightly. A Canadian accountant with experience in expat matters should be part of your team.

On the date of your arrival, take a screen shot of your brokerage account. Note the current price for each of your stocks or ETFs (if you own an all-in-one portfolio ETF, this is far simpler because you'll have just one price to document).

During your first week back in Canada, open a Canadian brokerage account. Each of Canada's major banks has one: CIBC's Investor's Edge; RBC's Action Direct; TD's TD Direct Investing. One of my favorites is the independent brokerage, QTrade. They each charge lower commissions than any of the offshore brokerages (including Interactive Brokers) and they are far easier to use.

After opening your Canadian-based brokerage account, ask the brokerage representative to transfer the ETFs from your offshore brokerage. The Canadian brokerage will also ask you to fill out a form, listing your holdings and your offshore account details. Once you have filled out the form and signed it, the transfer can begin. The transfer itself costs about $50 for each stock or ETF. That's another good reason for an all-in-one ETF, instead of individual ETFs.

Having said this, if your account is large, try asking the brokerage to waive this transfer fee. They know you could select a different brokerage, so they'll often acquiesce to gain your business.

Sometimes, the transfer takes several weeks. During that time, you won't be able to trade your shares. But when the holdings show up in your Canadian-based brokerage account, the value will reflect the current market value.

You can continue to hold this money in your Canadian brokerage's non-tax advantaged account. By doing so, you won't pay any capital gains taxes until the day you sell. And when you sell, you'll only pay capital gains tax based on the gains you made after your date of repatriation.

For example, imagine you transfer a portfolio worth $1 million. Assume you sell 4 percent of your holdings to cover that year's living expenses ($40,000). If you sell that money on the day your money arrives, you won't pay any Canadian tax on that money. Now assume you sell another $42,000 one year later. If your portfolio didn't gain money during that year, you wouldn't have to pay capital gains tax on any of that sale, either. If, however, you gained 10 percent in that second year, then $4,200 of that $42,000 withdrawn would represent a capital gain. Based on Canadian tax laws, you would be responsible for paying capital gains taxes on half that amount: $2,220. As a result, if your marginal tax bracket in Canada were 40 percent (I'm just using that as an example) your capital gains tax bill would be 40 percent of $2,200. That's $880 in tax that you would pay for withdrawing $42,000 that year.

In case you're curious, if a Canadian resident sold $42,000 from a RRSP portfolio, they would have to pay tax at their full marginal tax rate. If their marginal tax bracket were 40 percent (most retirees would have a lower bracket, but I want to keep the comparisons consistent) then they would pay 40 percent of $42,000 in tax. That represents a massive tax hit of $16,800. Can you see why, as an expat, I sold my RRSP? I was happy to pay a 25 percent withholding tax, and then I invested the proceeds in my brokerage account overseas.

Once you move back to Canada, also consider investing the maximum allowed into a TFSA. You could buy any combination of stocks, bonds or ETFs (yeah, I recommend an all-in-one ETF) and you could pull that money out whenever you want, without paying tax.

Notes

1. Interview with Jonathan Ho. Email interview by author, June 15, 2021.
2. Dan Bortolotti, "More Swap-Based ETFs on the Horizon," Canadian Couch Potato RSS, October 15, 2013. Accessed July 3, 2014. http://canadian couchpotato.com/2013/10/15/more-swap-based-etfs-on-the-horizon/
3. PWC Worldwide Tax. Accessed August 15, 2021. https://taxsummaries.pwc .com/quick-charts/capital-gains-tax-cgt-rates
4. "European Countries That Are Not Members of The European Union," World Atlas. Accessed August 15, 2021. https://www.worldatlas.com/articles/ european-countries-who-are-not-part-of-the-european-union.html
5. "Elective Professional Status," Swissquote. Accessed August 15, 2021. https:// en.swissquote.lu/elective-professional-status

Chapter 11

Portfolio Models for British Expats

Forty-three year old Clare Willis knew she should start investing. As a teacher at a private school in Singapore, she can't contribute to a UK-based teacher's pension, so she decided to build her wealth with stock and bond market investments. "I'm pretty hot at Grade 3 Maths," she says, "but trying to figure out ETFs and what to do with them hurts my head. An all-in-one portfolio seemed much less complicated than managing individual ETFs. I like that I can just invest money each month [into the same fund] and let it do its thing over time."[1]

Vanguard UK allows British residents to build portfolios of index mutual funds directly. But the firm doesn't allow British expats to open accounts. Perhaps that's a good thing. By investing offshore,

British expats can avoid paying UK capital gains taxes. They also avoid risking their offshore residency status.

As of this writing, Swissquote is the only offshore brokerage allowing investors to buy Vanguard UK's LifeStrategy index mutual funds. When I mentioned Vanguard's LifeStrategy index mutual funds in this book's previous edition, investors required at least 100,000 GBP to get started in these funds. Many expats use Luxembourg-based, Swissquote Bank Europe (formerly Internaxx) which lowered the minimum to just 1000 GBP.

Like their American counterparts, each of Vanguard UK's Life-Strategy index mutual funds represents a globally diversified portfolio of indexes wrapped up in a single fund. For example, as shown in Table 11.1, Vanguard's LifeStrategy 60% Equity fund includes exposure to UK and global stocks. It's a "60% Equity fund" because 60 percent of the internal holdings are stock market indexes. The remaining 40 percent represent UK and global bond market indexes.

Vanguard rebalances each fund's internal holdings to maintain a consistent allocation. For example, when stocks fell in March 2020, Vanguard ensured its LifeStrategy 60% Equity fund maintained 60 percent in equities (stock indexes) and 40 percent in bond indexes. To do that, Vanguard sold some of the bond indexes, adding the proceeds to their stock indexes when stocks were low. This practice ensures that the fund maintains a consistent risk level, and as mentioned in Chapter 8, it can sometimes boost returns. Such rebalancing also follows the classic mantra of, "Buying Low and Selling High."

Vanguard charges a paltry 0.22 percent per year for its LifeStrategy index mutual funds. But these are not ETFs. As a result, Swissquote Bank Europe charges higher trading commissions for these products than it does for ETFs. Each time someone adds money to a Vanguard LifeStrategy Index Mutual Fund via Swissquote Bank Europe, the brokerage charges 0.5 percent of the amount deposited, or a minimum of 24.95 Euros (approximately 21.68 GBP). For example, if they chose to invest 2000 GBP every month, 0.5 percent of 2000 GBP would be 10 GBP. But because Swissquote Bank Europe's

Table 11.1 Vanguard LifeStrategy Indexed Mutual Funds: Approximate Fund Allocations*

Fund Composition	Very Conservative Vanguard Life Strategy 20% Equity	Conservative Vanguard Life Strategy 40% Equity	Balanced Vanguard Life Strategy 60% Equity	Assertive Vanguard Life Strategy 80% Equity
UK Stocks	5%	10%	15%	20%
Global Stocks	15%	30%	55%	60%
Global Bonds	55%	40%	30%	14%
UK Bonds	25%	20%	7%	6%
Fund Purchase Code	GB00B4NXY349	GB00B3ZHN960	GB00B3TYHH97	GB00B4PQW151
Minimum Starting Investment	1000 GBP	1000 GBP	1000 GBP	1000 GBP

*I listed four allocations above. But each fund actually comprises more than four index funds. However, based on each fund's internal holdings, the allocations above are accurate within 1 or 2 percentage points.

SOURCE: Vanguard UK.

minimum commission for these products is 24.95 euros (approximately 21.68 GBP) that would be the commission on a 2000 GBP purchase.

That's why some investors prefer to add money to these funds quarterly instead of monthly. By doing so, they can deposit larger sums and lower the commissions they pay. As of the date of this research (July 2021) Vanguard doesn't yet offer an all-in-one portfolio ETF that reflect the allocations shown in Table 11.1 (with the UK lean). If they did, investors could pay lower trading commissions for such funds, whether the investor chose to use Swissquote, Saxo Capital Markets, Interactive Brokers or any other offshore-friendly brokerage. After all, none of these brokerages charge fees as high as 0.50 percent to buy ETFs.

Are The Extra Commission Fees Worth It?

You might wonder whether paying trading commissions of 0.5 percent is worth the cost, compared to building a portfolio of individual ETFs. Until an equivalent, British all-in-one portfolio ETF becomes available the answer is likely, yes.

After all, Vanguard's LifeStrategy funds encourage investors to behave much better, compared to investors in individual index funds and individual (non-all-in-one) ETFs.

Morningstar's Mind The Gap study measured investors' performance in seven stock market fund categories over the 10 years ending December 31, 2019. These ten years should have been easy on the nerves. After all, stocks went up almost every year. But if we don't include investors who bought all-in-one portfolio funds, the typical investor underperformed the funds they owned by 0.93 percent per year.[2]

That means they bought more on highs and less on lows. In contrast, all-in-one portfolio investors earned better returns than the returns posted by their funds. Such investors, after all, never have to ask themselves, "Which fund should I buy this month?" Nor do they have to ask, "When should I rebalance?" Most of them, like Clare Willis does, added consistent sums to their all-in-one portfolio funds (known as dollar-cost averaging). As a result, over the 10 years ending December 31, 2019, investors in all-in-one funds outperformed the posted returns of their funds by an average of 0.40 percent per year.

So, individual fund investors **underperformed** their funds by 0.93 percent per year (as a result of bad behavior) and all-in-one fund investors **outperformed** by 0.4 percent per year (as a result of consistent dollar-cost averaging). That gave the all-in-one fund investors a behavioral advantage of about 1.33 percent per year. You can see even broader advantages for all-in-one fund investors over the 15-year period ending June 2019 (see Chapter 8 for details).

When doing the long-term math, despite paying 0.50 percent commissions on purchases, investors in such all-in-one funds should make more money than investors who buy individual ETFs.

For example, assume one of Vanguard's LifeStrategy funds averages 8 percent over the next 15 years. Let's also assume an equally diversified collection of ETFs earned the same return. Unfortunately, most investors will underperform the posted returns of their individual ETFs. They won't always rebalance when they should. They might switch ETFs if they believe they've found "a better one." Just being in a position to tinker with an allocation increases the odds that the investor will speculate.

Assume the individual ETF investor's behavior hampers their returns by about 1 percent per year. It's easy to say, "That wouldn't happen to me!" but most individual index fund investors shot themselves in the feet between June 2004 and June 2019 (as shown in Chapter 8). And I doubt any of those investors figured that would happen.

Now let's pretend the investor in individual ETFs had a brokerage that, not only didn't charge commissions, but paid them 10 GBP to invest each month. That would never happen, but please play along for a moment.

Now assume the investor in one of Vanguard's LifeStrategy funds beat the posted return of their fund by 0.2 percent per year. That's a much lower behavioral advantage than what Morningstar discovered over the ten years ending December 31, 2019 and over the 15 years ending June 30, 2019 (see Chapter 8 for an explanation of how this occurs).

Swissquote Bank Europe charges the investor 24.95 euros (about 21.68 GBP) for each 2000 GBP purchase. Given these assumptions, as shown in Table 11.2, expats paying 0.5 percent commissions to purchase Vanguard's LifeStrategy funds would beat the performance of the typical expat buying an equal-risk adjusted portfolio of individual ETFs.

In this example, investing 2000 GBP per month over 15 years could give the Vanguard LifeStrategy Investor an advantage of 59,856 GBP over 15 years or 143,804 GBP over 20 years, compared to the

Table 11.2 Vanguard LifeStrategy Fund Investors Likely Come Out Ahead

	Investor In A Vanguard Life Strategy Fund	Investor In An Equal-Allocated Portfolio of Individual ETFs
Amount Invested Per Month	2000 GBP	2000 GBP
Monthly Purchase Commission (or the bonus with this fantasy brokerage)*	−21.68 GBP*	+10 GBP***
Monthly Sum Invested after commissions or fantasy brokerage bonus	1,978.32 GBP	2010.00 GBP
Annual Sum Invested after commissions or fantasy brokerage bonus	23,739.84 GBP	24,120 GBP
Average Annual Fund Return*	8%	8%
Investors' Annual Return, Considering Behavioral Implications	8.2%	7%
15-Year Portfolio Value	708,395 GBP	648,539 GBP
20-Year Portfolio Value	1,201,832 GBP	1,058,028 GBP

*Rough equivalent commission of 24.95 euros.
**This is just as an example. Nobody knows how the markets will perform in the future.
***No brokerage actually pays people to make purchases, but we're having some fun with this.

typical investor in individual ETFs. That includes all commissions for the LifeStrategy fund and the bonus payment (which I just I made up) for each deposit into a portfolio of individual ETFs.

The Downside of Vanguard's LifeStrategy Index Mutual Funds

For UK-based British investors, there isn't a downside to these funds. Investors can buy them commission-free directly from Vanguard UK and sell them commission-free. That's in sharp contrast to British expats who have to pay commissions to Swissquote Bank Europe. But British expats can compound their money free of UK capital gains taxes. Depending on where the expats live, they might not have to pay any capital gains taxes as the money grows. But a unique element in the UK tax code does add a wrinkle.

When expats from most other countries repatriate, they don't have to sell their ETFs or funds. For example, Canadians or Australians can simply transfer the investments they purchased offshore to a brokerage in their home country after they repatriate. In other words, they could feasibly have millions of dollars with an offshore brokerage, and pay just $50 per fund to transfer it. If they own an all-in-one portfolio fund, $50 is all they would have to pay (because everything would be wrapped up into just one fund). Such nationalities wouldn't pay home-country capital gains taxes on the money they made while they lived abroad. In other words, any gains they made abroad might be tax-free (depending on where they lived, as an expat).

This is true for British expats, too, with one notable difference. British expats can't simply transfer their funds to a UK-based broker-age account without risking a huge tax bill. That's why it's best for British expats to sell before repatriating. They can then transfer the assets in cash to a UK bank then reinvest that money in a Vanguard LifeStrategy fund without paying commissions (Vanguard UK doesn't charge commissions when you buy their funds directly).

But before doing so, they would have to pay Swissquote Bank Europe that pesky commission to sell. Despite that fee, if Morningstar's evidence is any indication, British expats in Vanguard's Life-Strategy funds should still beat the performance of most investors who choose to build portfolios of individual ETFs . . . even if such investors (remember my fantasy brokerage scenario) weren't charged commissions and were actually paid to invest.

But because they would have to sell before repatriating, Swissquote would hit them with a 0.5 percent commission bill. Assume an expat has to sell 708,395 GBP (as shown in my 15-year example in Table 11.2). At a commission rate of 0.5 percent, that sale would cost 3,541.97 GBP. A British investor in individual ETFs should also sell before they repatriate. But doing so would only cost a fraction of that.

However, if you look carefully at Table 11.2, you'll see that the Vanguard LifeStrategy index mutual fund investor will likely still come out ahead—even after paying the 0.5 percent commission before they repatriate. That said, paying a commission of 3,541.97 GBP to sell 708,395 GBP could still leave a sour taste. And when Vanguard offers these funds in an ETF form (which I'm guessing they will, at some point) investors in these funds could avoid these higher commissions to buy and sell.

Portfolios of Individual ETFs: For Walking British Buddhas

If you're vehemently opposed to paying higher trading commissions for a Vanguard LifeStrategy index mutual fund, and you have a Buddha's disposition, you might prefer to build a portfolio with individual ETFs.

The British Couch Potato portfolios in Table 11.3 include ETFs that trade in British pounds. This makes it easier for investors to rebalance because their ETFs will be listed in a common currency. The following funds also distribute dividends, instead of accumulating them automatically within the funds themselves.

Table 11.3 British Couch Potato Portfolios

Fund Name	Ticker Symbol	Expense ratio	Conservative	Cautious	Balanced	Assertive	Aggressive
Vanguard UK FTSE 100 Stock Index	VUKE	0.09%	10%	15%	20%	20%	25%
Vanguard UK FTSE 250 Stock Index	VMID	0.10%	5%	5%	10%	15%	15%
Vanguard FTSE All–World ETF	VWRL	0.22%	15%	25%	30%	40%	50%
iShares UK Gilts 0–5yr ETF Or	IGLS	0.07%	70%	55%	40%	25%	10%
Vanguard UK Gilt ETF	VGOV	0.07%					

SOURCES: Vanguard UK, iShares UK.

With the funds below, dividends would be distributed into the cash component of the brokerage account. Investors can lump that cash with new cash deposits (from their savings) to make new purchases.

Vanguard's UK FTSE 100 Stock Index contains 103 of the largest stocks in the UK market. I've also included Vanguard's UK FTSE 250 Stock Index to diversify further. As of this writing, it contained 253 mid-sized and small-sized UK stocks.

I've also included a choice of two different bond market ETFs. I prefer the iShares UK Gilts 0–5yr ETF (IGLS) because it comprises short-term bonds. But those who want more pop for their bond market pound might choose Vanguard's UK Gilt ETF (VGOV). It contains government bonds with slightly longer terms and slightly higher yields. Just remember that its price won't be as stable. Also, if inflation rears its head, it won't perform as well as the short-term bond market index.

If this confuses you, just flip a coin. Choosing one of these bond ETFs over the other won't make or break your portfolio. The difference will be negligible.

How Important Is UK Stock And Bond Market Exposure?

When Vanguard creates all-in-one index portfolios (like Vanguard UK's LifeStrategy funds) they include a slight bias towards the relative home country's market. For example, Vanguard's all-in-one funds on the Australian stock exchange contain global stocks and a relatively high exposure to Aussie stocks and bonds. It's much the same with Vanguard USA's all-in-one funds. They include global stocks and a relatively high exposure to US stocks and bonds. Vanguard Canada's all-in-one funds do likewise, containing global stock exposure and relatively high exposure to Canadian stocks and Canadian bonds.

As previously mentioned, this reduces home currency risk. But how important is that? Some experts say it isn't important at all. They prefer to build portfolios without a home-country bias. Without a working crystal ball, nobody will know what would perform better: It might be portfolios with some of your home country's bias. It might not. But one truth is paramount. Neither you, nor anyone you know, can predict what markets will do well in the future. That's why you shouldn't shun or embrace home country exposure based on economic predictions or past results.

And if you choose to invest in a portfolio without a home country bias, you would be sidestepping something called, global market capitalization risk. If you like the sounds of that, you could buy a globally diversified all-in-one ETF such as Vanguard LifeStrategy ETFs. They trade on the Italian and German stock exchanges, priced in euros. This doesn't, however, mean your future profits would be pegged to the fortunes of the euro. As mentioned in Chapter 7, the listed currency of your fund is completely irrelevant.

Vanguard rebalances the internal holdings of these funds, shown in Table 11.4, to maintain a consistent allocation. The funds' total expense ratio charges are just 0.25 percent per year.

Table 11.4   Vanguard LifeStrategy All-In-One ETFs: (With No UK Stock Or UK Bond Bias)

Fund Composition	Very Conservative	Conservative	Balanced	Assertive
	Vanguard Life Strategy 20% Equity UCITS ETF	Vanguard Life Strategy 40% Equity UCITS ETF	Vanguard Life Strategy 60% Equity UCITS ETF	Vanguard Life Strategy 80% Equity UCITS ETF
Global Stocks	20%	40%	60%	80%
Global Bonds	80%	60%	40%	20%
Fund Purchase Code on **Xetra****	V20A	V40A	V60A	V80A

**Xetra represents a Frankfurt stock exchange and is the commonly used exchange for this ETF.
Note: Technically, these funds have a very slight bias to the United States, beyond US global market capitalization and the bond allocations are hedged to the euro.
Source: Global.Vanguard.com.

One added benefit of these funds, compared to Vanguard UK's LifeStrategy mutual funds (in Table 11.2) is that they're cheaper to buy and sell. The drawback to the funds listed in Table 11.4 (at least for some British expats) is that they don't have much UK exposure. But whether British stocks beat global stocks over the next one, 10, or 15-year period will matter little. Over a 30-year period, all-in-one funds with a British lean will likely perform similarly to all-in-one portfolios without a British lean. If you try to guess which will perform better, well . . . that makes you human. But the effort is a waste of time. We humans are a silly bunch.

Socially Responsible Investing For British Expats

British investors might be some of the world's most socially conscious. Whenever I get a question on my blog about Socially Responsible Investing (SRI), it often comes from a British person.

Fund companies, like BlackRock noticed the demand. That's why they created all-in-one SRI funds that trade on the London Stock Exchange. These are much like the funds listed in Table 11.4, but BlackRock culled companies that didn't comply with socially responsible practices. Their annual expense ratios are just 0.25 percent.

As of June 2021, BlackRock didn't have an SRI all-in-one fund ETF with the popular 60 percent global stock and 40 percent global bond allocation. Although it defeats the simplicity of an all-in-one fund, investors who want about 60 percent exposure to global stocks and 40 percent exposure to global bonds could buy two of the funds below: The Blackrock ESG Multi-Asset Growth Portfolio (with 80 percent stocks and 20 percent bonds) and the Blackrock ESG Multi-Asset Moderate Portfolio (with about 53 percent in stocks and 47 percent in bonds). By investing an equal sum in each, you would end up with about 66 percent stocks, 34 percent bonds.

If you want a single all-in-one portfolio of socially responsible funds with 60 percent stocks and 40 percent bonds, it might be available by the time you read this. Check the BlackRock UK website and search under iShares ETFs: https://www.blackrock.com/uk

The funds in Table 11.5 are priced in euros. BlackRock also offers versions priced in GBP, with one significant difference. Recall that many investors like exposure to their home market to reduce home currency risk. As a result, most of Vanguard's all-in-one portfolios reflect respective home country bias (as previously mentioned with Vanguard's all-in-one funds for Brits, Americans, Canadians and Australians).

The GBP priced equivalents of the funds in Table 11.5 don't reflect home country British bias. But they are currency-hedged in an attempt to reduce currency risk for British investors. Here's an example of what that means. Within each of these all-in-one ETFs there's a US stock market ETF. Assume the US stock market, priced in USD, gains 10 percent in a given year. If the US dollar drops

Table 11.5 BlackRock's All-in-One Portfolios of Socially Responsible ETFs

Fund Composition	Very Conservative	Moderately Conservative	Assertive
	BlackRock ESG Multi-Asset Conservative Portfolio UCITS ETF	BlackRock ESG Multi-Asset Moderate Portfolio UCITS ETF	BlackRock ESG Multi-Asset Growth Portfolio UCITS ETF
Global Stocks	20%	53%	80%
Global Bonds	80%	47%	20%
Fund Purchase Code on London Stock Exchange	MACV	MODR	MAGR

Source: https://www.blackrock.com/uk.

10 percent that year, compared to the pound, then that US stock market index wouldn't gain a penny, when measured in pounds. However, if that US stock index were hedged to the pound, then a 10 percent gain, measured in USD, is supposed to represent a 10 percent gain measured in GBP.

There are just two problems with hedging stock market investments. First, currency swings aren't always bad. For example, if a non-hedged US stock index gained 10 percent in a given year, in USD, and if the USD gained 10 percent that year, compared to the pound, that US stock index would have gained 20 percent, measured in GBP.

What's more, currency hedging isn't an exact science, and it always comes with a hidden cost. As mentioned in Chapter 7, currency-hedged stock market funds typically create a drag of at least 1 percent per year. That's why I don't recommend currency-hedged stock market funds. Fortunately, none of the SRI funds listed in Table 11.5 include currency-hedged stock market exposure.

Are You Really Ready To Do This?

It's now time to be brutally honest. If you're like most people, you'll eventually stab yourself in the foot if you build a portfolio of individual ETFs. Most people look at funds and try to figure out which have earned the best historical returns. They try to second-guess whether they can time the stock market. They sweat over "the perfect" allocation of stocks and bonds and they want to make sure they own "the perfect" combination or the "perfect ETF." Too often, they make selections based on past results. Unfortunately, that's like putting drops of snake venom into your oatmeal every morning. Sure, some science-deprived people might believe that's healthy. But it isn't.

Maintaining a Couch Potato portfolio is simpler than riding a bike. But plenty of people overthink the process. They tweak things. They act on their thoughts (or the thoughts of others). The more analytical investors are usually the worst. They almost always screw things up. If that describes you, check your ego at the door. Heck, even if that doesn't describe you, strongly consider the advantages of an all-in-one portfolio fund over individual ETFs.

Notes

1. Interview with Clare Willis. Email interview by author, July 20, 2021.
2. Amy C. Arnott, "How Do Investors' Returns Stack Up Against Total Returns," Morningstar. August 18, 2020. Accessed August 18, 2021. https://www.morningstar.com/articles/998339/how-do-investor-returns-stack-up-against-total-returns

Chapter 12

Portfolio Models for Australian Expats

S hane Musarra is a trivia king. The 34-year old owns a quiz night company and he plays trivia regularly in Dubai. This contrasts with his day job; it smacks of serious stuff. Shane, who's originally from Perth, Australia, is Senior Manager in Procurement at Dubai Airports.[1]

As someone who wants the best odds of investment success, he selected two all-in-one portfolio ETFs that trade on the Australian stock exchange. As described in Chapter 8, most investors in all-in-one funds earn better returns than those who buy individual ETFs. But you might be asking, "Why would Shane buy two of them when just one of them should do?"

Vanguard Australia offers four all-in-one portfolio ETFs. But none of them reflect the asset allocation Shane wanted: 80 percent

213

stocks and 20 percent bonds. That's why he bought Vanguard's Diversified Growth Index ETF (VDGR) and Vanguard's Diversified High Growth Index (VDHG). VDGR includes 70 percent global and Australian stocks and 30 percent bonds, while VDHG includes 90 percent global and Australian stocks and 10 percent bonds. By investing equal amounts in both, Shane has 80 percent in stocks and 20 percent in bonds.

Shane uses Interactive Brokers. Transaction fees are low, so he can afford the low-cost commissions to buy both of these each month. Or, if he wanted to save money on trading commissions, he could buy one of them one month, followed by the next ETF the following month. What's more, in a few years, if the 34 year old wants to simplify things further, he could sell VDHG (90 percent stocks, 10 percent bonds) and roll the entire proceeds into VDGR, with 70 percent stocks and 30 percent bonds. As explained in Chapter 8, investors in all-in-one funds typically perform better than those who buy individual ETFs.

Below, I've shown Vanguard Australia's two other all-in-one portfolio ETFs in Table 12.1. They include Vanguard Australia's Diversified Conservative Index ETF (VDOC), comprising about 70 percent in bonds with the remaining 30 percent allocated to Australian and global shares. Vanguard Australia's Diversified Balanced Index (VDBA) comprises about 50 percent bonds, with the remaining 50 percent invested in global and Australian shares. Each of Vanguard Australia's all-in-one portfolio ETFs cost 0.27 percent per year.

Socially Responsible Investing For Australians

In August 2020, Vanguard Australia launched a series of socially responsible (SRI) ETFs. They're much like broad stock market ETFs with several companies' shares removed. As explained on Vanguard's website, these ETFs do not include companies with significant business activities involving fossil fuels, nuclear power, alcohol,

Table 12.1   All-In-One Portfolios For Australian Expats

Very Conservative	Conservative/ Balanced	Assertive	Aggressive
70% Bonds and Cash 30% Stocks	50% Bonds 50% Stocks	30% Bonds 70% Stocks	10% Bonds 90% Stocks
Vanguard Australia's Diversified Conservative Index ETF (VDOC)	Vanguard Australia's Diversified Balanced Index (VDBA)	Diversified Growth Index ETF (VDGR)	Vanguard's Diversified High Growth Index (VDHG).
Best suited for investors looking for high stability and low returns.	Best suited for investors looking for some stability, coupled with moderate long-term growth.	Best suited for investors looking for slightly more growth. Such investors can emotionally handle market declines.	Best suited for investors looking for high growth. But such investors require strong stomachs. If it would upset them to see this fund not make money for half a decade, they shouldn't invest in it.

*Each of the above trades on the Australian Stock Exchange.

tobacco, gambling, weapons, adult entertainment. Vanguard also omits companies embroiled in extreme controversy. As explained in Chapter 7, investors in such funds don't get punished for sidestepping so-called "sin stocks." Research suggests that, long-term, SRI funds perform just as well as plain vanilla index funds.

As of this writing, Vanguard Australia hadn't yet launched all-in-one SRI portfolio ETFs trading on the Australian stock market. But I have no doubt they will. Check Vanguard Australia's website to see if they've recently been launched. Until then, you could build SRI portfolios with the ETFs in Table 12.2. Each portfolio represents a different tolerance for risk.

Table 12.2 Australian Socially Responsible Investment (SRI) Portfolios

Fund Name	Ticker Symbol	Expense ratio	Listed Currency	Conservative	Cautious	Balanced	Assertive	Aggressive
Vanguard Ethically Conscious Australian Shares ETF	VETH	0.16%	AUD	15%	20%	30%	35%	45%
Vanguard Ethically Conscious International Shares Index ETF	VEFI	0.26%	AUD	15%	25%	30%	40%	45%
Vanguard Ethically Conscious Global Aggregate Bond Index Hedged ETF	VEFI	0.26%	AUD	70%	55%	40%	25%	10%

Source: Vanguard Australia.

What If You Don't Want High Exposure to Australian Shares?

According to statistica.com, Australian shares comprise just 2.4 percent of the world's global market capitalization.[2] To get a sense of what that means, assume you owned every share of every company in the world. In that case, people like Jeff Bezos and Bill Gates might wear loincloths and catch spare change in tin cups. Now assume you sold every share of every company you owned. In that case, 2.4 percent of the trillions of dollars you stuffed into your Sri Lankan-sized mattress would have come from Australian shares.

In other words, the Australian stock market isn't very big. Some Australian investors (especially those who don't want to retire in Australia) prefer that their portfolios represent global market capitalization. That isn't because Aussie shares haven't done well. According to the Credit Suisse Global Investment Return Yearbook, Australian shares beat inflation by an average of 6.8 percent annually from 1990–2020. Not even the United States managed to match that. Over the same time period, US stocks averaged 6.6 percent above their country's inflation rate.[3]

From January 2000 to May 31, 2021, Australia's MSCI index of Australian shares averaged a compound annual return of about 9.1 percent per year (measured in USD). That compares to 7.1 percent per year for the US stock market. I can hear the chanting now: Aussie! Aussie! Aussie! Oi! Oi! Oi!

Still, the past isn't a prologue to the future. And many Australian expats won't retire to their homeland. For that reason, a globally diversified, all-in-one portfolio ETF (without an Australian bias) might be more to their liking. Table 12.3 lists such funds with different tolerances for risk. Each fund trades on the Italian or German exchanges (Xetra, a Frankfurt stock exchange, is the most commonly used exchange for these ETFs).

Each of these funds is priced in euros, but as mentioned in Chapter 7, that doesn't mean investors in these funds peg their hopes

Table 12.3　Vanguard LifeStrategy All-In-One ETFs: (With No Australian Stock Or Australian Bond Bias)

Fund Composition	Very Conservative	Conservative	Balanced	Assertive
	Vanguard Life Strategy 20% Equity UCITS ETF	Vanguard Life Strategy 40% Equity UCITS ETF	Vanguard Life Strategy 60% Equity UCITS ETF	Vanguard Life Strategy 80% Equity UCITS ETF
Global Stocks	20%	40%	60%	80%
Global Bonds	80%	60%	40%	20%
Fund Purchase Code on **Xetra****	V20A	V40A	V60A	V80A

**Xetra represents a Frankfurt stock exchange and is the commonly used exchange for these ETFs.
NOTE: Technically, these funds have a very slight bias to the United States, beyond US global market capitalization but their bond allocations are hedged to the euro.
SOURCE: Global.Vanguard.com.

on the euro. In this case, the listed currency is irrelevant. Such funds provide exposure to the world's stocks, bonds and currencies.

The Repatriation Benefit of Aussie-listed Shares

When choosing ETFs, Australians who plan to repatriate should consider the benefits of owning Australian-listed ETFs, such as what I listed in Tables 12.1 and 12.2. Australians, for example, can simply transfer their ETFs to an Australian brokerage of their choice. This process is easiest with Australian-listed products.

For example, upon repatriating, you could open a brokerage account with Vanguard Australia. Then ask them to send you a transfer form. From that point, you could pay a nominal fee to transfer the ETFs you bought from an offshore brokerage, such as Swissquote, Saxo Capital Markets or Interactive Brokers. Interactive Brokers is available to resident Australians, but compared to Vanguard Australia's interface, it's like trying to drive a car with four steering wheels. In fact, when it comes to ease of operation, Vanguard Australia's brokerage puts the offshore firms to shame.

What's more, if your portfolio includes Vanguard Australia's listed ETFs (as shown in Tables 12.1 and 12.2) you won't have to pay commissions to buy or sell.

Tax Laws: Created By The Rich For The Rich?

In most cases, people with money created tax laws. How else could you explain how wealthy people (in almost every country) pay far lower taxes as a percentage of their wealth? This benefit doubles for Australians, like Shane Musarra, who would return home from a capital-gains free jurisdiction with a large investment portfolio. After all, as a resident of Dubai, Shane's portfolio would have grown almost entirely tax-free (with the exception of dividend withholding taxes) as long as he were deemed a non-resident over the duration he held these funds. What's more, Shane would pay paltry taxes when selling pieces of his portfolio after repatriating.

For example, assume Shane repatriated with $1 million. None of the capital gains he made, while living overseas, would be taxable in Australia. And from the date he repatriates, the Australian government presses a taxable re-set button.

Imagine Shane repatriates to Australia and then downshifts from trivia and airports to a part-time job walking dogs. Let's assume he's in a 30 percent marginal tax bracket (a relatively high tax bracket, but he's one hell of a dog walker). He then sells $40,000 of his portfolio 12 months after repatriating. If his portfolio gained 10 percent over those 12 months, he would record a $4000 capital gain. Because he doesn't sell anything within his first 12 months, Shane would pay capital gains taxes on just half of that profit. In other words, $2000 would be taxable at his marginal tax rate (30 percent). In that case, Shane would have to pay just $600 in capital gains taxes after withdrawing

$40,000. In other words, he would pay a tax rate of 1.5 percent of what he withdrew (600 is 1.5 percent of 40,000).

Over time, Shane's portfolio would likely continue to grow, and an increased percentage of what he withdraws (assuming he withdraws every year) would come from his portfolio's gains. But despite that fact, his tax rate would be paltry compared to the tax rate applied to regular working income.

Everyone's tax situation, however, is unique. There's much more to consider. That's why you should research and hire a great tax accountant. Forget about getting tax help from a well-meaning (but likely ignorant) person on Reddit or Facebook. When it comes to professional tax advice, it rarely pays to be cheap. That's why, if you don't have a professional accountant today, hire one before you repatriate. You might be surprised how much money and hassle this could save.

Now Look Deeply Into That Mirror

If you're like most people, you'll try to take something simple and make it really complicated. Most people will look at the portfolio allocations in this chapter and try to figure out which have earned the best historical returns. They will try to second-guess whether they can time the stock market. They will sweat over "the perfect" allocation of stocks and bonds and they will try to make sure they own "the perfect" ETF. They also waste their time thinking about the economies that represent the countries they're invested in.

However, maintaining a Couch Potato portfolio is like peeing in a cup. It's easy. But plenty of people (especially men) overthink the process. They tweak things. They act on their thoughts or the thoughts of others. That's like trying to pee from an angle or upside down. The more analytical investors are usually the worst. They almost always make a mess.

That's why investing in one of Vanguard Australia's all-in-one portfolios of ETFs makes so much sense.

Notes

1. Interview with Shane Musarra. Email interview by author, July 22, 2021.
2. "Distribution of countries with largest stock markets worldwide as of January 2021, by share of total world equity market value," Statistica.com. Accessed August 14, 2021. https://www.statista.com/statistics/710680/global-stock-markets-by-country/
3. Credit Suisse Reports and Research, Accessed August 15, 2021. https://www.credit-suisse.com/about-us/en/reports-research/csri.html

Chapter 13

Portfolio Models for Europeans and Other Nationalities

Yasmin Tahira Sewgobind lives in Abu Dhabi, where she works as a (Brazilian) Jiu Jitsu coach. The 38-year old single mother of a 4-year old daughter is originally from Amsterdam, The Netherlands. She also draws parallels between how she invests and Brazilian Jiu Jitsu.

"Yasmin says, "Brazilian Jiu Jitsu is a highly efficient martial art that uses physical leverage. I've trained most of my life with men who are physically stronger. But as a smaller female player this didn't mean I would get destroyed on the mat. Several times, I've dominated and forced bigger, physical opponents to tap out. With the right kind of physical leverage a smaller person can beat a stronger opponent.

It's much the same with investing. A small individual investor can beat a big hedge fund manager with an all-in-one portfolio ETF."[1]

As explained in Chapter 8, most investors in all-in-one portfolio ETFs outperform most people who build portfolios with individual ETFs. All-in-one funds work a bit like efficiency on a mat. Yasmin, for example, never has to worry about shifting her portfolio's allocation. She owns the Vanguard LifeStrategy 80% Equity UCITS ETF. It includes 80 percent global stocks and 20 percent global bonds. Vanguard maintains a consistent allocation so Yasmin doesn't have to. It charges a total expense ratio fee of just 0.25 percent.

"There's beauty in simplicity," says Yasmin, "and that aligns with my life philosophy."

The 49-year old father of two children, Stephen Bourne, selected the same fund as Yasmin. The MRI Technologist at Cleveland Clinic Abu Dhabi first began investing with the full-service firm, AES International. But he didn't feel his financial needs were complicated, so he switched to building a portfolio of individual ETFs. With help from the firm, PlanVision, he bought a global stock ETF and a global bond ETF. But when Vanguard offered all-in-one ETFs trading in euros, Stephen jumped at the chance to switch.[2] And it's the last jump he'll need to make.

Table 13.1 shows four Vanguard LifeStrategy ETFs. They each comprise several individual ETFs with the general allocations shown below.

The Home Currency Bias

Yasmin's and Stephen's all-in-one ETFs trade in euros. But as mentioned in Chapter 7, that doesn't mean they're fully invested in euros. The listed currency of an ETF, after all, doesn't represent the fund's internal holdings. In the case of these specific Vanguard LifeStrategy ETFs, there's less home currency bias. The internal holdings represent exposure to the world's stock and bond markets. As a result, their funds are invested in several global currencies.

Table 13.1   Vanguard LifeStrategy All-In-One ETFs: (With No Home Country Bias)

Fund Composition	Very Conservative	Conservative	Balanced	Assertive
	Vanguard Life Strategy 20% Equity UCITS ETF	Vanguard Life Strategy 40% Equity UCITS ETF	Vanguard Life Strategy 60% Equity UCITS ETF	Vanguard Life Strategy 80% Equity UCITS ETF
Global Stocks	20%	40%	60%	80%
Global Bonds	80%	60%	40%	20%
Fund Purchase Code on **Xetra****	V20A	V40A	V60A	V80A

**Xetra represents a Frankfurt stock exchange and is the commonly used exchange for this ETF.
NOTE: Technically, these funds have a very slight bias to the United States, beyond US global market capitalization.
SOURCE: Global.Vanguard.com.

Some investors, however, prefer a home market/currency bias. If you look at Chapters 9–12, you'll notice that Vanguard created all-in-one funds for Americans, Canadians, Brits and Australians that represent home market/currency bias. For example, Vanguard Canada's all-in-one portfolio ETFs include exposure to global stocks and bonds, but they also include relatively high exposure to Canadian stocks and Canadian bonds.

In his book, *Reboot Your Portfolio*, Dan Bortolotti explains why. The DIY advocate and financial advisor with PWL Capital says a Canadian investor without a home market/currency bias would have just 3 percent of her stock market holdings in Canadian markets (that's because Canada's stock market represents 3 percent of global market capitalization).

If such an investor also had global bond market exposure (instead of a high percentage of Canadian bond exposure) then just a small portion of her portfolio would be allocated to Canadian dollars. In this case, the vast majority of her portfolio would be in foreign currencies. Bortolotti explains that some foreign currency exposure is a good thing, but 97 percent is too much, considering that most Canadians' future expenses will be in Canadian dollars.

Then he asks us to consider fees and taxes. International stock ETFs tend to charge higher fees than domestic stock ETFs. In many cases, dividends coming from a home country market are taxed more favorably than dividends coming from abroad.[3] This would be the case after the expat has repatriated.

Having said this, if a European investor's portfolio represented global market capitalization, they would not have a whopping 97 percent of their portfolio invested in foreign markets and foreign currencies. That's because Europe makes up a far higher percentage of global market capitalization than Canada, Australia or the UK.

Consequently, the Vanguard LifeStrategy Funds that Yasmin and Stephen own include about 13 percent exposure to European stocks with the other 87 percent in international shares. What's more, all of their international bond market exposure is hedged to the euro. For example, if the fund's US bond market component gained 2 percent in USD, and the USD fell hard compared to the euro (as it did in 2003) then the European investor wouldn't be affected. The US bond market index, when measured in euros, would earn close to 2 percent.

As explained in Chapter 7, it's fine if bond market indexes are currency-hedged. But you shouldn't own a currency-hedged stock market fund. Fortunately, based on the holdings within these Vanguard LifeStrategy funds, Vanguard hasn't included currency-hedged equity ETFs among these funds' internal holdings.

Investors Who Might Not Want Any Home Currency Exposure

A few years ago, my wife and I were traveling in a camper van in Guatemala when we met two Argentinians: Diego Montagna and Natalia Fredes. They were exploring Central America in a Toyota Dolphin motorhome after investing their savings in a diversified portfolio of Argentinian stocks. But their home currency crashed. In July

2016, one Argentinian peso was worth about 60 US cents. By July 2021, it had fallen to just 10 US cents.

Emerging market currencies can fall really hard. That's one reason why investors shouldn't stuff a lot of money in emerging market bank savings accounts. In some cases, such accounts might pay high interest. But if that currency crashes and local inflation soars (the two typically go hand-in-hand) the investor can lose a lot. That's what happened to Diego and Natalia...but worse, because Argentinian stocks crashed, too.

If, however, an investor from an emerging market country owns a portfolio of global stocks and global bonds, they are less likely to get hammered by runaway inflation. For example, from January 2016 to July 2021, a global stock market index gained about 103 percent, measured in USD. But measured in Argentinian pesos, because of that currency's crash, that same index gained about 600 percent. That's a compound annual return of about 54 percent. It also compensated for inflation in Argentina and the currency's crash. According to Statistica .com, inflation in Argentina was 41.2 percent in 2016; 25.68 percent in 2017; 34.28 percent in 2018; 53.55 percent in 2019 and 42.02 percent in 2020.[4]

Investors from emerging market countries, however, aren't the only people who might prefer to sidestep home country bias. Those from small countries or those who don't know where they plan to retire often select portfolios with global market capitalization. The portfolio models in Table 13.2 have similar allocations compared to Vanguard's LifeStrategy funds in Table 13.1. But the bond components of these two-fund portfolios aren't hedged to the euro.

It's important to remember, however, that investors in all-in-one portfolios typically perform better than those who use individual ETFs. That's why, if I were a betting man, I would wager that most investors in Vanguard's LifeStrategy funds (in Table 13.1) will beat the long-term performance of those who choose two fund portfolios, such as those in Table 13.2. After all, once you have a globally diversified, low cost portfolio, how you behave will impact

Table 13.2 Portfolio Models Based on Global Market Capitalization

Fund Name	Ticker Symbol	Expense ratio	Listed Currency	Conservative	Cautious	Balanced	Assertive	Aggressive
Vanguard FTSE All-World UCITS ETF	VWRA	0.22%	USD	30%	45%	60%	75%	90%
iShares Core Global Aggregate Bond ETF	AGGG	0.10%	USD	70%	55%	40%	25%	10%

SOURCES: iShares UK; Vanguard UK.

your performance more than anything else. And the best way to harness your inner investment Jiu Jitsu master is with an all-in-one portfolio fund.

Socially Responsible Investing

As of this writing, there isn't yet an all-in-one portfolio ETF based on global market capitalization. iShares Canada has some with higher Canadian stock and bond market exposure, so they wouldn't suit non-Canadians. However, investors who want something similar could replace Vanguard's FTSE All World UCITS ETF (VWRA) shown in Table 13.2 with the iShares MSCI World SRI UCITS ETF (SUWS). This is priced in USD, with a euro-priced version trading under the symbol, SUSW.

As explained in Chapter 7, SRI funds should perform as well as their non-SRI equivalents when measured over long time periods. Sometimes, over short periods, SRI funds will lag their traditional counterparts. During other short periods, they will beat traditional ETFs. Just don't chase your own tail. Too many investors base their fund decisions on recent past performance. And "recent" could be as short as a ten-year period. It's human nature to do this and a foible that costs us money.

Notes

1. Interview with Yasmin Tahira Sewgobind. Email interview with author, July 27, 2021.
2. Interview with Stephen Bourne. Email interview with author, July 28, 2021.
3. Dan Bortolotti, *Reboot Your Portfolio* (Toronto, Canada, Milner & Associates, 87).
4. Inflation in Argentina, Statistica.com. Accessed August 21, 2021. https://www .statista.com/statistics/316750/inflation-rate-in-argentina/

Chapter 14

Setting Your Bulls Eye

I once had dinner with a financial advisor in Qatar. Over a delicious spinach salad, the advisor told me that one of his clients earns £450,000 a year. Over the previous decade, his total salary earnings had exceeded £3 million.

As a British expat in Qatar, the lawyer doesn't pay income tax. His employer pays for his housing costs *and* provides him with a car to use.

"Unfortunately," said the advisor, "unless my client makes some drastic changes, he'll never be able to retire." I almost choked on a crouton. "How is that possible?" I asked. But I already knew the answer. He spends almost every penny he makes. His investment portfolio was valued at just US$20,000.

It's tough to know who's wealthy and who's living a fantasy. Plenty of high-salaried expats are metaphorically flying over the ocean in private jets with near-empty fuel tanks. Their salaries might exceed a million dollars a year or more. They might drive Ferraris. They might own homes in Spain and France (with eye-watering mortgages). They might travel first class. But many aren't much different from professional football players.

Sports Illustrated estimates that 80 percent of professional (NFL) football players go broke within three years of their retirement. Their average salaries exceed $2 million a year. But when their salaries dry up, they end up broke.[1]

Such boneheaded blunders aren't just reserved for professional athletes. Plenty of expats suffer too. Sam Instone says it's more common than we think. "I see this all the time," says the CEO of AES International. "I've met plenty of professionals who earn millions of dollars a year. They live luxurious lives. But many of them are swimming in debt or they spend almost everything they have. So many of these people can be brilliant in one capacity of their lives, but completely clueless when it comes to planning for their futures."[2]

Thomas Stanley, author of *The Millionaire Next Door*, *The Millionaire Mind* and *Stop Acting Rich*, researched the habits of America's wealthy from 1973 until his death in 2015 when a drunk driver hit his car. His research found that some wealthy people drive high-end, expensive cars. But most rich people prefer Fords and Toyotas. He said non-millionaires drive most of the high-end cars we see on the roads. They usually have really big incomes and high levels of debt.

At the time of his death, Thomas Stanley and his daughter, Sarah Stanley Fallaw, were working on a new book. She continued their research and in 2019, she published *The Next Millionaire Next Door*, listing her father as the co-author.

Their research found that plenty of wealthy people live in million-dollar homes. But most millionaires live in homes that are worth less than a million dollars. What's more, millionaires don't own most million-dollar homes. Once again, high salaried people with big debts make up the majority of people living in seven figure homes.

When my wife and I get invited to a wealthy person's home for dinner, she often worries about what kind of wine to bring. "I know they're really rich," she will say, "so I want to make sure we bring something worthy." Over time, however, she is learning that wealthy people usually prefer the same drinks as middle-class wage earners. Thomas Stanley's research found the same thing.

In *Stop Acting Rich*, Dr. Stanley revealed statistics on people who collect and drink expensive wines. As with most people who drive flashy cars and live in million-dollar homes, most wine snobs aren't millionaires. More often, they're just high-salaried people with very expensive tastes.

What's a Better Definition of Wealth?

Many people define a person's wealth by their salary, what they wear, or what they own. But if a person can't live indefinitely without a paycheck, they aren't wealthy at all. I define wealth differently. In my view, if a person can survive without a paycheck, and if their investments can generate more than twice the median household income in that person's home country, then that person is wealthy.

For example, assume the median household income in your home country were $65,000 a year. If a person's investments could indefinitely generate *at least two times* that amount each year (that's $130,000), then I would say they are wealthy. In contrast, if someone earned $5 million per year and if she had a net worth of $1 million, she might be in trouble. Her net worth would only be one-fifth her annual salary. She might be addicted to a lifestyle of consumption. I call that a high *burn rate*. Such people suffer from expatitis.

What's This Ailment Expatitis?

Expatitis isn't a common medical term. But if you're an expatriate, chances are either you or someone you know is infected. It's easily diagnosed. Symptoms get posted on Facebook. Fortunately, it doesn't hurt—at least not in its early stages.

Unlike bronchitis, arthritis, appendicitis, or colitis, expatitis is rather pleasant. Afflicted individuals get addicted to five-star holidays, manicures, pedicures, massages, expensive dining, and entertainment. But expatitis creates delusions. It's much like drinking champagne underwater without checking your air supply.

Symptoms creep up. The better the expat's financial package, the greater the risk of contracting the condition.

I've been giving financial seminars to expatriates for almost two decades. When I ask people to estimate their retirement expenses, their needs vary. And I expect that. But here's the irony. Those reporting they need the most money are usually saving the least. They're like 500-pound men saying, "I want to run a marathon in less than 3 hours."

You don't need to be rich to retire. But much like a marathon, when preparing for retirement, you will require a training plan. The first step is to track everything you spend, so you can prioritize your spending and invest more money. Second, you'll need to invest effectively. And finally, you'll require a rough idea how much money you'll need. That's where the 4 percent rule comes in.

Three Decades And Counting With The 4 Percent Rule

I sat with Billy and Akaisha Kaderli at a bakery in Chapala, Mexico when Billy separated a piece of cheesecake with his fork. That's when he turned to me and smiled. "A financial reporter recently interviewed me," he said. "I explained that we live off the proceeds of our investment portfolio. She was surprised when I told her we have more money now than we did when we first retired."

That might not sound unusual, until we realize that Billy and his wife, Akaisha, have been retired for 30 years. They quit their jobs in

1991 when they were just 38-years old. Billy worked as an investment broker. Akaisha ran their restaurant. But in a quest for a lower stress life, they sold their business, their home, and nearly all of their possessions. Then they retired, with $500,000, decades before conventional wisdom says they should.

The 4 percent rule is more of a rule of thumb than an actual rule. Back-tested studies suggest that if a retiree withdraws an inflation-adjusted 4 percent per year, they shouldn't run out of money during a 30-year retirement. Historically, inflation-adjusted withdrawals would have lasted at least 30 years, even if someone retired in 1929, on the eve of history's biggest market crash.[3]

Billy and Akaisha were flexible, with respect to the 4 percent rule. In other words, they often sold less. To stretch their money, they spent most of their time outside the United States, in low-cost countries. But I wanted to see what would have happened if they withdrew an inflation-adjusted 4 percent from a globally diversified portfolio of index funds, beginning January 1991.

In 1991, the first year of their retirement, they would have withdrawn $20,000 because $20,000 is 4 percent of $500,000. In 1992, during their second year of retirement, they would have given themselves a raise to cover inflation. Inflation was 3.06 percent the previous year, so they would have withdrawn $20,612 ($20,612 is 3.06 percent more than $20,000). In 1993, they would have withdrawn 2.90 percent more than $20,612 because inflation was 2.9 percent in 1992. As such, Bill and Akaisha would have withdrawn $21,209 in 1993.

Now let's fast-forward to January 2021. After 30 inflation-adjusted annual withdrawals, the Kaderlis would have taken a total of $871,564 from their portfolio. It's mind-boggling to think they would have withdrawn more money than their portfolio was worth when they initially retired.

And if that portfolio comprised 60 percent in a global stock index and 40 percent in a US intermediate government bond index, it would have been worth about $2.4 million by July 2021. That doesn't include dividend taxes or any capital gains taxes resulting from the slight internal trading of the index holdings. But because index funds (even in a taxable account) are very tax-efficient, that value wouldn't be too far off. That's why Billy Kaderli told the reporter their portfolio was worth a lot more than when they first retired, despite all those withdrawals.

At first brush, you might say, "If they still have so much money, perhaps I could withdraw more an inflation-adjusted 4 percent per year." But don't count on that. True, the 4 percent rule was back-tested to 1926. However, when it comes to money, it's smart to be somewhat cautious. Billy and Akaisha retired at the beginning of a strong market for stocks. On the other hand, if you face a massive market crash during your first retirement year and if stocks remain low for several years, you wouldn't likely be as flush as Billy and Akaisha after 30 years.

One fascinating resource is Vanguard's Retirement Nest Egg calculator. It asks you to input how many years you want your savings to last; your current savings balance today; and how much you plan to withdraw from your portfolio each year (which Vanguard adjusts for inflation). Then the calculator asks you to determine your portfolio's allocation of stocks and bonds. After doing so, Vanguard runs a Monte Carlo simulator to determine how long your savings might last at that rate of withdrawal. This isn't a simple, back-tested model. The Monte Carlo calculation generates more than 100,000 scenarios based on what has happened in the past.

For example, from 2000–2002, global stock markets fell hard. Anyone retiring in 2000 would have seen their portfolio value plunge while they withdrew an inflation-adjusted 4 percent per year. But inflation was low over those three years. What if stocks plunged, as they did from 2000–2002, and inflation ran like a pack of wild dogs, as it did in the late 1970s and early 1980s? If that occurred the retiree would have been withdrawing hugely increasing sums every year to contend with double-digit inflation rates. Vanguard's Retirement Nest Egg calculator runs every historical simulation, blending more than 100,000 variables.

For example, based on every blended historical possibility (such as the scenario above) someone withdrawing an inflation-adjusted 4 percent from a portfolio comprising 60 percent stocks and 40 percent bonds has a 91 percent probability of not running out of money over a 30-year retirement. If, on the other hand, they withdraw an inflation-adjusted 5 percent per year, they have a 77 percent chance of not running out of money. If they try to withdraw an inflation-adjusted 6 percent, the odds of the money lasting drop to 59 percent.[4]

You and Your Money Can Both Last Longer

Nobody knows how stocks and bonds will perform after they've retired. Current interest rates and recent stock market performances don't mean a thing. The future, as always, is completely unknown. But if you want to boost the odds of not running out of money, there are three things you could do:

1. Withdraw slightly less than an annual inflation-adjusted 4 percent
2. Don't adjust withdrawals to match inflation during years when your portfolio value drops
3. Work part-time during retirement

To be cautious, some people withdraw less than an inflation-adjusted 4 percent. But retirement spending tends to be highest when we're young, so plenty of people figure they can always cut back later (if they must). After all, as retirees age, most tend to spend less money. They take fewer trips, eat out less and (even the adventurous ones) jump out of fewer airplanes. For these reasons, if you want to increase the odds that your money will last, you might start with an inflation-adjusted 4 percent withdrawal and not give yourself inflation-adjusted raises every year. Instead, you could give yourself raises every second or third year.

Or, you could withdraw an inflation-adjusted 4 percent each year, except during years when your portfolio's value drops. In fact, if you tucked in your tummy and withdrew slightly less during market down-years, you'll dramatically boost the odds that your money will last.

My third suggestion is to work part-time as a retiree. There are two reasons for this. Assume you earn $10,000 at a part-time job. Based on the 4 percent rule, this is equivalent to having an extra $250,000 in your investment account ($10,000 is 4 percent of $250,000). But there's an even bigger benefit. Research suggests you'll live a lot longer.

Harvard Medical School referenced a study published in the *Journal of Epidemiology and Community Health* suggesting that people who worked even just one year past traditional retirement age had a 9 percent to 11 percent lower risk of dying over the 18-year study, regardless of their initial health. Harvard also references a study of 83,000 adults published in the CDC journal, *Preventing Chronic Disease*. This research found that people who worked past the age of 65 were three times more likely to be in good health, compared to those who retired earlier.[5]

And research published in the National Library of Medicine reveals that older people who continue working also have lower odds of suffering from dementia.[6]

Genetics play a role, of course. But our brains are like a muscle. We either use it or we lose it. And part-time work keeps us social, often providing opportunities for us to spend time with different age demographics. And social connections are a key ingredient for longevity, as outlined in science journalist, Marta Zaraska's thoroughly researched book, *Growing Young*, and in Dan Buettner's book, *The Blue Zones*.

Plenty of expats also employ another strategy to make sure they don't run out of money, while ensuring they maintain a good standard of living. After retiring from their full-time jobs, they often move to low-cost countries. We'll focus on that, next.

Part II Retirement or Semi-Retirement In A Low-Cost Country

I once spoke to a British man whom I'll call Tony. He spent much of his career working overseas. After building a diversified portfolio of ETFs, he decided to retire to his old hometown. But he describes the scene as a time warp. "When I left England, my mates regularly went to the local pub and sat on the same stools. When I went back 20 years later, those same guys were still sitting in the same places."

Their conversations focused on football (which Tony enjoyed) but his old friends didn't ask Tony questions about what he had seen or done while living overseas. That doesn't mean his friends were selfish. They just couldn't relate. If you've been an expat for several years, you've likely faced the same thing. Many of your old friends don't ask you questions, either.

Being an expat doesn't make you better than anyone else. But it typically enhances your curiosity. When my wife and I visit popular expatriate retirement destinations, we notice something about the people. They're interesting . . . and interested. It's easy to establish emotional bonds with such people.

And because many of the retirees come from different countries (or different parts of the same country) they offer a wider range of conversational topics than Tony would get with his hometown mates.

That's one of the reasons Tony pivoted, to retire in Portugal. He can learn a new language and embrace a different culture. He can also seek like-minded expats. Many of them, much like Tony, have lived in several different countries. And whenever he chooses to, he can fly back to England to visit his old mates. What's more, Tony can enjoy a higher standard of living in Portugal than he could afford in the UK because it costs less to live in Portugal.

This Personal Decision In Not For Everyone

Retiring abroad will always be a personal choice. Some people would miss their children or grandchildren, and they might prefer living full-time in the town or city they grew up. Other expat retirees that retired to low cost countries in the sun report that they see their families more often than they would if they moved back to their home country.

I spoke to a retired couple in Costa Rica whose children and grandchildren are scattered throughout the United States. But these retirees live in a tropical paradise near the beach, so their families now take long vacations there every year. What's more, the lower cost of living in Costa Rica allows these expat grandparents to spend less on day-to-day living than they would if they lived in the United States. And with their extra savings, they can afford to fly to different parts of the US to visit their children and grandchildren.

I've also met several working expats who don't like their jobs. They want to retire or work part-time, but they say they don't have enough money. By moving to a low-cost country, however, they could accelerate their retirement date by ten years or more. Assume an Australian couple has $600,000. They set a goal to retire with $1.5 million. Based on the 4 percent rule, they could withdraw $60,000 a year from a $1.5 million portfolio. But it might take them longer than a decade to build a portfolio that big. And by the time they build a portfolio that size, it won't have the same buying power (inflation is relentless) so they'll need more than that to reach their retirement income goal. However, instead of slaving away at jobs they might hate for several more years, they could retire or semi-retire in a country like Malaysia, today.

After all, according to numbeo.com, someone who spends about $2,600 per month in Penang would require roughly $6,800 per month for the same standard of living in Melbourne, Australia. Of course, there are cheaper cities in Australia than Melbourne. But there are also cheaper destinations in Malaysia than Penang. What's more, an

Australian living in Malaysia wouldn't have to pay capital gains taxes on their investment portfolio because Malaysia doesn't charge capital gains taxes on equities.

I'm not suggesting everyone should retire to a low-cost country. But if you don't like what you're doing, this might help you quit a lot sooner than you think. In the case of my hypothetical Australians with a portfolio valued at $600,000 AUD, they should have enough money to retire in Penang today, while enjoying the same standard of living that a portfolio valued at $1.5 million AUD would afford them in Melbourne.

When It's Not About The Money

Plenty of expats retire to low cost countries, not so they can spend less money, but so they can live better with the money they have. Assume someone set a goal to retire with $1.5 million in Australia, New Zealand, the US or Canada. Based on the 4 percent rule, they could sell $60,000 a year, indexed to inflation. But what if they retired in Portugal, Mexico or Malaysia? That same $60,000 would go a heck of a lot further.

I've met some expats, however, who retired to low cost countries and complain that it isn't as cheap as they were led to believe. In most cases, these people haven't lived abroad before. They often buy the same things they were used to in their home country. Such people often pay through the nose to buy US peanut butter brands. Or they insist on American breakfast cereals like Fruit Loops or Captain Crunch (truly, nobody should eat that crap).

If you want to buy exactly what you bought at home, then yes, you might pay a small fortune. But consider what the locals buy. They rarely buy packaged brands shipped from halfway around the world. It's cheaper and healthier to buy local fish, fruit and vegetables instead. You'll often find great, fresh deals at the local farmer's market.

There are several other benefits to living more like a local. For example, most of the residents in low-cost countries don't earn a lot of money. As a result, they don't typically chase the high consumption habits of Mr. and Mrs. Jones. Unless you live in a swanky, isolated gated community far from the locals, your neighbors won't be buying fancy cars or continually renovating their homes. They won't be getting new boats, jet skis or subtly boasting about their new beach house. As a result, you won't feel the urge to spend as much.

Your lifestyle will shift. Your priorities will shift. And that's a good thing: for your pocketbook and for the environment (the more crap we buy, the more the environment suffers).

So in the following chapters, I'll introduce several low-cost regions where you could stay year-round, or just for the winter. Such places might offer you much needed, diverse social circles. They could also help you retire early, or help you live better. What's more, your location could improve your relationship with money, especially if you live in a community without big wage earners who are always pining for more stuff.

I've also profiled several expat retirees. Some spend a lot, but by living in low-cost countries, they can afford lifestyles they could never afford at home. Others spend so little you might be tempted to say, "There's no way anyone could live on such a paltry income!" Years ago, I stopped telling people what they could or could not do. If they suggested they could live on a relatively small sum, my instinct was to say, "You can't live on that. You're going to need more." But so many of these people proved me wrong. That's why I can't tell you how much it would cost you to live in any low-cost country. I will offer a bit of guidance, but nobody should try to tell you how much money you will spend.

Notes

1. Leigh Steinberg, "5 Reasons Why 80% of Retired NFL Players Go Broke," *Forbes*, February 9, 2015. Accessed August 15, 2021. https://www.forbes.com/sites/leighsteinberg/2015/02/09/5-reasons-why-80-of-retired-nfl-players-go-broke/?sh=3fcd585f78cc

2. Interview with Sam Instone. Interview by author, November 12, 2017.
3. Philip L. Cooley, Carl M. Hubbard and Daniel Walz, "Sustainable withdrawal rates from your retirement portfolio," Researchgate publication. Accessed August 15, 2021. https://www.researchgate.net/publication/228707593_Sustainable_withdrawal_rates_from_your_retirement_portfolio
4. Vanguard's Retirement Nest Egg Calculator: https://retirementplans.vanguard.com/VGApp/pe/pubeducation/calculators/RetirementNestEggCalc.jsf
5. Chenkai Wu, Michelle C. Odden, Gwenight G. Fisher and Robert S. Stawski, "Association of retirement age with mortality: a population-based longitudinal study among older adults in the USA," BMJ Journals. Accessed August 15, 2021. https://jech.bmj.com/content/70/9/917.short?g=w_jech_ahead_tab
6. "Old age at retirement is associated with decreased risk of dementia," National Library of Medicine, May 29, 2014. Accessed August 15, 2021.

Chapter 15

Retire A Decade Early In Latin America

After spending 17 months driving our camper van around Mexico and Central America, my wife and I came to an important conclusion: people who haven't lived in or spent significant time in Latin America don't know much about it. The general public, after all, has a voracious appetite for shocking headlines, whether that's a stock market crash, dire economic prediction or warring drug cartels in Mexico. Hollywood movies strengthen stereotypes, as do anecdotal examples of violence on TV. They confirm what so many people believe they know about Latin America. And most of those people are wrong.

Most of Latin America is safer than you might think. It's also cheap. Fortunately, if you're already an expat, I probably don't have to convince you. You've likely traveled extensively. You appreciate different cultures. And most importantly, you aren't looking to assert your own values and priorities on a different country. Instead, you see the beauty of differences and you like adventure.

While there's no shortage of great countries in Latin America to choose from, I've focused on Mexico, Costa Rica, Panama and Ecuador.

Mexico: Hot Beaches, Cool Mountains And The World's Best Expat Social Scenes

Americans Terry and Jon Turrell dreamed of retiring early. Terry was a traveling pharmacist in southern Oregon. Jon was a builder. They worked hard, maxed out their IRAs (tax-deferred retirement contributions) and bought investment real estate. They also bought land and a home they could sell.

With Jon's building experience, they figured they could sell the property at a profit. The strategy worked, so they kept doing it. "We built dozens of homes and condos on speculation over a period of 15 years that we sold at a good profit," says Jon. "We decided to develop a six lot sub-division and build the first two homes on spec."[1]

That's when disaster struck. The financial crisis hammered real estate prices. With looming mortgage payments, the couple had to sell their two newly built homes at a loss.

Their dream of early retirement was slipping away ... until they shifted their plans. Terry and Jon sold everything, bought a RV and drove it through much of the United States and then down to Mexico. They figured they could retire there. The couple spent time in nine different locations, including popular expat locations like San Miguel de Allende, Guanajuato and Puerto Vallarta.

They spent several years in the beachside town of Sayulita, where they lived well on about $2,400 a month. They had their own gardner, house cleaner, and they dined at restaurants about 14 times a month.

Weather

International Living magazine estimates that about 1 million Americans live in Mexico.[2] Many of them live in hot, beachside locations like Puerto Vallarta. Others prefer mountain towns like Ajijic, in the Lake Chapala region, and San Miguel de Allende, where year-round daytime temperatures average about 23 degrees Celsius (74 degrees Fahrenheit). I've met plenty of retirees who spend the winter in beachside regions and then flee for the mountains in the summer, where the air is cooler.

Medical and Dental Care

Private medical insurance costs far less in Mexico than it does in most countries, and if you live in the right region, you can find top quality medical and dental care. I'm not, however, a cheerleader for every Mexican clinic or dentist. I've seen such offices that (at least from the outside) look like a mad mechanic's shop. Old man Antonio's dental clinic might be OK, but if his front door is dirty, peeling paint and practically hanging on a single hinge, you really have to wonder. Over the past several years, my wife and I have spent more time in Mexico than in any other country. We've also visited several dentists.

The top doctors and dentists are as good in Mexico as they are in Canada and the United States. But the average doctor or dentist in Canada and the US adheres to higher standards than the average doctor or dentist in Mexico. That's why, when in Mexico, seek out the best practitioners you can. I haven't always done that, and on one occasion when I didn't, I ended up running from a dentist's chair.[3]

Another time, I paid $24 for a filling that, just one year later, was redone in Canada because it was rotting underneath (the dentist in Mexico didn't use Novocain because she said the cavity was a shallow one).

However, if you're willing to do some research, and ask a lot of long-term expats, you can find US or Canadian trained dentists and doctors in Mexico who do amazing work. Guadalajara, for example (a 45 minute drive from Lake Chapala) has some top-quality hospitals, as does Mexico City. And you can find other fabulous health care professionals in popular expat regions such as Mérida, Mexico City and Puerto Vallarta.

My wife found a great physiotherapist near Ajijic, for example. She had torn her rotator cuff doing a flip into the water on the Yucatan peninsula about a month before we were scheduled to travel to Singapore. She ignored the pain and we flew to Singapore, a city renowned for first class medical services. While in Singapore, a physiotherapist and a surgeon recommended surgery. But we would soon be returning to Mexico again, so we didn't have time.

Upon arriving back in Mexico, we met a highly recommended physiotherapist in Ajijic. He examined Pele's shoulder and asked a Guadalajaran-based surgeon for his assessment. To our surprise the surgeon said, "Let's not jump to surgery as the first option. Do physiotherapy first." Pele and her physiotherapist focused on an intensive therapy schedule—and it worked. She visited her physiotherapist three times a week for three months, and her shoulder is now perfect. Best of all, he charged just $15 per visit.

Community

Plenty of expats say, "I wouldn't want to live in a region of Mexico with a high expat population because I want something more authentic. I refuse to be surrounded by gringos." While that's a legitimate complaint, there are plenty of perks to living in a popular expat community. You can attend movies in English. Local restaurants cater to a variety of different tastes. You'll find more clubs and organized health activities, like hiking clubs, kayaking clubs and writing clubs. And as I've mentioned, most expats are interesting and interested. Like you, they've made the leap to try something different. Rich conversations are an added benefit.

That said, to enhance your experience in Mexico, take Spanish lessons. Find some Mexican friends so you don't just isolate yourself with an expat crowd. And if you decide to live in a more "authentic" part of Mexico, consider towns that aren't far from popular expat locations. After all, you can dip in and out whenever you choose.

Safety

It's best not to label countries as safe or dangerous. It's better, instead, to consider regions. Mexico has some toe-curling spots you might want to avoid. They include plenty of the areas along the US border and several of the port towns. The homicide rate in Mexico, per 100,000, is far higher than it is in Europe, Canada or the United States. For example, according to World Bank data, in 2018 there were about five homicides in the US per 100,000 people. In Mexico, there were 29.[4]

I asked 47-year old family psychologist Annette Boyer what she thought. She was born in Guadalajara and has lived in Mexico her entire life. "Mexico is dangerous, yes," she says. "But most of the shootings aren't random."

Annette adds, "Relatively few innocent people are killed. It's often rival drug dealers who are killed, or those speaking out against the cartel, or those speaking out against the political establishment. I'm not saying this is good. But it's possible to live in peace in Mexico."

I asked if any of her friends or family members were ever kidnapped. "I knew somebody who knew somebody who was kidnapped once," she says. "But that was 30 years ago."[5]

One of the first things you might notice, however, are the bars on house windows. This is common almost everywhere in Mexico. They're to prevent petty theft, which can be an issue, especially if you look like a rich, easy target.

Affordability

Some expats in Mexico spend as little as $300 a month. That's an extreme example, but I've met several creative people living on a shoestring (it takes creativity to spend that little). One such trio shares a house they bought together in Ajijic, on Lake Chapala. In 2021, YouTube host Jerry Brown interviewed them, which you can watch at the following link: https://www.youtube.com/watch?v=t1bkIT9q8Ds

Janet Blaser, who moved to Mexico as a 50 year old single woman, now lives in Mazatlán. The 65-year old recently began renting an apartment about a block from the ocean. The regular surfer is paying more for her rent in Mazatlán than she has ever done in Mexico before: $420 per month. Profiled in *CNBC's Make It*, Janet says she earns between $1,200 and $1,400 per month. The following video link shows off her apartment and her gorgeous ocean surroundings.[6]

Janet's income (approximately $16,800 per year) comes from Social Security payments and from book royalties. If you want to enjoy the same lifestyle as Janet in Mazatlán, and you don't qualify for a defined benefit pension or Social Security, you would require a diversified portfolio of stocks and bonds worth about $420,000. Based on an inflation-adjusted withdrawal rate of 4 percent, such a portfolio would provide about $16,800 of annual "income."

Other expats spend $5000 a month or more. One thing is certain, it costs far less to live in Mexico than it does to live in Canada, the US, and western Europe. Living in Mexico also costs far less than it does in Costa Rica or Panama. But asking people, "How much does it cost you to live?" doesn't account for regional tastes and personal differences. *International Living* magazine is a popular source of information for people who are interested in retiring abroad. Two of their writers Suzan Haskins and Dan Prescher also wrote a couple of decent books. My personal favorite is *International Living's Guide To Retiring Overseas on a Budget* (Wiley 2014). They also wrote *Live Richer, Spend Less: International Living's Ultimate Guide to Retiring Overseas* (International Living Publishing 2019). As much as I like them, their books (and *International Living* magazine) exuberantly cheerlead low-cost retirement destinations—tending to avoid comparative safety and crime levels for different regions.

Plenty of expats have also given them the unflattering title, "International Liars." Such expats claim the reported costs of living touted by *International Living's* writers are dramatically understated. But after spending long periods of time in low-cost regions and speaking to retired expats around the world, I disagree. The range of costs people pay will always be as varied as fingerprints, no matter where you live.

So, when *International Living* says a couple can live comfortably in Mexico on anything between $1,800 and $2,500 a month, they aren't stretching the truth at all. However, one of the best ways for you to get a personal sense of affordability in a specific city or town is to compare it to a place you know, using numbeo.com. Numbeo provides crowdsourced costs for different places around the world. The only downside, however, is that they haven't been able to collect enough data from people in smaller towns. Having said that, comparing equal-sized large cities can provide an excellent idea of general, comparative country costs.

For example, according to numbeo.com, a standard of living that would cost about 5000 euros a month in Amsterdam would cost about 2000 euros a month in Mexico City for the same standard of living. Mexico City is also half the cost of Dubai, UAE; Toronto, Canada; Rome, Italy and Dallas, Texas. And if you've never been to Mexico City (at least for a visit) you really should check it out. It's one of the most beautiful cities on Earth.

Seventy-five year old Jerry Brown and his wife, Lori, have lived in Ajijic for the past 13 years. "We rent a beautiful, 2000 square foot home in a gated community," he says. "It has a swimming pool and a view of the lake." They pay $1,700 a month for rent. Their total monthly living costs, including rent, are $4000 a month. Jerry and Lori pay out of pocket for medical costs, which have crept up over the years. "We pay $300–$500 a month for doctor visits and medication," he says. "We've both been in the private hospital here in Mexico and have had excellent medical care with very updated, state of the art hospital equipment." [7]

While living in Sayulita Mexico for six years, Terry and Jon Turrell spent about $2,400 a month, including rent. Their cost savings, coupled with Terry's Social Security payments (which she began to receive a few years after arriving in Mexico) allowed them to recently push their lifestyle standard up. They bought a gorgeous, two bedroom, two bathroom condominium in Puerto Vallarta for $465,000. "It has a rooftop infinity pool with a swim-up bar and restaurant," says Terry. "It also has a gym." Property taxes in Mexico are consistently low. Terry and Jon's property taxes are a paltry $178 a year. Their monthly condo fees (HOA fees) are $525 US per month. That includes water, gas, trash, pool maintenance and internet services in the condo's recreational areas.[8]

Costa Rica: Happiest People, Best Wildlife And Environmental Leaders

International Living magazine rated Costa Rica the world's best country to retire in 2021.[9] We understand why, after my wife and I spent six weeks cycling around the country on our tandem. You can learn a lot from the seat of a bicycle, especially when you're curious.

We've ridden our tandem in more than two dozen countries, and we're pleased to say the drivers in Costa Rica are more courteous than drivers in most other places.

Costa Rica is also surprisingly clean. We saw plenty of signs that read, in Spanish, "Garbage doesn't go away on its own." The government aims to wean itself from fossil fuels by 2050 and while deforestation runs rampant through the world, Costa Rica has bucked the trend. They have doubled their forest coverage over the past 30 years and 80 percent of their energy comes from hydro-electricity.[10]

Locals recycle and you can safely drink water from the taps.

According to the Happy Planet Index, Costa Ricans are also among the happiest people on the planet.[11] And if you're looking for a peaceful place, you'll like that fact that the Costa Rican government disbanded its military in 1948. They haven't had armed forces since.

Weather

Much like Mexico, Costa Rica has plenty of climates to choose from. You could live on the Atlantic or Pacific coasts, where the weather is hot, year-round. In contrast, the popular Central Valley region has the mildest climate in the country, with average temperatures ranging from 22–24 degrees Celsius (72–75 degrees Fahrenheit).

Medical and Dental Care

Costa Rica's universal health care system is one of the best in the world. Costa Ricans also have the second-longest life expectancy in the Americas (only Canadians live longer).[12]

After obtaining legal residency, you'll be required to sign up for *La Caja Costarricense de Seguro Social*, known as *Caja*. Ten of Costa Rica's major public hospitals and most community clinics participate in the Caja health care program.

Sixty-two year old Mark Richardson and his 57-year old wife, Sylvia moved to Costa Rica from Texas in 2019. They pay about $65 a month for Caja, and a total of $500 a month for medical, dental and optical private insurance. "It's fully international," says Mark, who lives in the mountain town of La Fortuna. "We can go back to the US or anywhere else in the world for any kind of treatment." If that sounds like a spectacular deal, it is. Mark's former employer offered that benefit for the first five years of his retirement, through Aetna International.

Some of his friends, however, are trying to convince him that he might not need private insurance. "Caja works well for them," he says, "so we might drop our private plans after we've gained more experience."[13]

Fran Teaster and her husband, Chuck Gleason, are also impressed by Costa Rica's low-cost medical care. The couple lives in San Rafael de Heredia, after moving from Portland, Oregon in 2012.

Fran says the socialized system meets most of her needs, but she doesn't enjoy waiting for appointments. That's why she sometimes pays out-of-pocket for private care. "I see the top rated cardiologist in Costa Rica," she says. "My consultation with him costs about $120 and that includes an EKG, ultrasound or stress test." She adds that dental care costs three times more in the United States, compared to similar treatment in Costa Rica.[14]

Community

Because so many expats live in Costa Rica, it's relatively easy to find a sense of community. But because only about 8 percent of Costa Rican adults speak English, if you want to get the most out of your retirement experience, it's best to learn their language.

As with retiring in any Latin American country, expats will also need to be patient. Costa Ricans, for example, don't place the same emphasis on punctuality that most people in western cultures do. Instead, they tend to put their close relationships first. For example, a Costa Rican might be late for work before he or she might be late for their son's soccer game. That means, if you're getting work done on your home, and a local worker says he'll arrive around 10 am, don't hold your breath. They might show up at noon, or at noon the next day. "Sometimes it can take weeks and several appointments to get someone to fix a door," says Mark Richardson. "It took me three visits of 2–3 hours each time, just to open a bank account."

If that would drive you crazy, forget about living in Central America. Satisfied expat retirees learn to bend with Costa Rican culture. They don't try to force their own culture on Costa Ricans.

Safety

According to WorldBank figures compiled by Statistica.com, Costa Rica is twice as safe as Mexico. Over the five-year period ending 2018, Mexico's homicide rate averaged 21.8 homicides per 100,000 people. Over the same time period, Costa Rica averaged 11.3. That's higher than the five murders per 100,000 each year in the United

States. But after Panama (with 9 murders per 100,000 people) Costa Rica's homicide rate is the lowest in Central America. And the crime rate is far lower outside the capital city of San Jose.[15]

After nine years in Costa Rica so far, Fran Teaser says, "We have had only one incident. Someone stole an extension ladder from our yard when we were on vacation one year." It's wise, however, to be prudent and respectful. Most expats have far more money than the average Costa Rican. That's why it's always best to be careful, and not flaunt your relative wealth.

Affordability

As previously mentioned, if you plan to buy the same brand names in Costa Rica that you bought at home, you'll end up paying a lot of money. One expat told me that a jar of Jif peanut butter, for example, costs as much as $15. But local fruits and vegetables are much cheaper in Costa Rica than they are in Europe and North America.

You'll only find American fast food restaurants, such as McDonald's, in the larger cities. But you can find healthier, lower cost meals everywhere. The best values are at local family-run establishments called *Sodas*. You'll pay as little as $4 USD for a large plate of chicken, salad, rice, beans and plantains. If you include a fresh fruit smoothie, you'll pay about $6 for the total meal.

Plenty of people also live part-time in Costa Rica. They include Bob and Debbie Davis, who have spent 3 to 6 months in Costa Rica each year for the past 8 years. "We own a condo at the beach [in Samara] of about 1000 square feet," says Debbie. "We have a 145 degree view of the ocean." The couple got a great deal on their apartment because it was a foreclosure. But Debbie says similar units are priced between $170,000 and $220,000.

Even during the high season, some people can rent simple homes at the beach for as little as $1000 a month. But Debbie says if people want to live in luxury with a view and a pool, they'll have to pay at least $2,800 a month.[16]

But as always, to maximize the experience, it's best to relax and accept the differences in pace. Fran Teaser offers three suggestions that echo the sentiment of almost every happy expatriate. "Have patience, a sense of humor and a sense of adventure. Always remember that you are the visitor here. You are the one who needs to adapt, not the Ticos [Costa Ricans]."

Panama: Idyllic Islands, Popular Mountain Towns and Retirement Discounts Galore

Sixty-two year old Jean Munroe (I've changed her name to protect her privacy) stood in front of the counter while a Panamanian restaurant worker asked what she wanted for lunch. She selected chicken, rice, beans, vegetables and a soft drink. I chose a similar meal, and after paying $6 USD each, we sat down to eat while I peppered her with questions.

Jean has lived in several countries, including Spain, New Zealand, England, Democratic Republic of Congo, Dominican Republic, and most recently, Uzbekistan. But she chose to retire in Panama.

"I considered all the usual suspects for people on a budget wanting to make this [early retirement] happen: Thailand, Malaysia, Cambodia, Mexico . . . I ruled out the hot ones because I don't fare well in the heat . . . The mountains of Panama have a lovely temperate climate."

Weather

Jean chose the popular expat retirement town of Boquete. It's about 4000 feet above sea level, at the base of a volcano (it last erupted between 400 and 500 years ago). To get to Boquete from Panama City requires a 45 minute flight to the city of David, and then a 45 minute drive into the mountains. Temperatures range from about 15 to 26 degrees Celsius (55 to 78 degrees Fahrenheit). It's far warmer in coastal regions, such as Panama City, David or the Caribbean islands of Bocas del Toro, all of which are also popular among expat retirees.

Plenty of wealthy (or just big-spending!) expats live in large secluded homes in the oceanside region of Coronado, about a one-hour drive west of Panama City. But after walking around these homes, I noticed they're culturally isolated, and likely very expensive. Different strokes for different folks.

Although not as popular as Boquete, several expats also live in the smaller mountain town of El Valle de Antón. It's only a 1 hour drive from Coronado. At about 2000 feet in elevation, it's far cooler than the beachside regions (yet a bit warmer than Boquete). It doesn't, however, have Boquete's range of restaurants and it gets busy on the weekends as locals drive up from Panama City.

Medical and Dental Care

In 2021, I went cycling with 62-year old Maureen (Muzz) Laverty. I marveled as she powered her bicycle up a 20 percent grade, about 15 kilometers from her home in Boquete. When she was younger, Muzz was a competitive runner. But over the years, her body began breaking down. Doctors diagnosed that she needed a new hip.

Muzz had her surgery at Punta Pacifica hospital, a Johns Hopkins affiliate in Panama City. "It was a level of personal care that I never saw in the US. The care was fantastic and the surgeons were skilled. The operation gave me back my life since I could barely walk with a cane going in." Muzz says her US-based insurer promised to cover the cost, but when it came time to pay up, they balked. Fortunately for Muzz, her new hip cost far less than it would have in the United States. She paid $11,000.

After plenty of research, Muzz changed her medical insurance policy. She and her husband Mike Webber, who's also 62, pay a combined $5,800 a year in medical premiums. Doctor visits cost just $16, so Muzz and Mike pay out of pocket for those. "It's quite common for doctors to give you their cell phone numbers and correspond with you directly," she says, "They'll either call you on the phone or connect with you on WhatsApp to see how you're feeling."[17]

Community

If you plan to retire in a different country, connect with expats on Facebook. Just enter "Expats in [and name your country or region]" You'll find reams of helpful people willing to share—and several grumpy farts who were likely born cranky. Pro-tip: always be gracious to jerks on Facebook. Others will jump to your defense and provide you with even more help and info than they ordinarily might.

At one point, while in Panama City, I connected with an expat Facebook group and mentioned that I would be taking my road bike to Boquete. I wondered if anyone could connect me with someone to ride with. That was how I met Muzz Laverty and several of her friends. On my second day in Boquete, I joined a group of keen cyclists comprising expats and locals. We cycled into the mountains while they shared information on the best places to buy fruits and vegetables, as well as their favorite restaurants. I also asked about safety and their overall living costs.

Safety

Panama is one of the safest countries in Latin America. Petty crime is also low. Of course, theft can occur anywhere. But a tell-tale sign is the number of homes with bars on the windows and fortress-like gates blocking homes from the streets. While traveling around Mexico for several months, I noted the homes: bars on every window, locked gates and broken glass embedded in the tops of concrete walls to dissuade would-be burglars. You'll also see plenty of barking dogs on flat roofs. And no, these aren't always pets.

Panama, however, has a different vibe. Sure, some people have bars on windows and locked gates, but plenty of people don't. My friend, Mario Sylvander, has lived in Panama City for several years. He keeps his expensive bicycles locked in an open carport beneath his condominium's building. I said, "Mario, I can't believe you leave your bikes down here. I'm amazed nobody has stolen them." He replied, "Theft isn't that high in Panama City, and there's a guard at the entrance of the parking garage." I'm not stealth-like. But I told Mario (and I would bet him money on this) that I could stroll into that garage in broad daylight with a pair of bolt cutters and steal several bikes without that "guard" even knowing. That's how vigilant he appeared.

This is in sharp contrast to my condominium in Victoria B.C. We have a locked parking garage. Residents lock their bikes to metal rings in locked rooms and cages. My wife and I even locked our bikes in a locked cage within a locked cage ... in the locked basement garage. But still, thieves stole our bikes in the middle of the night ... twice. In Canada, bicycle theft is the national sport. And you thought it was hockey?

While in Panama City, I bought a new Cannondale racing bike. Mario convinced me to lock it beside his, suggesting it would still be there when I returned four months later. If we ever meet, make sure you ask, "Andrew, was your bike still there when you returned?" Mario, who (as I'm writing this) has left Panama for several months, assures me that it will be. He's either deluded or, as several expats have told me, theft in Panama isn't as high as you might think.

Affordability

Panama isn't cheap. Compared to Mexico or Colombia, Panama might as well be Switzerland. But it still costs less to live in Panama than it does in most of Europe, Canada, New Zealand, Australia or the United States.

Jean Munroe banks on that. She found a cute, 1,100 square foot home a few kilometers from Boquete, which she rents for just $550 a month. On clear days, she can see the Pacific Ocean, about 35 km away. At 62 years of age, Jean earns about $1000 a month from US Social Security payments. Anyone who can guarantee income of $1000 a month (from a pension or annuity) would qualify for

Panama's Pensionado residency program—after a criminal record check. There's only one drawback. This visa won't allow you to work in Panama. That's why Jean acquired Panama's Friendly Nations Visa, instead.

Jean, who moved to Panama a few days before we met, expects to spend about $1,500 a month. Her investment portfolio of ETFs is worth about $250,000, so based on the 4 percent rule she should be able to withdraw an inflation-adjusted $830 a month ($10,000 a year). When combining her Social Security payments with her investment income, Jean should have pre-tax income of about $1,830 a month. One factor that's drawing an increased number of expats is that Panama doesn't charge income taxes on money that residents earn online. "I will start by teaching English online," says Jean. "But I plan to find something more lucrative and interesting. If I can earn about $2000 a month, I'll be able to afford some traveling."

Jean is American, and she'll likely earn less than the US foreign income exclusion, which was $108,700 a year in 2021.[18]

As a result, Jean won't have to pay US taxes on her Panama-based income either. (Note: for expats of other nationalities, Panama's capital gains taxes on equities is a flat 10 percent).

Muzz Laverty and her husband wisely document every penny they spend. They retired to Panama in 2016. Including their $5,800 annual medical insurance and income tax payments, their living costs total about $45,000 a year. The couple, formerly from New Jersey, say that's about one-third of what they would pay for the same standard of living in their old hometown.

"We paid $125,000 for a 2 bedroom, 2 bathroom 2 story furnished home on a small plot. It's a single family home in a neighborhood with locals and expats." There's no limit to what people can pay for real estate in Boquete, but a quick online search in 2021 reveals you can still buy a modest home for less than $200,000 USD. My friend Mario, who owns a two-bedroom condominium with a swimming pool in Panama City is just one block from the ocean. In 2021, he estimated its market value is less than $300,000 USD.

Panama also treats "old people" well. They offer discounts for women over the age of 55 and men over 60:

50 percent off movies, theaters, concerts and sporting events

50 percent off the closing costs when purchasing a home

50 percent off hotel stays from Monday through Thursday

30 percent off hotel stays from Friday through Sunday

25 percent off airline tickets originating in Panama (I spoke to a couple that received this discount on several connecting flights to and around Europe because they flew from Panama).

25 percent off restaurant meals

15 percent off dental and eye exams

15 percent off hospital bills (if the patient is uninsured)

10 percent off prescriptive medications

Panamanians also use the US dollar as their main currency and unlike several countries in Latin America, you can safely drink water from the taps. If, however, you believe Panama is too expensive, Ecuador offers living at a fraction of the cost.

Ecuador: Friendly People, Great Climate, And An Ultra-Low Cost Of Living

Let's assume you've worked overseas your entire career. You didn't contribute to a government or defined benefit pension. You also contracted a wicked case of expatitis. That meant you lived large and didn't save as much as you should have. And then your employer cut you loose. The thought of retirement or semi-retirement sounds appealing, but you don't believe you have enough money. If that applies to you, or someone you know, Ecuador offers salvation.

In fact, you could buy an apartment in the popular expat retirement town of Cuenca for about $110,000. Then, if you have an investment portfolio of $450,000, you and a partner could live off the proceeds for the rest of your lives, based on the 4 percent rule.

If you can expect some form of government pension, you might not need an investment portfolio at all. Assume you and a partner earned a combined monthly income of $1,500 from US Social Security. In that case, you could retire in Ecuador with a portfolio of . . . zero.

Nancy and Stephen Turpin, aged 67 and 70 respectively, have lived in Cuenca for the past nine years. At first, they rented accommodation, paying an average of about $350 a month. But recently, they bought a 2 bedroom, 2.5 bathroom condominium for $110,000 USD, including their legal closing costs. Their building offers 24-hour security and the monthly condominium (HOA) fees are $84 a month. Because they own their own home, the couple's annual expenses are about $15,000. That's an average of just $1,250 per month.[19]

Weather

Because Ecuador is on the equator, the country receives about 12 hours of sunlight every day, year-round. It also offers a variety of climates, considering that the Andes Mountains run north to south through the entire country. The capital city of Quito sits at 9,250 feet above sea level (2,900 meters) so it rarely gets hot. At night, temperatures are about 10 degrees Celsius (69 degrees Fahrenheit) and it rarely exceeds 21 degrees Celsius (69 degrees Fahrenheit) during the day. Cuenca, where Nancy and Stephen Turpin live, is slightly lower in elevation, and a little bit warmer.

Coastal towns, of course, are hotter. The most popular seaside towns for expats include Salinas, Manta, and Bahía de Caráquez. Temperatures range between 26 and 32 degrees Celsius (80–90 degrees Fahrenheit).

Medical

Every resident of Ecuador must enroll in the IESS Social Security program. Plenty of expats also buy private medical insurance. According to International Living, IESS costs the primary enrollee 17.6 percent of their declarable income and an additional 3.41 percent for each additional family member.[20]

Valerie and Bill (they asked me not to use their last names) have lived in Ballenita, Santa Elena, Ecuador for the past eight years. As with most of the expats I connected with, they said IESS is acceptable for emergencies, but those who acquire private care insurance (or pay out of pocket for private care) report higher levels of service. Valerie and Bill pay $25 for doctors' visits and just $70 to see a specialist.

They also, unfortunately, had to put the medical system to a test when Bill had a heart attack. As with any country, medical facilities are far less comprehensive in smaller towns. But that emphasis doubles in developing countries. "We live on the coast, so we can't expect an ambulance," explained Valerie. "We drove to a free hospital that evaluated and stabilized Bill but that clinic couldn't do everything, so they got IESS to pay for private care. We were transported to a larger city and spent a week in a hospital. Bill underwent several tests, saw plenty of specialists, spent three days in the hospital and had surgery, getting three stents. The total cost was $1,500 because the doctor was not part of the IESS network. But that price was cheaper than most stateside insurance deductibles."

Nancy and Stephen Turpin also had a good experience when Stephen required eye surgery. "[Stephen] had cataract surgery in both eyes," explained Nancy. "It went beautifully and we didn't have to pay a thing, except for the medicine." Nancy adds, "My adult daughter ended up having to have her gall bladder removed at a local hospital under the IESS coverage and it went as well or better than in the US, and we only had to pay for a stronger pain medication."

Despite being a developing country, you can find solid health care in major cities, such as Guayaquil, Quito, and Cuenca.

Community

The high number of expats in Ecuador are, in part, represented by the huge numbers on Facebook groups. As I write this, there are almost 30,000 members on Facebook's *Ecuador Expats* page. There are about 8000 members on the *Expats in Quito, Ecuador* page. If you have questions about living in Ecuador, or you're living in Ecuador and seeking interesting activities, these are great places to start. Keep in mind, some expats appear to sit around all day on their phones, criticizing others who ask "dumb questions." But there are no dumb questions, if you don't know the answers. As always, check out the FAQ (frequently asked questions) first, if they have such a section.

Curmudgeons will always represent the minority. And if you're kind, polite and curious, plenty of friendly expats will be willing to help (often putting curmudgeons in their place). Facebook groups are great starting points if you're looking for activities and social groups. They can even offer suggestions on dentists, doctors and legal firms. Just don't take legal advice or tax advice from people on Facebook. Instead, let Facebook be a starting point, and then do your own research with help from a qualified legal or tax professional.

Safety

You'll find petty crime anywhere, especially in countries where there's a high disparity of wealth. Larger cities, like Quito, tend to have higher crime rates (violent or otherwise) than most of Ecuador's smaller cities and towns. But common sense is important. Valerie echoes what many expats say: "Keep watchful of your surroundings and protect your belongings by not showing them in public. This can include fancy jewelry, phones, tablets, cameras, wallets. Don't make yourself a target. Never carry more than you can afford to lose. This means all original documents should be kept safe and not on your person unless needed for the task at hand. Carry copies. Less fortunate people will grab what they can and turn it into cash."

Plenty of other low-cost retirement destinations in Latin America attract a lot of expats. Some of them include Belize (an English speaking country); Colombia, famous for its low costs and great medical system; and Peru, which has one of the easiest retirement visas to acquire. But as always, you should spend several months in these countries, getting the lay of the land, before committing to live in one. And in the case of Latin America especially, residents should have patience. Respect the go-slow culture and embrace the beauty, color and differences.

Notes

1. Interview with Terry Turrell. Email interview by author, May 6, 2021.
2. "One Million Americans In Mexico Can't Be Wrong," *International Living*. Accessed August 19, 2021.
3. Andrew Hallam, "Should You Be Afraid To Get Dental Work In Mexico?" December 18, 2018. Accessed August 18, 2021. https://assetbuilder.com/knowledge-center/articles/should-you-be-afraid-to-get-dental-work-in-mexico
4. Intentional Homicides (per 100,000 people). The World Bank. Accessed August 19, 2021. https://data.worldbank.org/indicator/VC.IHR.PSRC.P5
5. Interview with Annette Boyer. Personal interview with author, April 5, 2018.
6. Janet Blaser, "This 65-year-old retiree just moved into a $420 per month apartment in Mexico 'steps from the beach'—take a look inside." CNBC Make-It, August 7, 2021. Accessed August 18, 2021. https://www.cnbc .com/2021/08/07/this-65-year-old-retiree-just-moved-to-a-420-a-month-apartment-in-mexico-by-the-beach-see-photos.html?fbclid=IwAR1VgtVR OFhG30DiHxLyc5AxXJPEk36TG7Iq NB2L9tv1y06KhUt_-l2EuM0
7. Interview with Jerry Brown. Email interview with author, July 2, 2021.
8. Interview with Terry Turrell. Email interview by author, May 6, 2021.
9. "The World's Best Places to Retire in 2021," *International Living*. Accessed August 18, 2021. https://internationalliving.com/the-best-places-to-retire/
10. Romini Sengupta and Alexander Villegas, "Tiny Costa Rica Has a Gren Deal Too. It Matters for the Whole Planet." New York Times, March 12, 2019. Accessed October 1, 2021. https://www.nytimes.com/2019/03/12/climate/costa-rica-climate-change.html?.?mc=aud_dev&ad-keywords=auddevgate& gclid=CjwKCAjw49qKBhAoEiwAHQVTo1d8RpgFQBexW_321TNgx70h w2xmW0mS76pue1DAdjYsX-3uB8QVgBoCEiUQAvD_BwE&gclsrc=aw.ds
11. Happy Planet Index. Accessed August 18, 2021. http://happyplanetindex.org/countries/costa-rica
12. "Life Expectancy of the World Population," Worldometer. Accessed August 18, 2021. https://www.worldometers.info/demographics/life-expectancy/
13. Interview with Mark Richardson. Email interview by author, August 6, 2021.
14. Interview with Fran Teaster. Email interview by author, February 8, 2020.
15. Intentional Homicides (per 100,000 people). The World Bank. Accessed August 19, 2021. https://data.worldbank.org/indicator/VC.IHR.PSRC.P5

16. Interview with Debbie Davis. Personal interview with author, February 2, 2020.
17. Interview with Muzz Laverty. Email interview with author, August 4, 2021.
18. "Foreign Earned Income Exclusion," IRS. Accessed August 18, 2021. https://www.irs.gov/individuals/international-taxpayers/foreign-earned-income-exclusion#:~:text=However%2C%20you%20may%20qualify%20to,deduct%20certain%20foreign%20housing%20amounts.
19. Nancy Turpin interview. Email interview with author, August 9, 2021.
20. "Healthcare In Ecuador," *International Living*. Accessed August 18, 2021. https://internationalliving.com/countries/ecuador/health/

Chapter 16

Retire A Decade Early In Europe

When North Americans take holidays in Europe, they often limp home with massive credit card bills. Trips to Paris, Rome and Switzerland are, to many, once-in-a-lifetime splurges that suck bank accounts dry. But Europeans know a secret. If you know where to look, Europe offers some of the world's best, low-cost retirement destinations.

Eastern Europe might be the best-kept secret. But Portugal and Spain still offer low costs, and some of the best weather in the world.

Portugal: Crashing Surf, Gorgeous Scenery and Europe's Best Weather

I took a bath in a Portuguese lake near the Odeleite Dam. I'm not a nudist, but nobody was around and I hadn't showered that day. You might think I was hours from civilization, but my wife and I were only about 25 kilometers from (arguably) Europe's most popular beach area: the southern Algarve region of Portugal.

It was about 4 p.m. The sun was still high and I was surrounded by clean lake water and rolling hills. The fresh smell of pine trees rolled in with the light breeze, and in the far distance, I could barely make out another camper van. Like us, they parked beside the lake. That's one of the things I love most about Portugal. They have campsites with amenities, but you can also freely camp almost anywhere.

Not far from the southern city of Faro, we also camped along a perfect beach for free, alongside dozens of other campers. Other times, we stayed on secluded cliff tops overlooking the Mediterranean Sea.

Fifty-year olds Heidi and Matthew Hill plan to do something similar. Heidi, who's originally from the UK, and Matthew, who's from Australia, moved to Portugal in December 2021 after working for several years in the United Arab Emirates. The couple doesn't want to buy property, at least not yet. For now, they want to rent a home in the Algarve region in the winter and rent on Portugal's Silver Coast during warmer months. They're also keen to buy an RV and explore Portugal and the rest of Europe, with their visa providing free, permanent access to the Schengen region's countries.

"We chose Portugal mostly due to the friendly tax regime here," says Heidi. "It's called NHR [non habitual resident]."

Heidi and Matthew acquired residency through the D7 Visa program. "The requirements are very simple," says Heidi. "When we gained residency in 2021, we needed to show income or savings covering our first year that matched whatever the minimum wage in Portugal was, so that year, that equated to €1000 per month between us. If I were single, I would have needed to prove income of just €665 per month. This visa gives us the same rights as a local citizen with access to free government healthcare among other benefits."[1]

They spend about €3000 per month, including rent. When I asked about rental prices in the Algarve, Heidi sent me several online listings. They tempted me to leave for the country's southern coast right away. A single bedroom, single bathroom villa, costing €900 a month, is located just 300 meters from the large sandy beach of Praia da Lota. Heidi also sent me a listing for a three bedroom villa with access to a swimming pool and a weight room for €1,300 a month.

Portugal might be the most popular country in Europe for retirees on a budget. But I think it would still attract a sizable number of expat retirees, even if it were expensive. After all, it might offer the best weather in Europe.

It has plenty of golf courses and water sport activities; the entire west coast faces the Atlantic Ocean. The Algarve region is popular among expats, including cities along the Mediterranean, such as Faro, Albufeira and Lagos. The Alentejo region, north of the Algarve, is also a favorite.

Plenty of expats also live along the Silver Coast between Porto and the capital city of Lisbon. The seaside towns of Nazaré and São Martinho are popular, as is the municipality of Cascais.

Generally, Portugal is cheap. But there are a few exceptions. For starters, real estate in popular regions is getting more expensive. Friends of ours bought a tiny one-bedroom, one-bathroom condominium in Cascais for €300,000. It doesn't have a view, and the street in front isn't pretty. After leaving our friends' apartment, I searched online for homes to purchase or rent in Cascais. They cost much more than I thought they would.

Cascais is a beautiful seaside city, so for some international context, I compared Cascais' real estate to that of another beautiful seaside city: Victoria, British Columbia. Victoria is one of Canada's most expensive cities. As such, I thought it would cost much more to live in Victoria. But that isn't true. According to Numbeo.com, one-bedroom apartments in each city center rent at similar monthly rates: roughly €1,116 ($1,660 CAD). Outside their respective city centers, rentals in Cascais are about 15 percent cheaper than rentals in Victoria: about €785 ($1,167 CAD) per month versus €925 ($1,375 CAD) per month.

To buy an apartment in either Cascais or Victoria costs about the same per square foot. However, you'll pay about 80 percent more for a car in Cascais, compared to Victoria, and gym memberships cost about 43 percent more in Cascais.

That said, the cost of fruits and vegetables, restaurant meals, beer, and coffees at a café are significantly cheaper in Portugal. Based on Numbeo's data, if you're renting accommodation in Cascais, total living costs (including food, utilities and everything else) are just 14 percent lower in Cascais than Victoria, BC, so expats should be wary of costs in Portugal's different cities.

Having said this, cities like Lisbon (and especially smaller towns) offer lower-priced homes. For example, you can still buy a modest home in a smaller town for less than €150,000.

Home Sweet Home

Thirty-six year old Luis and his 38 year old wife, Ana, (they requested that I not reveal their last names) have worked in the United Arab Emirates for several years. Luis, a cardiovascular technologist and Ana, a radiography technologist, are originally from Portugal. They plan to retire in their early 40s, and the relatively low cost of living in Portugal will help them do that.

Luis says, "We plan to live in the suburbs of Lisbon, in a small village called Santo Estevao. This is near to where family and friends live. It has easy access to Lisbon's city center, its airport and it also has convenient road links to the north and south of Portugal."

In 2021, the couple's globally diversified portfolio of ETFs was worth about €800,000. "We plan to retire with a nest egg of

€1.2 million," says Luis. They're also conservative, with respect to how much they plan to withdraw each year. Luis and Ana will withdraw an inflation adjusted 3 percent from their portfolio each year. "This will give us €36,000 in income during the first year of our retirement," says Luis. Over time, they'll be able to adjust those withdrawals upward to cover the rising cost of living. And with a mortgage-free home, it will give them more than enough money to live.

From Canada to Portugal for an Easier Pace of Life

Forty-eight year-old Andre Oliveira and his 46 year old wife, Hellen de Paula realized they could cut back on how much they work if they took advantage of Portugal's low cost of living. The couple was born in Brazil but spent most of their adult lives in Canada (23 years). "After visiting Spain and Portugal several years ago, we decided to change our pace of life," says Andre. "We already speak the language, so Portugal was the easiest choice."

They rent an apartment in a trendy area of Lisbon for €950 a month. Andre says, "Lisbon is the biggest city and has the most amenities, providing us a lifestyle similar to what we had in Toronto. We have access to a variety of restaurants, parks and shows." Andre and Hellen carefully track everything they spend. Hellen also documents their costs at *Viva Happy Blog, Good Food & Good Vibes*. https://tinyurl.com/eej64zts

"Including our rent, we spend an average of about €2,400 a month," says Andre, "which is half what we spent each month in Toronto." The couple isn't retired, but Portugal's lower cost of living allows them to work far fewer hours. "My job in Canada allowed me to work remotely even before the pandemic," says Andre. "But I've put in far fewer hours since moving here."[2]

For the first 10 years of their residency, Andre can also take advantage of the Non-Habitual Residency (NHR) tax codes. One such perk is that he won't have to pay Portuguese income taxes on money he earns overseas from his Canadian employer.

Safety

While it costs more to live in Portugal, compared to most Latin American countries, this European gem has something the others don't: one of the lowest homicide rates in the world. According to The World Bank data, Portugal recorded just one intentional homicide per 100,000 people in 2018. That compares to two in Canada; five in the United States; 29 in Mexico; nine in Panama and 11 in Costa Rica. In fact, Portugal's homicide rate is on par with Germany's, France's and the UK's.[3]

The World Bank also compiles reported crime rates for different countries. Portugal's crime rate is a fraction of any Latin American country. It also has lower crime rates than even France and Germany.[4]

Medical

Okay, so Portugal's a safe country. But is the medical system good? You might breathe easier knowing that The World Health Organization's country rankings of the best medical systems gave Portugal a solid 12th out of 191 countries. It beat several countries you might expect to come out ahead, including Netherlands (17th); Switzerland (20th); Sweden (23rd); Germany (25th); Canada (30th); the United States (37th) and New Zealand (41st).

(Note: several publications reference this data with years as recent as 2021, but they link to the original, and still latest, WHO research paper from 2000).[5]

Life expectancy in Portugal is on par with most developed European countries, with the average Portuguese person living an average of 81 years. That's two years longer than the average American lives.[6]

Andre and Hellen don't have private medical insurance, relying instead (as most people in Portugal do) on the national public health care system. "The cost of medical exams and consultations aren't entirely free," says Andre, "But they are heavily subsidized. Consultations sometimes cost less than three euros. Even going to a private specialist for a serious eye care diagnostic cost me less than €150 for the most expensive exam. I currently take a medication that used to cost me $10 to $15 in Canada, and we pay less than 50 cents in Portugal."

Community

Portugal has long been a favorite low-cost destination for European retirees. You'll find the Algarve, especially, also floods with tourists in the summer. You can easily spot British tourists on beaches. They glow brightly after frying their pasty flesh (as a born Brit, I relate).

Sun-smart retirees—with the British making up the highest percentage of retired expats—are scattered throughout the Algarve region. More densely populated regions, such as Lisbon and Porto also include large expat numbers.[7]

But as with anyone retiring to a foreign country, it's tough to maximize your experience without learning the local language. English is commonly spoken in high tourist areas (especially within the service industry) but it's best to know some Portuguese if you're planning to live in one of the smaller, lower cost towns. Even if you can "get by" with English, it's disrespectful to move to a different country and not learn at least some of the local language. Taking language classes will enhance your sense of community. And according to the Glasgow Memory Clinic, learning a foreign language is also a great way to ward off dementia.[8]

As for challenges, every expat I've spoken to in Portugal and Spain say the same thing. Local and national bureaucracy can be challenging. That stands for government and private run enterprises. "Learn to manage your expectations regarding customer service," says Andre Oliveira. "It's not unusual to contact a business requesting information on a product or service and getting no reply, an incomplete reply, or a reply three months later."

Spain: Spectacular Beach Walks and Skiing In The Same Day

As I lay in a hammock, Eduardo emerged from his house and walked over to chat. He and his wife split their home into three separate units. They live in one, and they rent out two others that face an outdoor eating area surrounded by mango trees. "Did the mangoes keep you up last night?" Eduardo asked. We were in the tiny town of San Carlos, Panama, just one block from the beach. If you've never lived (or slept) beneath mango trees, you won't know that they can pound a tin roof hard when they fall.

"In a couple of months, we'll be moving to Malaga, Spain," he said. When we think about people moving to low-cost countries, we often consider those moving from first world countries to cheaper countries, so they can stretch their retirement euros, dollars or pounds. But this man, who had lived in Panama most of his life, was moving to Spain. "I don't plan to spend less money in Malaga," he said. "But if I spend the same amount of money as I spend here, I can improve my standard of living."

Spain was hard-hit by the economic recession from 2008–2014. Properties that were once far more expensive than equivalent homes in Portugal, for example, plunged in value, and many popular regions are still attractively priced today. For example, property in the ocean-side city of Malaga, with its long sandy beach and its fabulous mountain backdrop costs less to rent or buy than equal-sized properties in Lisbon, Portugal.

According to Numbeo.com, Malaga's rental prices are about 22 percent lower than in Lisbon. To buy an equal-sized apartment in Malaga costs about 23 percent less than it does in Lisbon and about 40 percent less than it does in Cascais, Portugal.

Even the gorgeous, iconic city of Seville costs less to live in than Lisbon. In Seville, a standard of living that costs €2,700 a month would cost about €3,100 in Lisbon.

And much like Portugal, if you're willing to live in smaller towns, the cost of living drops considerably.

Aerobatics Pilot Chooses To Fly

Sixty-one year old Alan Cuthbertson and his 62-year old wife, Heather aren't afraid to try new things. When Alan was about 35 years old, he and Heather were at a British airshow, watching an aerobatics team. Alan didn't even know how to fly an airplane, but he turned to Heather and said, "I want to try that!" Three years later, he was a qualified aerobatics pilot and a commissioned officer in the RAF reserves.

When Alan was 45 years old, he decided to retire. No, he wasn't a trust fund baby, nor did he have millions of pounds. Instead, he and his family had a sense of adventure and they knew where living costs were low. They sold their home, all their possessions, and drove to Ventorros De La Laguna, about 20 miles west of Granada.

The couple also brought their two adult daughters (aged 20 and 21). Alan hilariously explained the story of their move in his book, *Fiestas and Siestas Miles Apart*. In 2005, they paid €190,000 for their home in Spain. By mid 2021, the home's value was just €140,000, a lingering casualty of Spain's economic crisis.

As a 45-year old, Alan and Heather lived off the proceeds of the home and business, which they sold before leaving the UK. "Currently, my wife and I live on about €14,000 a year," says Alan.

"We also go to Barbados or Mexico for a month every winter," he says. "And we have a couple of other holidays each year. Our money will last until we can draw our [UK] state pensions. Even then, we'll still have a tidy sum for holidays, so I can't complain."[9]

Couple Enjoys Life on Less Than €9000 a Year

Sixty-year old Jane Dunbar and her 68-year old husband, Ian, have lived in Martos, Jaen, Spain since 2015. "I suffered from SAD [Seasonal Affective Disorder] when living in the UK," says Jane. But we get a lot more sunlight here in Spain." The couple bought what Jane describes as "a typical Spanish townhouse," where she and Ian have to duck a bit to get under some of the doorways. But they love their location, and the price was right.

"We paid €24,000 for the three-bedroom, one-bathroom home," says Jane, "But today [2021] a similar home would probably cost between €35,000 and €40,000." Writing about their decision to move to Spain, Ian says, "Jane ended up getting cancer [in the UK] and while she was recovering, she spent a lot of time watching [the television program] Life in the Sun. When we dug deeper, we found that we could afford to retire in Andalucia." That's a large region of hills and farmlands, ranging from the southern coast to north of the region's capital city, Seville.

Jane and Ian's city of Martos includes about 24,000 residents. About 65 of them are British expats. "We usually meet [expat friends] at least once a month for tostados and coffee," says Jane. But she and Ian are happy to be living far from some of the more popular expat regions. For starters, this has helped them learn Spanish and connect with more of the locals. It's also far more cost-effective.

Ian and Jane live on an average of €750 a month. That includes Jane's two trips to the UK each year to visit her family. Ian typically stays in Spain, but the couple also enjoys a hotel vacation to the Spanish coast at least once a year. They also enjoy take-out dinners at least twice a month, plus a restaurant meal at least once a month.

"The fresh fruits, vegetables and high quality meats have really helped my health," says Jane. "They cost a lot less here than they do in the UK, and they are far fresher. With the added sunshine, I've also spent more time outside walking, and I've lost 9 stone [57 kg]. Ian jokes that he should get a refund, because I'm only half the woman he married."[10]

The added sunshine, lower stress and more outdoor activities lead plenty of expats to see improvements in their health. Several of my friends who retired in Mexico, for example, looked younger five years after they retired. In many cases, they had also weaned themselves off medications.

Jane and Ian live on Ian's government pension. In a few years, Jane should receive pensionable income of her own which will give them even more money for vacations, dining out, or whatever they chose.

If You Don't Have A Pension, How Much Money Would You Need?

Let's assume you wanted a lifestyle in Martos, equivalent to Jane and Ian's. You should expect to pay about €40,000 for a home. And if you'll be living off the proceeds of a diversified portfolio of ETFs, you'll need about €260,000 ($308,000 USD). That's based on a 4 percent inflation-adjusted withdrawal rate, plus some wiggle room to cover capital gains and dividend taxes. You'll need more money if you live in more expensive cities, enjoy dining out, traveling and skiing. And in case you're curious, yes, you can ski in Spain!

Weather

Spain is a large country with dramatic differences in geography and climate. The coastal areas can be hot in the winter, and temperatures in the country's prolific mountain regions can be cold in the winter. Many people don't realize, in fact, that Spain offers world class skiing, especially in the Pyrenees near the border with France. What's more, it's far cheaper to ski in Spain than in most European ski resorts.

There are also ski resorts in the south of Spain, in the Sierra Nevada region and near Madrid, in the northwest (including Galicia, Leon and Cantabria, as well as La Rioja and Teruel). And if you get hurt doing a flip off an epic ski jump (I write that for people who are wired like my wife) take comfort knowing Spain has good medical services.

Medical

The testing requirements to become a physician in Spain are epic. It's one of the reasons Spain's medical is so darn good: ranked 7th in the world by the World Health Organization. Spanish residents' life expectancy reflects in this ranking. With the average person living 83 years, the average Spaniard lives longer than most Europeans and significantly longer than those who live in the United States.[11]

Safety

According to the World Bank's data on intentional homicides, Spain is also one of the world's safest countries, recording less than one homicide per year for every 100,000 people. That's even safer than Belgium, Canada and the UK.[12]

So, as with Portugal, if you can handle the often head scratching bureaucracy and the slow (sometimes non-existent) customer service, Spain offers a healthy lifestyle that, depending on where you live, costs far less than you might expect. And if you're wondering where you can live better on even less, Eastern Europe could be the world's best secret.

Eastern Europe: The World's Best Low-Cost Secret

Diana Rosberg has lived in plenty of different countries. She and her Swedish husband, Bengt, have worked as educators in international schools their entire careers. "I started in Nicaragua in the early 1990s," says Diana. "Then I moved to Kuwait, Latvia, Qatar, Malaysia and now Russia."

People like Diana and Bengt are typically far better suited to retiring abroad, compared to those who have lived and worked in their home countries all their lives. People who have had exposure to different cultures, languages and traditions, after all, tend to be far more accepting of differences. They don't tend to be looking for a "little England" or "little America" when they move abroad.

That's why Diana and Bengt are excited to retire and spend their time volunteering in Latvia. "Our retirement will need to be funded entirely by our savings," says Diana. "I've never worked in the US (my home country) other than when I was a teenager or had jobs while going to university. I never amassed enough credits to qualify for Social Security payments."

What pleases Diana, especially, is that she won't have to pay for expensive, private medical insurance. When they retire, Diana and Bengt will enroll in Latvia's socialized health program and, eventually gain citizenship.

As for Riga itself, Diana (who has lived in Latvia before) says, "It's a very liveable city, with everything we think of for an old European city: cafes, everything within walking distance, beautiful architecture and parks, gorgeous opera house with world-class performances." The couple plans to buy their dream apartment for about €300,000 and spend about €28,000 a year, not including vacation expenses.[13] And to live on €28,000, they won't need to scrimp. After all, you could afford a high standard of living in Latvia for far less than you might think. According to numbeo.com, a standard of living that would cost about €3,100 a month in Lisbon, Portugal would cost about €2,400 a month in Riga, Latvia. That's also significantly cheaper than Malaga, Spain, a city of similar size.

Climate and Safety

Latvia, which is flanked by Lithuania to its south and Estonia to its north, sits at about the same latitude as Scotland. Winter temperatures rarely drop below minus 6 degrees Celsius (21 degrees Fahrenheit), with daily summer temperature highs rarely rising above 25 degrees (77 degrees Fahrenheit). And according to the World Bank Data on intentional homicides, it's safer than the United States, with about 4 intentional homicides per 100,000 people per year.

Why Georgia's Becoming The New Hot Spot

While eastern European countries like Latvia are gaining more attention, the country of Georgia might be the biggest draw. As of this writing, foreign-earned income is tax-free in Georgia, so you could feasibly work online and not pay income tax. What's more, Georgia wouldn't levy capital gains taxes on the sale of ETFs (for example) if held in one of the brokerage accounts I suggested in this book.[14]

With a population of about 4 million people, Georgia sits roughly 42 degrees north of the equator. Northern Turkey is to its south, the Black Sea to its west, with Russia to the north. Google, "images for the country of Georgia" and the scenery will astound you. It includes beautiful old architecture, gorgeous hiking in the Caucasus Mountains, snow-capped peaks and rolling hills with sleepy rivers.

The capital city of Tbilisi is also a hot spot for Digital Nomads. *The Digital Nomad Handbook*, published by *The Lonely Planet* says, "A low cost of living is matched by a comfortable quality of life, and a liberal visa regime—with free, visa-free travel for a year for most nationalities." That flexibility might be one of the best parts. You could stay a full year and sample every season before applying for residency.

Fifty-one year old Patrick Ammann moved from Switzerland to retire in Tbilisi, Georgia. "I wanted to live in a country that offered me the same standard of living that I was used to in Switzerland, but at a much lower price," he says. "I also wanted to feel safe and Georgia is one of the safest countries in the world."

Based on the World Bank's most recent data on intentional homicides, Patrick is right. In 2018, there were just two intentional homicides per 100,000 people. That makes Georgia about as safe as Canada and most of Western Europe, while significantly safer than Latin America.[15]

At the time of writing, you could find modern apartments in the city for less than $100,000 USD. Prices for rental units start at about $350 a month.

Patrick Ammann bought two apartments in Tbilisi, so he receives rental income and doesn't pay rent. "It costs me about €12,000 [$14,100 USD] a year to live here," he says. "With this amount, you can live like a king."

When comparing living costs of different cities using Numbeo .com, you'll see that Patrick is right. Tbilisi is an extremely low-cost city. In fact, it's almost half the cost of Riga, Latvia. To put this in an international context, the data at numbeo.com suggests that for an equal standard of living, Victoria, B.C. is 200 percent more expensive than Tbilisi, Georgia. Omaha, Nebraska is about 180 percent more expensive than Tbilisi. Nottingham, England is about 185 percent more expensive and Perth, Australia is about 190 percent more expensive than Tbilisi. In other words, if you needed a retirement portfolio worth $1 million in Victoria, BC, you would need just $300,000 to provide the same standard of living in Tbilisi.

Fifty-seven year old Lesley Koch and her 69 year old husband, Chris, love Georgia. For about 10 years, the South African couple came to the country for annual vacations. They love the lush landscape, rich history and the blended mix of old and new architecture. Four years ago, they moved to Georgia. "We live in a small village in Chakvi, Adjara Region, Georgia," says Lesley. "It is about 10km from Batumi, a city on the Black Sea." The couple initially bought an apartment with an ocean view, but they now rent their apartment to a tenant and live in a place surrounded by much more greenery. Lesley explains: "Chris being a horticulturist, missed working in his garden and miraculously found land to buy in the village. It is difficult to buy land as a foreigner. There is a law prohibiting foreigners from buying agricultural land and most of the land in Georgia is still classified as agricultural."

Because they don't pay for rent, the couple's annual living costs are about $12,000 USD. That includes Lesley and Chris' local medical insurance. "It's fully comprehensive with a few limitations," Lesley says. "It costs about $57 USD for both of us each month."

In cases when their medical tests or procedures aren't fully covered, Chris and Lesley know they won't break the bank. "At one time, Chris had a severe headache," recalls Lesley. "I panicked and thought he might have a stroke or encephalitis. I took him to hospital where they took a CT Scan and he was under observation for about 6 hours. The CT Scan cost about $90 USD."

They're also impressed with the region's dental service. "Chris had a toothache and I had two cavities re-done," says Lesley. Chris' bill came to about $6, including x-rays, and mine, which also included x-rays, cost about $20 USD. "We both were impressed and received good treatment—very professional, ultra-modern, clean and efficient and very informative options and advice."[16]

Patrick Ammann chose a medical insurance plan that was valid for any country in the world. As is typically the case, insurers base premiums on their assessments of medical costs in the country where the policyholder lives. In Patrick's case, he pays just $1,500 USD per year. The insurance, he says, is for big emergencies. In such cases, people often pay higher deductibles if they require significant medical care, but the policyholder covers the cost of smaller medical procedures (as Patrick does) out of pocket.

There is something, however, to consider. *The Digital Nomad's Handbook* profiles several countries and cities. In each case, they suggested whether the cities were LGBT-friendly. In each of the profiled cases, they were, with just one exception: Tbilisi, Georgia. Expats also say the language is tough to learn and Georgians don't use the same alphabet we do.

And if you don't want four seasons, preferring year-round summers instead, the next chapter is for you.

Notes

1. Interview with Heidi Hill. Email interview by author, July 30, 2021.
2. Interview with Andre Oliveira. Email interview by author, July 26, 2021.
3. Intentional Homicides (per 100,000 people). The World Bank. Accessed August 19, 2021. https://data.worldbank.org/indicator/VC.IHR.PSRC.P5

4. "Portugal Crime Rates and Statistics," Macrotrends.com. Accessed August 19, 2021. https://www.macrotrends.net/countries/PRT/portugal/crime-rate-statistics

5. Ajay Tandon, Christopher JL Murray, Jeremy A Lauer and David B Evans. "Measuring Overall Health System Performance for 191 Countries," World Health Organization. Accessed August 19, 2021. https://www.who.int/healthinfo/paper30.pdf

6. "Live Expectancy at Birth (total years)," The World Bank. Accessed August 19, 2021. https://data.worldbank.org/indicator/SP.DYN.LE00.IN

7. "Leading nationalities as a share of total expats living in Portugal 2018," Statistica.com. Accessed August 21, 2021. https://www.statista.com/statistics/915177/top-nationalities-of-expats-living-in-portugal/

8. "Can learning language help prevent dementia?" Glasgow Memory Clinic. Accessed August 19, 2021. http://glasgowmemoryclinic.com/news/learning-language-prevent-dementia/

9. Interview with Alan Cuthbertson. Email interview by author, July 20, 2021. http://glasgowmemoryclinic.com/news/learning-language-prevent-dementia/

10. Interview with Jane Dunbar. Email interview July 28, 2021.

11. "Live Expectancy at Birth (total years)," The World Bank. Accessed August 19, 2021. https://data.worldbank.org/indicator/SP.DYN.LE00.IN

12. Intentional Homicides (per 100,000 people). The World Bank. Accessed August 19, 2021. https://data.worldbank.org/indicator/VC.IHR.PSRC.P5

13. Interview with Diana Rosberg. Email interview by author, August 8, 2021.

14. "Tax rates in Georgia (country)," TPsolution audit company. Accessed August 19, 2021. https://tpsolution.ge/tax-rates-in-georgia-country/

15. Intentional Homicides (per 100,000 people). The World Bank. Accessed August 19, 2021. https://data.worldbank.org/indicator/VC.IHR.PSRC.P5

16. Interview with Lesley Koch. Email interview by author, August 15, 2021.

Chapter 17

Retire A Decade Early In Southeast Asia

*I*nternational Living magazine recommends several low-cost retirement destinations in Southeast Asia. But in this chapter, I focus on two. I based this choice on one important question: "If I were to have open-heart surgery in Southeast Asia, where would I be comfortable having it?" After living in Southeast Asia for 13 years, I would be most comfortable with Singapore, Malaysia or Thailand. Singapore is one of the world's most expensive places, so this chapter focuses on Malaysia and Thailand.

Several fabulous surgeons could do the work in Indonesia, the Philippines, Vietnam, Laos or Cambodia, but most expats living in these regions would agree that if they had the financial means, most would fly to Singapore, Malaysia or Thailand to have such an important procedure done. (Note: India, which is considered southern Asia, has among the best surgeons in the world).

Retiring In Malaysia: Beauty In The Sun

Before my wife and I were even dating I told her, "If I ever disappear and go completely off the grid, you'll find me on Pulau Tioman. It's an island in the South China Sea, about a 90-minute boat ride from the mainland town of Mersing. If you can remember the old TV series, *Fantasy Island*, Tioman looks like that, but far prettier: gorgeous blue waters, jagged mountain peaks and in several cases, boutique seaside accommodations that you can only access by boat.

There's a limited road network on Tioman, and several times a year, I hiked over the mountain to stay at the village of Juara on the island's east coast. Pulau Tioman is just one of thousands of islands off Malaysia's coast. If you're choosing a holiday destination, you can take your pick: everything from busy islands to uninhabited little gems.

But Malaysia offers more than idyllic islands. Cities like Kuala Lumpur provide low-cost, cosmopolitan living with world class medical. English is also widely spoken in Malaysia, making it perhaps the most popular retirement destination in Southeast Asia.

Can You Handle The Heat?

Malaysia, however, isn't for everyone. For starters, the weather can be oppressive. It's true that the Cameron and Genting Highlands offer cool temperatures. But most of the country is hot and humid. As someone who lived in the bordering city-state of Singapore for many years, I liked the heat. But if you hate hot weather, cross Malaysia off your list.

One of the saving graces is the regular, tropical rain. Unlike countries like England or the rainforest area of Canada's west coast, you'll rarely experience constant drizzle. When it rains in Malaysia it's more like someone dumped a lake on your head. That's why, if you like hot weather but dislike rain, don't discount retiring in a Malaysian city because of its year-round precipitation levels. After all, the rain usually comes all at once, and it typically ends within an hour or two.

Top Quality Medical

Malaysia is becoming a popular medical tourism destination. That doesn't mean you'll find top-notch medical facilities in every town, but cities like Kuala Lumpur offer world-class service and care. I once stayed with an American friend in Kuala Lumpur who had recently had open-heart surgery. We had worked together in Singapore and I asked if he flew to Singapore for his procedure. "There wasn't any need for that," he said, "Kuala Lumpur has top-notch medical care."

This surprised me. I asked, "Would your medical insurance have covered this procedure in Singapore or the United States?" He replied, "Yes, but my wife and I did a lot of research. We found an amazing hospital in Kuala Lumpur and a top-notch surgeon to perform the operation."

Community

Because so many expats have flocked to Malaysia for the lifestyle and low-cost of living, you'll find expat communities thrive. Some of the more popular destinations for expats include the capital city of Kuala Lumpur, the island of Penang, the European-like seaside city of Malacca, the island of Langkawi as well as the cities of Ipoh and Johor Bahru (a city that borders Singapore, via a bridged causeway).

Safety

Countries with broad disparities of wealth tend to have more crime. Such is the case with several Latin American countries. But Southeast Asian countries tend to buck that trend. Of course, crime exists in every country. But despite the wealth disparity in Malaysia, crime rates are low. According to The World Bank data on intentional homicides, Malaysia is about as safe as Canada and most of Europe. It's far safer than Latin America and the United States.[1]

Affordability

If you're comparing costs of living in different countries, it's good to juxtapose capital cities. After all, these provide some of the best apples-to-apples comparisons. And Malaysia is cheap. For example, according to numbeo.com, Kuala Lumpur is about 8 percent cheaper than Mexico City. Malaysia's capital city is also about 30 percent cheaper than Lisbon, Portugal and 40 percent cheaper than Madrid, Spain.

Sixty-four year old Peter Bendheim and his 51-year old wife, Adele, left South Africa in 2019 to retire in Penang. Known as the "Pearl Of The Orient," Penang is popular among expats. Peter and Adele live about 12 kilometers from Georgetown in an area called Batu Ferringhi. "Penang is an island with a rich and diverse culture," says Peter. "It's relatively laid back, compared to the busy city of Kuala Lumpur." As with most retired expats in Malaysia, they gained their residency from the Malaysia My Second Home Program: a ten-year renewable residency visa with more than 57,000 members.

The program was temporarily suspended in 2020 while changes were being made. As of this writing, the Malaysian government plans to tighten several of the requirements for the residency permit. And unless the program reverts to its previous financial requirements (which it might) it will be far more difficult to retire and remain in Malaysia. For example, one of the proposed changes is for retirees to require a minimum income of $10,000 USD per month.[2]

Malaysia is a capital gains free jurisdiction, so the government might be aiming to attract fewer (but wealthier) foreign retirees. But that would be a shame because Malaysia has always been such a low-cost gem.

Peter and Adele bought a seaside condominium for about $160,000 USD. Their condo is 1,100 square feet in size. It has three bedrooms, two bathrooms, a balcony and an ocean view. Their facility includes a swimming pool, a gym and undercover parking. Peter says they pay about $1,066 USD in annual maintenance fees and about $237 USD in annual property taxes.

When doing an online search for rental properties in Penang, I found 3-bedroom, 2-bathroom condominiums renting for about $950 USD per month with an ocean view. Of course, there's no limit to what you could pay, if you're seeking a really high-end place.

Peter and Adele's annual living costs are about $28,000 USD. The couple will likely spend more when they can resume traveling, once COVID-19 is under control. Peter recommends that anyone who retires in Malaysia should get private medical insurance. Peter and Adele's total health insurance costs are about $1,800 USD per year. But as Peter says, the premiums will increase as they age.[3]

For updates on the Malaysia My Second Home program, check the website at http://www.mm2h.gov.my/ and ask other expats on the Facebook group, Expats Malaysia. At the time of writing, many of the group's 37,600 members have residency agents and were discussing changes to the program. By the time you're reading this, there's always a chance the Malaysian government has changed its mind and relaxed the financial requirements for residency, once again.[4]

Retiring In Thailand: The Land of Smiles

My wife and I pulled our rental scooter onto our favorite beach. We bought a couple of coconuts from a beachside vendor and a woman made us a Pad Thai noodle meal from her portable kitchen on wheels (it was a tiny trailer that she pulled with her scooter). After paying about $2.50 USD for each delicious meal and $1 USD for each ice-cold coconut, we sat at a small table and watched the clean ocean water lap against the sand.

You might imagine a busy resort and several sun burned tourists. But we were alone. We walked along the beach at the tip of the island of Phuket (a small bridge connects it to the mainland) and took goofy photos performing handstands and cartwheels.

Two hours later, we drove down the west side of Phuket and stopped for a foot massage. For an hour, skillful hands rubbed our calves and feet while we drifted in and out of sleep. This hour of luxury cost about $7 USD each.

Thailand has almost everything: gorgeous islands, busy nightlife, remote beaches, bustling beaches, a world class city (Bangkok) and hill tribe villages near the northern city of Chiang Mai and the mountain towns of Pai and Mae Hong Son. In fact, even most expats in Thailand have limited knowledge of what the country offers (yes, I'm annoying because I'm always asking them).

One of our closest friends is Thai. During one visit, she recommended we fly from Bangkok to Nan province, which borders the country of Laos.

"That's where Thais like to go for holidays," she said. And we could see why. We rented a motorbike and rode along the gorgeous mountain roads. If you've been a tourist in Thailand, and you believe the popular regions of Bangkok, Chiang Mai and Phuket are cheap you'll be amazed at the prices off the expat tourist track. In fact, if you decide to retire in Thailand, you might not need to vacation in any other country. The Land of Smiles offers far more than any brochure could show.

Weather

Much like Malaysia, Thailand experiences year-round hot weather. Fifty-six year old expat, Nick Spray, enjoys the temperature, but when it gets overwhelming, he likes to escape. "The area where we live is an almost flat valley that lies between two large mountain ranges," he says. "At the top of the mountains it is around 10 degrees cooler than the valley, so on hot days we can escape the heat."[5] He and his girlfriend, Aom, live in Lom Sak, Phetchabun province, about 350km north of Bangkok.

Medical

While spending a few months in Thailand, I met a retired British couple in the town of Pai whose daughter was involved in a terrible car accident. The young woman was in her 20s, and her face had taken a horrible beating. The couple heard whispers of plastic surgery wizards in Thailand, and they wanted to see if some Thai surgeons could help their daughter.

Thailand might not be the first place you consider when seeking medical treatment, especially cosmetic-related magic. But several Thai hospitals are famous for their high-quality, low-cost work. The British couple whipped out their iPhone and showed me before and after pictures of their daughter. I was amazed at the surgery's success.

This doesn't mean you'll find top-quality care in every Thai town or city. But hospitals like Bangkok's Bumrungrad International have famous reputations. The hospital's website is also impressive, allowing people to receive quotes for a variety of procedures. It might be Thailand's most expensive hospital, but out-of-pocket expenses for procedures at Bumrungrad International are far lower than you would pay at most (if not all) other world-class hospitals.[6]

It attracts patients from all over the world, and friends who have received care at Bumrungrad say it feels (even looks) more like a five-star resort than a hospital.

Hospitals in smaller areas can also be effective. Sixty-year old Richard Nikoley lives in Rawai Beach, in southern Phuket. "I have had elevated blood pressure since I was a teenager," he says. "But one day, out in the village, I was feeling way, way off. They wanted to take me to a private hospital in Surin city, an hour and a half away. I said, 'let's try the Khukhan County hospital just minutes away.'" When Richard arrived at the hospital, his blood pressure was a sky-high 220/130. "They treated me like The King," he says. "Four hours of intensive care, including IV and two doses of oral meds. My blood pressure went down, and I was released with two prescriptions that I still take. I can get them at any pharmacy and they keep my blood pressure down." The total cost of Richard's hospital visit, including his first month of medication was 800 Baht (about $20).[7]

Low medical costs in Thailand is one of the reasons many expat retirees choose to "self insure." They don't pay medical insurance premiums because the out-of-pocket costs tend to be low. But major procedures, like heart bypass surgery, could still knock you back between $9,600 USD and $42,000 USD. While cheap by US standards, this could send plenty of retirees into a financial tailspin.[8]

Community and Safety

According to World Bank data on intentional homicides, Thailand ranks among the world's safest countries. Petty crime is also significantly lower in Thailand than in most (if not all) of Latin America. Thai culture also tends to be warm and friendly, one of the reasons Thailand is known as, "The Land of Smiles." While it's difficult for many westerners to learn the language, mastering a few common phrases can go a long way.

Affordability

One 75-year old retired expat named David (who asked me to keep his last name private) bought a home with his Thai girlfriend in the seaside city of Hua Hin for about $56,000 USD. A city that's popular among expat retirees, the last time I visited Hua Hin, I was invited to join a group of Hash House Harriers (they call themselves drinkers with a running problem).

Like David, many of those runners lived on pensions and US Social Security payments. "I have to keep about 1.6 million Baht ($48,000 USD) in the bank to maintain my retirement visa," says David. "But it doesn't cost a lot to live here. We live on my British pension of £505 a month (690 USD). Because David owns a home, he doesn't have to pay rent.

But Nick Spray does pay rent, and his living costs are still surprisingly low. "We spend around 400,000 baht, US$12,000 per year," he says. "That includes car payments, rent, Internet, phone, utilities, and we eat out between 4 and 5 times per week."

As always, for the best living cost comparisons, numbeo's data comparing capital cities is a good place to start. For an equal standard of living, Bangkok, Thailand costs about 30 percent more than Kuala Lumpur, Malaysia. But Bangkok is still far cheaper than any major European city, with the exception of those in Eastern Europe.

Besides Bangkok, some other popular expat retirement regions include the island of Phuket (connected to the mainland by a land bridge); the coastal city of Pattaya; the northern city of Chiang Mai; the island of Koh Samui and the seaside city of Hua Hin. If you're looking for a younger vibe, Chiang Mai is especially popular with Digital Nomads and young, budget conscious backpackers. Backed against a series of mountains, it's also a gateway to incredible hiking and cycling. Temperatures are a little cooler than in Bangkok, and costs of living in Chiang Mai are about 30 percent lower than in Thailand's capital city.

But as with any place, if you're thinking about retiring to Thailand, thoroughly check it out first. Rent a home for several months. Also be aware of seasonal weather changes. For example, if you dislike torrential rain of any kind, it might be a mistake to buy a home in southern Thailand where summer rains are often constant and heavy.

Furthermore, don't base decisions entirely on cost. Community, after all, is much more important. Find a place where you can fit in. Build friendships with expats and locals. After all, as science journalist Marta Zaraska describes in her bestselling book, *Growing Young: How Friendship, Optimism and Kindness Can Help You Live to 100*, relationships are the greatest key to longevity and happiness. That's important to remember when you're living in the land of smiles.

Notes

1. Intentional Homicides (per 100,000 people). The World Bank. Accessed August 19, 2021. https://data.worldbank.org/indicator/VC.IHR.PSRC.P5

2. Mazwin Nik Anis, "Malaysia My Second Home to be reactivated with changes, says Home Ministry." The Star, August 11, 2021. Accessed August 27, 2021. https://www.thestar.com.my/news/nation/2021/08/11/malaysia-my-second-home-to-be-reactivated-with-changes-says-home-ministry?fbclid=IwAR34do JQJkSkB6CQ3uKFtofn81eSx8pgV9K-4BPztKgZU6YuhbqLoNg3Dws

3. Interview with Peter Bendheim. Email interview with author, August 18, 2021.

4. Facebook Expats Malaysia: https://www.facebook.com/groups/123696805080

5. Interview with Nick Spray. Email interview with author, August 15, 2021.

6. Bumrungrad International Hospital. Accessed August 21, 2021. https://www.bumrungrad.com/en

7. Interview with Richard Nikoley. Email interview with author, August 14, 2021.

8. Health Tourism. Accessed August 21, 2021. https://www.health-tourism.com/bypass-surgery/thailand-c-bangkok/

Conclusion

Time is the only nonrenewable resource you have. That's why you shouldn't waste it. If you haven't started to invest in a portfolio of low-cost index funds or ETFs, you will never be younger than you are right now. Start today. And if you have a job, keep adding money. Ignore the stock market's daily, weekly, monthly and annual movements. Consider economic news as the investor's Anti-Christ. These distractions threaten to take you off course.

Staying on track is important if you want the best odds of investment success. After all, if you must work longer because you speculated or got sucked into a dodgy investment scheme, your employer will be buying more of your life. That might be OK, if you enjoy your job. But the choice to quit, work part-time or take long unpaid sabbaticals won't be available if you don't have the funds.

Fortunately, you're now aware of choices: low cost destinations from which you could work online, retire to full-time, or escape to for several months every winter. Based on your location, you could save more money as an online worker or triple your retirement portfolio's annual buying power. Most importantly, be generous with your time and knowledge and squeeze every ounce out of life that you can.

Discount Book Orders and Speaking

If you would like to hire me for a speaking engagement (live or on Zoom) please connect with me at millionaireteacherspeaks@gmail.com.

Likewise, if you're part of an organization that would like to order bulk copies of *Millionaire Expat (3rd edition)* at a discount, I can liaise with the publisher and help make that happen.

Please connect with me on LinkedIn and check out my website at www.andrewhallam.com

Low-Cost Retirement Country Resources

Climate Choices

Some people thrive on year-round warm weather and sunshine. Others prefer seasons. You might believe you've found a perfect place, but then it pours with rain three months after you arrive, or you're hit with searing heat for several months at a time. Compare average monthly sunshine, humidity levels, precipitation, temperature highs and lows for regions you're interested in at https://en.climate-data.org/

Social Considerations

As previously mentioned, it's important that we feel part of a community. Consider this when choosing where to retire. Cultures differ. For example, if 100 people spent one year retired in Eastern Europe and another 100 people spent one year in Latin America, most of those who retired in Latin America would likely report far more warmth from the locals. That doesn't mean Eastern Europeans aren't nice people. But on average, they take far longer to warm up and build relationships. In contrast, Latino families will often quickly invite you to weddings, children's school performances and picnics with warm, open arms. To understand cultural differences, I recommend Erin Meyer's superb book, *The Culture Map: Breaking Through The Invisible Boundaries of Global Business*. It may be a business book, but Meyer's researched assessments of different cultures is impressive and likely to be helpful.

Cost of Living Comparisons

Numbeo.com

Residency Requirements

Residency rules can change. Consult with the country's embassy or consulate. Most of them have websites offering detailed residency requirements, but they aren't always up-to-date. To maximize efficiency, seek legal council in your country of choice. The right lawyer can improve the process dramatically. Join a Facebook group for expats in the country you want to live in. Just search, "Expats in [name your country]."

Then ask the Facebook group to recommend a law firm for residency help. My wife and I did this for Panama. We received plenty of recommendations, with the majority recommending a firm called Kraemer & Kraemer. It wasn't as cheap as some of the other firms, but our experience with them was efficient and highly professional. Our residency process was also completed far faster than many other applicants who were employing lower-priced (and less well-known) law firms at the time. Plenty of countries (Panama included) also offer different residency visas from which you could choose.

Most countries will require a criminal record report and proof of your income or assets. Often, they'll need to be notarized or apostilled (a special form of authentication). You might also require a health check and blood work done at a clinic or hospital in the country you want to move to.

Temporary Visas For Digital Nomads

If you want to "test" a country before applying for residency (which is an excellent idea) you might not need a residency visa. Depending on the country, they could grant you up to 180 days with a tourist visa. This is typically the case with Mexico, Panama and Colombia. Countries such as Ecuador will give you a 90-day tourist visa with the option to extend for an additional 90 days.

Other countries aren't as generous, but with some creativity, you could test your country with an extended stay, such as with Thailand's Hand-to-Hand Combat Visa or language courses. Other countries, including Panama, Portugal and Georgia (to name just three) now offer Digital Nomad visas giving people an opportunity to work online while sampling their country.

Visa List: https://visalist.io/
Thailand's Hand-to-Hand Combat Visa:
   https://hand2handcombat.com/
Panama's Digital Nomad Visa:
   https://kraemerlaw.com/en/immigration/panama-digital-nomad-visa/

Co-Working Spaces

CoWorker: coworker.com
Croissant: getcroissant.com

Accommodation Sites

HomeAway (VRBO): vrbo.com

HolidayLettings: holidaylettings.com
GoBeHere: gobehere.com
Airbnb: airbnb.com

Nomad Resources:

Entrepreneur: entrepreneur.com
Nomad Gate: nomadgate.com
Nomad List: nomadlist.com

Co-Living

CoLiving: coliving.com
Digital Nomad House: digitalnomadhouse.net
Outside: outsite.co

Apps for Safety

BSafe: getbsafe.com
CDC Apps: cdc.gov
CityMapper: citymapper.com
SmartTraveler: travel.state.gov

International Health Insurance Companies

International Medical Group (IMG)
Foyer Group
AXA
Cigna
Aetna International
Bupa Global
GeoBlue
ExpaCare Global HealthCare
A Plus International

Online Local News In English

You might find local, online English news sources helpful to get a feel for specific expat cultures. Here are a few examples.

Mexico

El Ojo del Lago (Lake Chapala)
El Universal
The Guadalajara Reporter
Mexico Daily News
PVDA (Puerto Vallarta Daily)
Riviera Maya News
Yucatan Expat Life
The Yucatan Times

Panama

Panama Today
Newsroom Panama
Today Panama
The Visitor

Costa Rica

AM Costa Rica
Tico Times
Today Costa Rica

Ecuador

Cuenca Highlife
Ecuador Times

Portugal

Algarve Daily News
The Portugal News
Portugal Resident

Spain

The Local
El Pais

Georgia

Georgia Today

Estonia, Latvia, Lithuania

The Baltic Times

Thailand

Bangkok Post
Chiang Mai City Life
The Nation

Malaysia

The Star
Malay Mail
New Straits Times
The Straits Times Malaysia

Index

Page numbers followed by *f* and *t* refer to figures and tables, respectively.